OUTLINES OF ROMAN [

BY
William C. Morey

OUTLINES OF ROMAN HISTORY

Published by Palatine Press

New York City, NY

First published 1900

Copyright © Palatine Press, 2015

All rights reserved

ABOUT PALATINE PRESS

Ancient Rome forged one of the greatest and most influential empires in history, and books written by and about them continue to be popular all over the world over 1500 years after its collapse. Palatine Press is a digital publishing company that has reproduced the greatest works ever written by Romans, from the poetry of Virgil to the philosophy of Marcus Aurelius, as well as histories of Rome written by historians like Edward Gibbon.

INTRODUCTION.—THE LAND AND THE PEOPLE

The Character of Roman History, I.—The Geography of Italy, II.—The Peoples of Italy, III.

I. THE CHARACTER OF ROMAN HISTORY

Importance of Roman History.—As we begin the study of Roman history, we may ask ourselves the question, Why is this subject important and worthy of our attention? It is because Rome was one of the greatest powers of the ancient world, and has also exercised a great influence upon nearly all modern nations. There are a few great peoples, like the Hebrews, the Greeks, and the Romans, who have done much to make the world what it is. If these peoples had never existed, our life and customs would no doubt be very different from what they are now. In order, then, to understand the world in which we live to-day, we must study these world-peoples, who may have lived many centuries ago, but who have given to us much that makes us what we are—much of our language, our literature, our religion, our art, our government and law.

Rome and the Ancient World.—We often think of the Romans as the people who conquered the world. But Rome not only conquered the most important countries of the old world; she also made of these different countries one united people, so that the ancient world became at last the Roman world. The old countries which bordered. upon the Mediterranean Sea-Carthage and Egypt, Palestine and Syria, Greece and Macedonia—all became parts of the Roman Empire. The ideas and customs, the art and institutions, of these countries were taken up and welded together into what we call Roman civilization. We may, therefore, say that Rome was the highest product of the ancient world.

Rome and the Modern World.—If Rome held such an important relation to the ancient world, she has held a still more important relation to the modern world. When the Roman Empire fell and was broken up into fragments, some of these fragments became the foundation of modern states Italy, Spain, France, and England. Rome is thus the connecting link between ancient and modern history. She not only gathered up the products of the ancient world, she also transmitted these products to modern times. What she inherited from the past she bequeathed to the future, together with

3

what she herself created. On this account we may say that Rome was the foundation of the modern world.

Phases of Roman History.—As we approach the study of Roman history, we shall find that we can look at it from different points of view; and it will present to us different phases.

In the first place, we may look at the external growth of Rome. We shall then see her territory gradually expanding from a small spot on the Tiber, until it takes in the whole peninsula of Italy, and finally all the countries on the Mediterranean Sea. Our attention will then be directed to her generals, her armies, her battles, her conquests. We may trace on the map the new lands and new peoples which she gradually brought under her sway. Looked at from this point of view, Rome will appear to us as the great *conquering* nation of the world.

The Mediterranean World

Again, we may look at the way in which Rome ruled her subjects, the way in which she built up, from the various lands and peoples that she conquered, a great state, with its wonderful system of government and law. We shall then see the work of her statesmen and lawgivers, her magistrates, her senate, and her assemblies. From this point of view she will seem to us the great *governing* nation of the world.

Finally, we may look at the way in which the Romans were themselves improved in their manners and customs, as they came into contact with other peoples—how they learned lessons even from those whom they conquered, and were gradually changed from a rude, barbarous people to a highly civilized and cultivated nation. We shall see the straw-thatched huts of early times giving place to magnificent temples and theaters and other splendid buildings. We shall see the rude speech of the early Romans growing into a noble language, capable of expressing fine, poetic feeling and lofty sentiments of patriotism. We shall also see Rome giving the fruits of her culture to the less favored peoples whom she takes under her control; and when she passes away, we shall see her bequeathing her treasures to future generations. From this point of view Rome will appear to us as the great *civilizing* nation of the world.

In order to understand the Romans well, we should look at them in all these phases we should study their conquests, their government, and their civilization.

II. THE GEOGRAPHY OF ITALY

The Italian Peninsula.—The study of Roman history properly begins with the geography of Italy; because it was in Italy that the Roman people had their origin, and it was here that they began their great career. It was only when the Romans had conquered and organized Italy that they were able to conquer and govern the world. If

4

we look at the map (p. 10), we shall see that the position of the Italian peninsula was favorable to the growth of the Roman power. It was situated almost in the center of the Mediterranean Sea, on the shores of which had flourished the greatest nations of antiquity—Egypt, Carthage, Phoenicia, Judea, Greece, and Macedonia. By conquering Italy, Rome thus obtained a commanding position among the nations of the ancient world.

Boundaries and Extent of Italy.—In very early times, the name "Italy" was applied only to the very southern part of the peninsula. But from this small area it was extended so as to cover the whole peninsula which actually projects into the sea, and finally the whole territory south of the Alps. The peninsula is washed on the east by the Adriatic or Upper Sea, and on the west by the Tyrrhenian or Lower Sea. Italy lies for the most part between the parallels of thirty-eight degrees and forty-six degrees north latitude. It has a length of about 720 miles; a width varying from 330 to 100 miles; and an area of about 91,000 square miles.

The Mountains of Italy.—There are two famous mountain chains which belong to Italy, the Alps and the Apennines. (1) The *Alps* form a semicircular boundary on the north and afford a formidable barrier against the neighboring countries of Europe. Starting from the sea at its western extremity, this chain stretches toward the north for about 150 miles, when it rises in the lofty peak of Mt. Blanc, 15,000 feet in height; and then continues its course in an easterly direction for about 330 miles, approaching the head of the Adriatic Sea, and disappearing along its coast. It is crossed by several passes, through which foreign peoples have sometimes found their way into the peninsula. (2) The *Apennines*, beginning at the western extremity of the Alps, extend through the whole length of the peninsula, forming the backbone of Italy. From this main line are thrown off numerous spurs and scattered peaks. Sometimes the Apennines have furnished to Rome a kind of barrier against invaders from the north.

Mountains, Rivers, and Divisions of Italy

The Rivers of Italy.—The most important river of Italy is the Po, which, with its hundred tributaries, drains the fertile valley in the north, lying between the Alps and the Apennines. The eastern slope of the peninsula proper is drained by a large number of streams, the most noted of which are the Rubicon, the Metaurus, the Frento, and the Aufidus. On the western slope the most important river is the Tiber, with its tributary, the Anio.

Climate and Products.—The climate of Italy varies greatly as we pass from the north to the south. In the valley of the Po the winters are often severe, and the air is chilled by the neighboring snows of the Alps. In central Italy the climate is mild and agreeable, snow being rarely seen south of the Tiber, except on the ranges of the Apennines; while in southern Italy we approach a climate almost tropical, the land being often swept by the hot south wind, the *sirocco*, from the plains of Africa.

The soil of Italy is generally fertile, especially in the plains of the Po and the fields of Campania. The staple products in ancient times were wheat, the olive, and the vine. For a long period Italy took the lead of the world in the production of olive oil and wine. The production of wheat declined when Rome, by her conquests, came into commercial relation with more fertile countries, such as Egypt.

The Divisions of Italy.—For the purpose of convenience and to aid us in our future study, we may divide ancient Italy into three divisions: northern, central, and southern.

(1) *Northern* Italy comprised the whole continental portion from the Alps to a line drawn from the river Macra on the west to the Rubicon on the east. It contained three distinct countries: Liguria toward the west, Cisalpine Gaul in the center, and Venetia toward the east.

(2) *Central* Italy comprised the northern part of the peninsula proper, that is, the territory between the line just drawn from the Macra to the Rubicon, and another line drawn from the Silarus on the west to the Frento on the east. This territory contained six countries, namely, three on the western coast,—Etruria, Latium (*la'shi-um*), and Campania; and three on the eastern coast and along the Apennines,—Umbria, Picenum, and what we call the Sabellian country, which included many mountain tribes, chief among which were the Sabines, the Frentani, and the Samnites.

(3) *Southern* Italy comprised the rest of the peninsula and contained four countries, namely, two on the western coast, Lucania and Bruttium, extending into the toe of Italy; and two on the eastern coast, Apulia and Calabria (or Iapygia), extending into the heel of Italy.

III. THE PEOPLES OF ITALY

The Settlement of Italy.-Long before Rome was founded, every part of Italy was already peopled. Many of the peoples living there came from the north, around the head of the Adriatic, pushing their way toward the south into different parts of the peninsula. Others came from Greece by way of the sea, settling upon the southern coast. It is of course impossible for us to say precisely how Italy was settled. It is

6

enough for us at present to know that most of the earlier settlers spoke an Indo-European, or Aryan, language, and that when they first appeared in Italy they were scarcely civilized, living upon their flocks and herds and just beginning to cultivate the soil.

The Italic Tribes.—The largest part of the peninsula was occupied by a number of tribes which made up the so-called Italic race.1 We may for convenience group these tribes into four divisions the Latins, the Oscans, the Sabellians, and the Umbrians. (1) The *Latins* dwelt in central Italy, just south of the Tiber. They lived in villages scattered about Latium, tilling their fields and tending their flocks. The village was a collection of straw-thatched huts; it generally grew up about a hill, which was fortified, and to which the villagers could retreat in times of danger. Many of these Latin villages or hill-towns grew into cities, which were united into a league for mutual protection, and bound together by a common worship (of *Jupiter Latiaris*); and an annual festival which they celebrated on the Alban Mount, near which was situated Alba Longa, their chief city (see map, p. 46).

A Temporary Village of Straw Huts in Modern Italy—supposed to be like an ancient Latin village

(2) The *Oscans* were the remnants of an early Italic people which inhabited the country stretching southward from Latium, along the western coast. In their customs they were like the Latins, although perhaps not so far advanced. Some authors include in this branch the Aequians, the Hernicans, and the Volscians, who carried on many wars with Rome in early times.

(3) The *Sabellians* embraced the most numerous and warlike peoples of the Italic stock. They lived to the east and south of the Latins and Oscans, extending along the ridges and slopes of the Apennines. They were devoted not so much to farming as to the tending of flocks and herds. They lived also by plundering their neighbors' harvests and carrying off their neighbors' cattle. They were broken up into a great number of tribes, the most noted of which were the Samnites, a hardy race which became the great rival of the Roman people for the possession of central Italy. Some of the Samnite people in very early times moved from then mountain home and settled in the fertile plain of Campania.

(4) The *Umbrians* lived to the north of the Sabellians. They are said to have been the oldest people of Italy. But when the Romans came into contact with them, they had become crowded into a comparatively small territory, and were easily conquered. They were broken up into small tribes, living in hill-towns and villages, and these were often united into loose confederacies.

7

The Etruscans.—Northwest of Latium dwelt the Etruscans, in some respects the most remarkable people of early Italy. Their origin is shrouded in mystery. In early times they were a powerful nation, stretching from the Po to the Tiber, and having possessions even in the plains of Campania. Their cities were fortified, often in the strongest manner, and also linked together in confederations. Their prosperity was founded not only upon agriculture, but also upon commerce.

Their religion was a gloomy and weird superstition, in which they thought that they could discover the will of the gods by means of augury, that is, by watching the flight of birds and by examining the entrails of animals. The Etruscans were great builders; and their massive walls, durable roads, well-constructed sewers, and imposing sepulchers show the greatness of their civilization.

The Greeks in Italy.—But the most civilized and cultivated people in Italy were the Greeks, who had planted their colonies at Tarentum, and on the western coast as far as Naples (*Neapolis*) in Campania. So completely did these coasts become dotted with Greek cities, enlivened with Greek commerce, and influenced by Greek culture, that this part of the peninsula received the name of Magna Graecia.[2]

The Gauls.—If the Greeks in the extreme south were the most civilized people of Italy, the Gauls or Celts, in the extreme north, were the most barbarous. Crossing the Alps from western Europe, they had pushed back the Etruscans and occupied the plains of the Po; hence this region received the name which it long held, Cisalpine Gaul. They held this territory against the Ligurians on the west and the Veneti on the east; and for a long time were the terror of the Italian people.

SELECTIONS FOR READING

Ihne, Early Rome, Ch. 1, "The Greatness of Rome" (5).[3]

Michelet, Ch. 2, "Description of Italy" (6).

Liddell, Introduction, "Physical Geography of Italy" (1).

How and Leigh, Ch. 2, "Peoples of Italy" (1).

Shuckburgh, Ch. 3, "Inhabitants of Italy" (1).

Mommsen, Vol. 1., Bk. 1., Ch. 3, "Settlements of the Latins" (2).

Mommsen, abridged, Ch. 5, "The Etruscans—The Greeks in Italy" (2).

SPECIAL STUDY

SOURCES OF ROMAN HISTORY.—Liddell, Ch. 16 (1); Ihne, Early Rome, Ch. 2 (5); Shuckburgh, pp. 54-60 (1); Mommsen, abridged, pp. vii.-xviii. (2); Dyer, Kings of Rome, Introductory Dissertation (5).

[1] Remnants of other early peoples may be seen in the Ligures and the Veneti in the north, the Iapygians in the southeast, and the Siculi in Sicily.

[2] It may be noticed here that the early Phoenician traders touched upon the coasts of Italy and the neighboring islands, and that Sardinia and western Sicily came to be occupied by Carthage, the greatest of the Phoenician colonies. Eastern Sicily was colonized by the Greeks.

[3] The figure in parenthesis refers to the number of the topic in the Appendix, where a fuller title of the book will be found.

CHAPTER II

THE BEGINNINGS OF ROME

Traditions of the Early Kings, I.—The Situation of Rome, II.—The Origin of the City, III.

I. TRADITIONS OF THE EARLY KINGS

The Early Legendary History.—In its beginnings, the history of Rome, like that of all other ancient peoples, is made up largely of traditions. But we must not suppose on this account that the early history of Rome is a mere blank. Like all other traditions, these stories have in them some elements of truth. They show to us the ideas and the spirit of the Roman people; and they show how the Romans used to explain the origin of their own customs and institutions. While we may not believe all these stories, we cannot ignore them entirely; because they have a certain kind of historical value, and have become a part of the world's literature.

Foundation of the City.—According to the Roman legends, the origin of the city was connected with Alba Longa, the chief city of Latium; and the origin of Alba Longa was traced to the city of Troy in Asia Minor. After the fall of that famous city, it is said that the Trojan hero, Aeneas, fled from the ruins, bearing upon his shoulder his aged father, Anchises, and leading by the hand his son, Ascanius. Guided by the star of his mother, Venus, he landed on the shores of Italy with a band of Trojans, and was assured by omens that Latium was to be the seat of a great empire. He founded the city of Lavinium, and after his death his son Ascanius transferred the seat of the kingdom to Alba Longa. Here his descendants ruled for

ÆNEAS (Coin)

ROMULUS AND REMUS AND THE WOLF

three hundred years, when the throne was usurped by a prince called Amulius. To secure himself against any possible rivals, this usurper caused his brother's daughter, Rhea Silvia, to take the vows of a vestal virgin. But she became the mother of twin children, Romulus and Remus; their father was Mars, the god of war. The wicked Amulius caused the children to be thrown into the Tiber; but they remained under the guardianship of the gods. Drifting

11

ashore at the foot of the Palatine hill, they were nursed by a she-wolf, and were brought up at the home of a neighboring shepherd. And when they had grown to manhood, they founded (B.C. 753?) the city of Rome on the Palatine, where they had been providentially rescued. In a quarrel between the two brothers, Remus was killed, and Romulus became the king of the new city.

The Reign of Romulus.—Romulus was looked upon by the Romans not only as the founder of their city, but as the creator of their social and political institutions. He is said to have peopled his new town by opening an asylum for refugees; and when he wanted wives for his people he captured them from the Sabines. After a war with the Sabines peace was made; and the two peoples became bound together into one city under the two kings, Romulus and Titus Tatius. After the death of Titus, Romulus reigned alone and gave laws to the whole people. He made many wars upon the neighboring towns, and after a reign of thirty-seven years he was translated to heaven and worshiped under the name of Quirinus.

Numa Pompilius.—After a year's interregnum a Sabine named Numa Pompilius was elected as the second king of Rome. He is said to have been a very wise and pious man, and to have taught the Romans the arts of peace and the worship of the gods. Numa is represented in the legends as the founder of the Roman religion. He appointed priests and other ministers of religion. He divided the lands among the people, placing boundaries under the charge of the god Terminus. He is also said to have divided the year into twelve months, and thus to have founded the Roman calendar. After a peaceful reign of forty-two years, he was buried under the hill Janiculum, across the Tiber.

Tullus Hostilius.—The third king, Tullus Hostilius, was chosen from the Romans. His reign was noted for the conquest of Alba Longa. In accounts of this war with Alba Longa, the famous story is told of the Horatii and the Curiatii, three brothers in each army, who were selected to decide the contest by a combat, which resulted in favor of the Horatii, the Roman champions. Alba Longa thus became subject to Rome. Afterward, Alba Longa was razed to the ground, and all its people were transferred to Rome. Tullus, it is said, neglected the worship of the gods, and was at last, with his whole house, destroyed by the lightnings of Jove.

Ancus Marcius.—After the reign of Tullus the people elected Ancus Marcius, a Sabine and a grandson of Numa Pompilius. He is said to have published the sacred laws of his grandfather, and to have tried to restore the arts of peace. But, threatened by the Latins, he conquered many of their cities, brought their inhabitants to Rome, and settled them upon the Aventine hill. He fortified the hill Janiculum, on the other side of the Tiber, to protect Rome from the Etruscans, and built across the river a wooden bridge (the *Pons Sublicius*). He also conquered the lands between Rome and the sea and built the port of Ostia at the mouth of the Tiber.

Credibility of the Legends.—These are in substance the stories which, decorated by many fanciful and miraculous incidents, the Romans were proud to relate as explaining the beginnings of their city and the work of their early kings. These traditions have been shown to be unworthy of belief in many particulars. It is of course impossible, in a small book like this, even to suggest the many and various opinions which have been expressed regarding the credibility of early Roman history. It is enough to say that, while we need not believe all the incidents and details contained in these stories, we may find in them references to facts and institutions which really existed; and with the aid of other means, we may put these facts together so as to explain in a rational way the origin and growth of the famous city on the Tiber.

II. THE SITUATION OF ROME

The Hills of Rome.—To obtain a more definite knowledge of the birth of Rome than we can get from the traditional stories, we must study that famous group of hills which may be called the "cradle of the Roman people." By looking at these hills, we can see quite clearly how Rome must have come into being, and how it became a powerful city. The location of these hills was favorable for defense, and for the beginning of a strong settlement. Situated about eighteen miles from the mouth of the Tiber, they were far enough removed from the sea to be secure from the attacks of the pirates that infested these waters; while the river afforded an easy highway for commerce.

Their Relation to One Another.—To understand the relation of these hills to one another, we may consider them as forming two groups, the northern and the southern. The southern group comprised three hills—the Palatine, the Caelian, and the Aventine—arranged in the form of a triangle, with the Palatine projecting to the north. The northern group comprised four hills, arranged in the form of a crescent or semicircle, in the following order, beginning from the east: the Esquiline, the Viminal, the Quirinal, and the Capitoline—the last being a sort of spur of the Quirinal.  These two groups of hills became, as we shall see, the seats of two different settlements. Of all the hills on the Tiber, the Palatine occupied the most central and commanding position. It was, therefore, the people of the Palatine settlement who would naturally become the controlling people of the seven-hilled city.

Their Relation to Neighboring Lands.—By looking at the neighboring lands about the Tiber we see that Rome was located at the point of contact between three important countries. On the south and east was Latium, the country of the Latins, already dotted with a number of cities, the most important of which was Alba Longa. On the north was the country of the Sabines, a branch of the Sabellian stock. On the northwest was Etruria, with a large number of cities organized in confederacies and inhabited by the most civilized and enterprising people of central Italy. The peoples of these three different countries were pushing their outposts in the direction of the seven hills. It is not difficult for us to see that the time must come when there would be a struggle for the possession of this important locality.

III. THE ORIGIN OF THE CITY

The Latin Settlement on the Palatine.—So far as we know, the first people to get a foothold upon the site of Rome were the Latins, who formed a settlement about the

Palatine hill. This Latin settlement was at first a small village. It consisted of a few farmers and shepherds who were sent out from Latium (perhaps from Alba Longa) as a sort of outpost, both to protect the Latin frontier and to trade with the neighboring tribes. The people who formed this settlement were called *Ramnes*. They dwelt in their rude straw huts on the slopes of the Palatine, and on the lower lands in the direction of the Aventine and the Caelian. The

HUT-SHAPED URN

outlying lands furnished the fields which they tilled and used for pasturage. In order to protect them from attacks, the sides of the Palatine hill were strengthened by a wall built of rude but solid masonry. This fortified place was called *Roma Quadrata*,1 or "Square Rome." It formed the citadel of the colony, into which the settlers could drive their cattle and conduct their families when attacked by hostile neighbors. What some persons suppose to be the primitive wall of the Palatine city, known as the Wall of Romulus, has in recent years been uncovered, showing the general character of this first fortification of Rome.

"WALL OF ROMULUS"

The Sabine Settlement on the Quirinal.—Opposite the Palatine settlement there grew up a settlement on the Quirinal hill. This Quirinal settlement seems to have been an outpost or colony of the Sabine people, just as the Palatine settlement was a Latin colony. The Sabines were pushing southward from beyond the Anio. The settlers on the Quirinal were called *Tities*; their colony formed a second hill-town, similar in character and nearly equal in extent to the Palatine town.

Union of the Romans and the Sabines.—The two hill-towns which thus faced each other naturally became rivals for the possession of the lands near the Tiber; but being

so nearly of equal strength, neither could conquer the other. If these settlements had not been so close together, they might have indulged in occasional strife and still remained separate; but being near to each other, they were obliged to be constantly at war, or else to come to some friendly understanding. They chose the latter course, and after forming an alliance, were united by a permanent league, and really became a single city. To celebrate this union, the intervening space was dedicated to the two-faced god, Janus, who watched the approaches of both towns, and whose temple was said to have been built by Numa. The Capitoline hill was chosen as the common citadel. The space between the two towns was used as a common market place (*forum*), and also as a place for the common meeting of the people (*comitium*). This union of the Palatine and Quirinal towns into one community, with a common religion and government, was an event of great importance. It was, in fact, the first step in the process of "incorporation" which afterward made Rome the most powerful city of Latium, of Italy, and finally of the world.

The Third Settlement, on the Caelian.—The union of the Romans (*Ramnes*) and the Sabines (*Titie* s) was followed by the introduction of a third people, called the *Luceres*. This people was probably a body of Latins who had been conquered and settled upon the Caelian hill—although they are sometimes regarded as having been Etruscans. Whatever may have been their origin, it is quite certain that they soon came to be incorporated as a part of the whole city community. The city of the early Roman kings thus came to be made up of three divisions, or "tribes" (*tribus*, a third part, from *tres*, three). The evidence of this threefold origin was preserved in many institutions of later times. The three settlements were gradually united into a single city-state with common social, political, and religious institutions. By this union the new city became strong and able to compete successfully with its neighbors.

SELECTIONS FOR READING

Merivale, Gen. Hist., Ch. 3, "The Earliest Legends" (1).[2]

How and Leigh, Ch. 3, "Legends of the Kings" (1).

Pelham, Bk. I., Ch. 1, "The Traditions" (1).

Parker, Arch. Hist., Ch. 2, "Roma Quadrata" (9).

Shuckburgh, Ch. 4, "Origin of Rome" (1).

Mommsen, Vol. I., Bk. I., Ch. 4, "Beginnings of Rome" (2).

Plutarch, "Romulus," "Numa" (11).

Livy, Bk. 1., Chs. 24-26, The Horatii and Curiatii (4).

SPECIAL STUDY

CREDIBILITY OF EARLY ROMAN HISTORY.—Liddell, Ch. 5 (1); Ihne, Early Rome, Ch. 4 (5); How and Leigh, pp. 34-37 (1); Leighton, Ch. 3 (1); Michelet, pp. 403-424 (6); Lewis, Credibility, *en passant* (5).

[1] This has been the generally accepted view; but some authorities say that the name was applied only to a square altar in the center of the city.

[2] The figure in parenthesis refers to the number of the topic in the Appendix, where a fuller title of the book will be found.

CHAPTER III

THE INSTITUTIONS OF EARLY ROME

The Early Roman Society, I.—The Early Roman Government, II.—The Early Roman Religion, III.

I. THE EARLY ROMAN SOCIETY

The Social Institutions.—We have thus far traced the origin of the Roman city, according to what seem to be the most reasonable and generally accepted views. Various writers on early Roman history, of course, differ upon many matters of detail; but they are fairly well agreed that the Roman city grew out of a settlement of Latin shepherds and farmers on the Palatine hill; and that this first settlement slowly expanded by taking in and uniting with itself the settlements established on the other hills. But to understand more fully the beginnings of this little city-state, we must look at the way in which the people were organized, that is, how they were arranged in social groups; how they were ruled; and how their society and government were held together and made strong by a common religion. Let us look first at the early social institutions.

The Roman Family.—The smallest group of Roman society was the family, which the early Romans regarded as the most important and sacred of all human institutions.

At its head was the household father (*paterfamilias*). He was supreme ruler over all the members of the household; his power extended to life and death. He had charge of the family worship and performed the religious rites about the sacred fire, which was kept burning upon the family altar. Around the family hearth were gathered the sons and daughters, grandsons and granddaughters, and also, the adopted children,—all of whom remained under the power of the father as long as he lived. The family might also have dependent members, called "clients," who looked up to the father as their "patron"; and also slaves, who served the father as their master. Every Roman looked with pride upon his family and the deeds of his ancestors; and it was regarded as a great calamity for the family worship to become extinct.

DOMESTIC ALTAR

The Roman Gens.—A number of families which were supposed to be descended from a common ancestor formed a clan, or *gens*. Like the family, the gens was bound together by common religious rites. It was also governed by a common chief or ruler (*decurio*), who performed the religious rites, and led the people in war.

18

The Roman Curia.—A number of *gentes* formed a still larger group, called a *curia*. In ancient times, when different people wished to unite, it was customary for them to make the union sacred by worshiping some common god. So the curia was bound together by the worship of a common deity. To preside over the common worship, a chief (*curio*) was selected, who was also the military commander in time of war, and chief magistrate in time of peace. The chief was assisted by a council of elders; and upon the most important questions he consulted the members of the curia in a common place of meeting (*comitium*). So that the curia was a small confederation of gentes, and made what we might call a little state.

The Roman Tribes.—There was in the early Roman society a still larger group than the curia; it was what was called the tribe. It was a collection of *curiae* which had united for purposes of common defense and had come to form quite a distinct and well-organized community, like that which had settled upon the Palatine hill, and also like the Sabine community which had settled upon the Quirinal. Each of these settlements was therefore a tribe. Each had its chief, or king (*rex*), who was priest of the common religion, military commander in time of war, and civil magistrate to settle all disputes. Like the curia, it had also a council of elders and a general assembly of all people capable of bearing arms. Three of such tribes formed the whole Roman people.

II. THE EARLY ROMAN GOVERNMENT

The Growth of the Roman Government.—It will now be easy for us to understand how the government of the whole united city came into existence. Each of the tribes, as we have seen, had its own king, its council of elders, and its general assembly. When the tribes on the Palatine and Quirinal hills united and became one people, their governments were also united and became one government. For example, their two kings were replaced by one king chosen alternately from each tribe. Their two councils of one hundred members each were united in a single council of two hundred members. Their two assemblies, each one of which was made up of ten curiae, were combined into a single assembly of twenty curiae. And when the third tribe is added, we have a single king, a council of elders made up of three hundred members, and an assembly of the people composed of thirty curiae.

The Roman King.—The Roman king was the chief of the whole people. He was elected by all the people in their common assembly and inaugurated under the approval of the gods. He was in a sense the father of the whole nation. He was the chief priest of the national religion. He was the military commander of the people, whom he called to arms in time of war. He administered law and justice, and like the father of the household had the power of life and death over all his subjects.

The Roman Senate.—The council of elders for the united city was called the senate (from *senex*, an old man). It was composed of the chief men of the gentes, chosen by the king to assist him with their advice. It comprised at first one hundred members, then two hundred, and finally three hundred—the original number having been doubled and tripled, with the addition of the second and third tribes. The senate at first had no power to make laws, only the power to give advice, which the king might accept or not, as he pleased.

The Comitia Curiata.—All the people of the thirty curiae, capable of bearing arms, formed a general assembly of the united city, called the *comitia curiata*. In this assembly each curia had a single vote, and the will of the assembly was determined by a majority of such votes. In a certain sense the *comitia curiata* was the ultimate authority in the state. It elected the king and passed a law conferring upon him his power. It ratified or rejected the most important proposals of the king regarding peace and war. The early city-state of Rome may then be described as a democratic monarchy, in which the power of the king was based upon the will of the people.

III. THE EARLY ROMAN RELIGION

The Growth of the Early Religion.—Like the Roman government, so the early Roman religion grew up with the union of the various settlements into one community. When the different tribes came together into the Roman city, they selected Jupiter and Mars as their common gods to be worshiped upon the Capitoline hill, together with Quirinus on the Quirinal. As the fire was kept burning on the family hearth, so the sacred fire of the city was kept burning in the temple of Vesta. The Roman people were filled with religious ideas. All power, from that of the household father to that of the king, was believed to come from above. In peace and in war they lived in the presence of the gods, and sought to remember them by worship and festivals.

TEMPLE OF JUPITER CAPITOLINUS (Medallion)

The Early Roman Deities.—To the ancestral gods which were worshiped in the family and gens, were added the gods of nature, which the Romans saw everywhere. These earliest deities were those which naturally sprang from the imagination of a pastoral and agricultural people. In their gods they saw the protectors of their flocks and herds, and the guardians of the weather, the seasons, and the fruits of the soil. Jove (Jupiter) was the god of the sky and the elements of the air, the thunder and the lightning. Tellus was the goddess of the earth, and the mother of all living things; Saturn, the god of sowing; and Ceres, the goddess of the harvest; Minerva, the goddess of olives; Flora, of flowers; and Liber, the god of wine.

The Religious Officers.—The king was the supreme religious officer of the state; but he was assisted by other persons, whom he appointed for special religious duties. To each of the three great national gods—Jupiter, Mars, and Quirinus—was assigned a special priest, called a *flamen*. To keep the fires of Vesta always burning, there were appointed six vestal virgins, who were regarded as the consecrated daughters of the state. Special pontiffs, under the charge of a *pontifex maximus*, had charge of the religious festivals and ceremonies; and the *fetiales* were intrusted with the formality of declaring war.

The Religious Observances.—The Romans showed their remembrance of the gods in their prayers, offerings, and festivals. The prayers were addressed to the gods for the purpose of obtaining favors, and were often accompanied by vows. The religious offerings consisted either of the fruits of the earth, such as flowers, wine, milk, and honey; or the sacrifices of domestic animals, such as oxen, sheep, and swine. The festivals which were celebrated in honor of the gods were very numerous and were scattered through the different months of the year. The old Roman calendar contained a long list of these festival days. The new year began with March and was consecrated to Mars and celebrated with war festivals. Other religious festivals were devoted to the sowing of the seed, the gathering of the harvest, and similar events which belonged to the life of an agricultural people such as the early Romans were.

SELECTIONS FOR READING

Arnold, Hist., Ch. 2, "Early History of Rome" (2).[1]

How and Leigh, Ch. 4, "The Regal Period" (1).

Pelham, Bk. I., Ch. 2, "The City and the Commonwealth" (1).

Mommsen, Vol. I., Bk. I., Ch. 5, "Original Constitution of Rome" (2).

Mommsen, abridged, Ch. 3, "Rome's Original Constitution" (2).

SPECIAL STUDY

THE ROMAN RELIGION.—Leighton, Ch. 4 (1); Ihne, Early Rome, Ch. 6 (5); Mommsen, Vol. I., Bk. I., Ch. 12 (2); Ramsay and Lanciani, Ch. 10 (8); Eschenburg, pp. 229-248 (8); Harper's Dict. Antiqq., "Religio," "Sacerdos," "Sacrificium" (8); Coulanges, Bk. I (20).

[1] The figure in parenthesis refers to the number of the topic in the Appendix, where a fuller title of the book will be found.

CHAPTER IV

THE ETRUSCAN KINGS OF ROME

The Traditions of the Later Kings, I.—The Etruscan Influence, II.—The Growth of the City, III.

I. THE TRADITIONS OF THE LATER KINGS

The Later Kingdom.—As we come to the later kingdom, we shall see that many changes took place which made Rome quite different from what it was in the early period. The history is still based upon legends; but these legends are somewhat more trustworthy than the older ones. We shall see that Rome now came under foreign princes; and that the city was greatly improved, and its institutions were changed in many respects. These new kings, instead of being Romans or Sabines, were Etruscans, who gave to Rome something of the character of an Etruscan city.

Tarquinius Priscus.—The first of these new kings, it is said, came from the Etruscan city of Tarquinii, from which he derived his name. The story is told that, as he approached the city, an eagle came from the sky, and, lifting his cap from his head, replaced it. His wife, who was skilled in the Etruscan art of augury, regarded the eagle as a messenger from heaven, and its act as a sign that her husband was to acquire honor and power. At the death of Ancus Marcius, Tarquinius became king. He carried on many wars with the neighboring peoples, the Latins and the Sabines. He was great in peace as well as in war. He drained the city, improved the Forum, and founded a temple to Jupiter on the Capitoline hill. After a reign of thirty-eight years, he was treacherously slain by the sons of Ancus Marcius.

Servius Tullius.—The next king was Servius Tullius, who is said to have been the son of a slave in the royal household, and whom the gods favored by mysterious signs. He proved a worthy successor to the first Tarquin. He made a treaty with the Latins, by which Rome was acknowledged as the head of Latium; and as a sign of this union, he built a temple to Diana on the Aventine hill. He enlarged the city and inclosed the seven hills within a single wall. After a reign of forty-four years, he was murdered by his own son-in-law, who became the next king.

Tarquinius Superbus.—Tradition represents the last king, Tarquinius Superbus, as a cruel despot. He obtained the throne by murder, and ruled without the consent of the senate or the people. He loved power and pomp. He continued the wars with the Latins. He also waged war with the Volscians on the southern borders of Latium; and with the spoils there obtained he finished the temple of Jupiter on the Capitoline hill. Although he scorned religion, it is related that he was induced to buy the Sibylline books from the inspired prophetess of Cumae. It is also said that later in life he was frightened by strange dreams, and sent his two sons, with his nephew Brutus, to consult the Greek oracle at Delphi. To one question asked the oracle, the response was given that the person who first kissed his mother should succeed to the power of Tarquin. Brutus showed that he was the person intended, by falling and kissing the earth, the common mother of all. The traditions tell us how at last the proud Tarquin was driven from the throne and the kingdom was ended.

Significance of the Legends.—We cannot of course accept these stories as real history. We can yet see in them the evidence that Rome was becoming different from what it had been under the early kings. We can see that Rome came under the power of the Etruscans; that it was much improved by the construction of great public works and buildings; and that it acquired a dominant power over the neighboring land of Latium.

II. THE ETRUSCAN INFLUENCE

The Kingly Power.—One of the most important features of the Etruscan dynasty was the increase of the kingly power. All the Etruscan kings were represented as powerful rulers. Although they could not change the spirit and character of the people, they gave to Rome a certain kind of strength and influence which it did not have before. This great power of the Etruscan kings was at first used for the good of the people; but finally it became a tyranny which was oppressive and hateful.

The Insignia of Power.—From the Etruscans came the royal insignia, that is, the symbols of power which were intended to make the person of the king more dignified and respected. These insignia consisted of a golden crown, an ivory scepter, an ivory chair called the "curule chair," a white robe with a purple border (*toga praetexta*), and twelve lictors, or royal attendants, each carrying a bundle of rods (*fasces*) inclosing an ax. This last symbol was a sign of the absolute power of the king.

The Haruspices.—From Etruria also came the art of the haruspices, or soothsayers, who interpreted the will of the gods. These persons were supposed to ascertain the divine will by observing the lightning and other phenomena of nature, and also by examining the internal organs of animals offered in sacrifice, and even by watching the sacred chickens as they ate their food. The Etruscan soothsayers were supposed to be better versed in divine things than the Roman augurs; and the senate is said to have provided for the perpetual cultivation of the Etruscan ritual.

Public Works.—The buildings and other public works of the later kings bear the marks of Etruscan influence. The massive and durable style of architecture, especially as seen in the walls and the sewers constructed at this time, shows that they were the works of great and experienced builders, The name of the "Tuscan Street" (*vicus Tuscus*) which opened into the Forum, preserved the memory of this foreign influence in the Roman city.

III. THE GROWTH OF THE CITY

The Servian Walls.—The expansion of the city under the Tarquins is shown, in the first place, by the construction of the new and larger walls which are ascribed to Servius Tullius, and which received his name. Previous to this time the principal city wall was on the Palatine. Some of the other hills were partly fortified. But now a single fortification was made to encircle all the seven hills, by joining the old walls and by erecting new defenses. The walls were generally built of large, rectangular blocks of stone, and so durable were they that they remained the only defenses of the city for many hundreds of years; and parts of them may be seen at the present day.

The New Temples.—Under the Tarquins, the temples of the city assumed a more imposing architectural appearance. Before this the places of worship were generally altars, set up on consecrated places, and perhaps covered with a simple roof. The Etruscan kings gave a new dignity to the sacred buildings. The most imposing example of the new structures was the temple dedicated to Jupiter Optimus Maximus, on the Capitoline hill, which contained shrines set apart for the worship of Juno and Minerva. Other new temples were the one dedicated to Saturn at the foot of the Capitoline near the Forum, and one dedicated to Diana on the Aventine.

The Cloaca Maxima.—Among the most remarkable works of the Tarquins were the sewers which were constructed to drain the city. The most important of these was the famous *Cloaca Maxima*, or great drain, which ran under the Forum and emptied into the Tiber. It was said to be large enough to admit a hay-cart, and one could sail down it in a boat. It was strongly built of stone, in the form of a semicircular arch, such as the Etruscans had used, and its mouth is still visible on the shore of the Tiber.

The Circus Maximus.—For the amusement of the people, games were introduced from Etruria, and a great circus, called the *Circus Maximus*, was laid out between the Aventine and the Palatine hill. Here the people assembled once every year, to witness chariot races and boxing and other sports, which were celebrated in honor of the gods who were worshiped on the Capitoline.

SELECTIONS FOR READING

Merivale, Gen. Hist., Ch. 4, "The Three Later Kings" (1).[1]
Liddell, Ch. 3, "Tarquinius Priscus and Servius Tullius" (1).
Parker, Arch. Hist., Ch. 5, "The City on the Seven Hills" (9).
Abbott, Ch. 2, "Monarchical Institutions" (13).

Livy, Bk. I., Chs. 34-39, Stories of Tarquinius Priscus (4).

SPECIAL STUDY

THE CITY UNDER THE KINGS.—Dyer, pp. 1-61 (9); Parker, Chs. 2-5 (9); Liddell, pp. 52-55 (1); Arnold. Chs. 3, 5 (2); Merivale, Gen. Hist., Ch. 78 (1).

[1] The figure in parenthesis refers to the number of the topic in the Appendix, where a fuller title of the book will be found.

CHAPTER V

I. THE INTRODUCTION OF THE PLEBEIANS

The Reforms of the Tarquins.—We must not suppose that the work of the Etruscan kings was simply to give to Rome better buildings and more durable public works. However important these may have been, the Tarquins did something which was of still greater benefit to the Roman people. The first Tarquin and Servius Tullius are described as great reformers, who made the little Roman state stronger and more compact than it had been before. Let us see why the Roman state needed to be reformed, and how this reform was brought about.

The Patrician Aristocracy.—We have already seen that the early Roman people was made up of three tribes, that is, the three old communities which were settled on the Roman hills. We have also seen that these tribes were made up of curiae; and these curiae of gentes; and lastly, that these gentes were composed of the old families. It is therefore evident that no person could be a member of the state unless he was a member of some old Roman family. It was only the descendants of the old families who could vote in the assembly or could be chosen to the senate. And it was they only who were called upon to serve in the army. These old families and their descendants were called patricians; and the state was in reality a patrician state. As all other persons were excluded from political rights and privileges, the patricians formed an aristocratic class, exclusive and devoted to their own interests.

The Growth of the Plebeians.—But in the course of time there grew up by the side of the patricians a new class of persons. Though living at Rome, they were not members of the old families, and hence had no share in the government. These persons were called plebeians. There were no doubt many of these persons under the early kings; but they became more numerous under the later kings. They consisted largely of people of other cities who had been conquered and brought to Rome, and of people who had escaped from other cities and found refuge at Rome. They thus became subjects, but not citizens. They could not hold office, nor vote; nor could they marry into the patrician families; although they were allowed to hold property of their own. But as they became more numerous, and as some of them became wealthy, they desired to be made equal with the patricians.

The New Plebeian Gentes.—It was Tarquinius Priscus, the first Etruscan king, who, it is said, took the first step toward introducing the plebeians into the state. He did this by introducing into each one of the tribes a number of the more wealthy plebeian families, under the name of lesser gentes (*gentes minores*); while the old patrician gentes were called by the more honorable name of greater gentes (*gentes maiores*). In this way the line of separation between the patricians and the plebeians began to be broken down, but it was many years after this time before the two classes became entirely equal.

II. THE REFORMED CONSTITUTION

The New Local Tribes.—More important than the reforms of Tarquinius Priscus were the reforms which are said to have been made by Servius Tullius. The previous changes had affected only a small part of the plebeian class; the great body of the plebeians remained just where they were before. Now Servius saw that Rome would be stronger and more able to compete with her enemies if the plebeians were called upon to serve in the army and pay taxes, just like the patricians. He therefore made a new division of the people, based not upon their birth and descent, like the old division into tribes, but upon their domicile, that is, the place where they lived. He divided the whole Roman territory, city and country, into local districts, like wards and townships. There were four of these in the city, and sixteen in the country, the former being called "city tribes" (*tribus urbanae*), and the latter "rural tribes" (*tribus rusticae*). All persons, whether patricians or plebeians, who had settled homes (*assidui*), were enrolled in their proper tribes and were made subject to military service and the tribal tax (*tributum*).

The New Classes and Centuries.—The next step which Servius took was to reorganize the Roman army, so that it should include all persons who resided in the Roman territory and were enrolled in the new local tribes. First came the cavalry (*equites*), made up of young wealthy citizens, and arranged in eighteen centuries, or companies. Next came the infantry (*pedites*), which comprised all the rest of the men capable of bearing arms. In ancient times every man was obliged to furnish his own weapons. Now as all the people could not afford to obtain the heavier armor, they were subdivided into "classes" according to their wealth, and according to the armor it was supposed they could afford to furnish. The first class consisted of eighty centuries, and was made up of the wealthiest men, who could afford a full armor—a brass shield carried on the left arm, greaves which covered the legs, a cuirass to protect the breast, and a helmet for the head, together with a sword and a spear. The second class had in place of the brass shield a wooden shield, covered with leather.

The third class omitted the greaves, and the fourth class omitted also the cuirass and the helmet, carrying only the wooden shield, spear, and sword. The fifth class was made up of the poorest citizens, who fought only with darts and slings. Each of these classes, except the first, was arranged in twenty centuries, or companies. One half of the centuries in each class were composed of the younger men (*iuniores*), who might be called out at any time. The other half were composed of the older men (*seniores*), who were called out only in times of great danger. Besides, there were fifteen centuries of musicians, carpenters, and substitutes, We may perhaps get a clearer idea of this new military arrangement by the following table:—

I.	Cavalry (*Equites*)	18 centuries.
II.	Infantry (*Pedites*)	
	1st class (40 *iuniores*, 40 *seniores*)	80 centuries.
	2d class (10 *iuniores*, 10 *seniores*)	20 centuries.
	3d class (10 *iuniores*, 10 *seniores*)	20 centuries.
	4th class (10 *iuniores*, 10 *seniores*)	20 centuries.
	5th class (10 *iuniores*, 10 *seniores*)	20 centuries.
	Musicians, Carpenters, Substitutes	15 centuries.
	Total	193 centuries.

The New Assembly, Comitia Centuriata.—This arrangement of the people was first intended for a military purpose; but it soon came to have a political character also. There was every reason why the important questions relating to war, which had heretofore been left to the old body of armed citizens, should now be left to the new body of armed citizens. As a matter of fact, the new fighting body became a new voting body; and there thus arose a new assembly, called the assembly of the centuries (*comitia centuriata*). But this new assembly did not lose its original military character. For example, it was called together, not by the voice of the lictor, like the old assembly, but by the sound of the trumpet. Again, it did not meet in the Forum, where the old assembly met, but in the Field of Mars (*Campus Martius*), outside of the city. It also voted by centuries, that is, by military companies. After a time the *comitia centuriata* acquired the character of a real political and legislative body, of greater importance than the old *comitia curiata*.

III. THE SUPREMACY OF ROME IN LATIUM

Conquests in Latium.—While Rome was thus becoming strong, and her people were becoming more united and better organized, she was also gaining power over the neighboring lands. The people with whom she first came into contact were the Latins. A number of Latin towns were conquered and brought under her power, and were made a part of the Roman domain (*ager Romanus*). She also pushed her conquests across the Anio into the Sabine country, and across the Tiber into Etruria. So that before the fall of the kingdom, Rome had begun to be a conquering power. But her conquests at present were limited, for the most part, to Latium, and it was from this conquered land in Latium that she had created the rural tribes already mentioned.

Rome and the Latin League.—Outside of this conquered territory were the independent Latin cities, united together into a strong confederacy. When Alba Longa was conquered, Rome succeeded to the headship of this confederacy of thirty cities. The people of these cities were not made Roman citizens; but they were given the right to trade and to intermarry with Romans. The Latin league was bound to Rome by a treaty, which made it partly subject to her; because it could not wage war without her consent, and it must assist her in her wars.

Review of the Roman Kingdom.—In the various ways which we have described, Rome had come to be a strong city, and was growing into something like a new nation, with a kind of national policy. If we should sum up this policy in two words, these words would be *expansion* and *incorporation*. By "expansion" we mean the extension of Roman power over the neighboring territory, whether by conquest or by alliance. By "incorporation" we mean the taking of subject people into the political body. For example, Rome had first incorporated the Sabine settlement on the Quirinal; then the Latin settlement on the Caelian; and finally the plebeian class, which had grown up by the side of the patrician class. By pursuing this kind of policy, Rome had come to be, at the end of the kingdom, a compact and quite well-organized city-state with a considerable territory of her own (*ager Romanus*) about the Tiber, and having a control over the cities of Latium.

SELECTIONS FOR READING

Ihne, Early Rome, Ch. 9, "People of the Regal Period" (5).[1]
Shuckburgh, Ch. 5, "The Regal Period" (1).

Granrud, pp. 19-26, "The Later Royal Constitution" (13).

How and Leigh, Ch. 4, "The Regal Period" (1).

Mommsen, abridged, Ch. 4, "Reforms of Servius Tullius—Supremacy of Rome in Latium" (2).

SPECIAL STUDY

THE SERVIAN CLASSES AND CENTURIES.—'Pelham, pp. 36-39 (1); Leighton, pp. 22-24 (1); Mommsen, Vol. I., pp. 132-141 (2); Ramsay and Lanciani, p. 96 *et seq.* (8); Niebuhr, Hist., Vol. I., pp. 212-236; Taylor, pp. 25-36 (1).

[1] The figure in parenthesis refers to the number of the topic in the Appendix, where a fuller title of the book will be found.

CHAPTER VI

THE STRUGGLE AGAINST THE KINGSHIP

The Expulsion of the Kings, I.—The New Republican Government, II.

I. THE EXPULSION OF THE KINGS

The Transition to the Republic.—We have seen how Rome came into existence, and how it gradually grew in extent and power under the regal government. We are now to consider how the Roman kingdom was changed into a republic; and to look at the different struggles by which this change was brought about. The change from the Roman kingdom to the republic was due to the tyranny of the last Tarquin; so that the first struggle for Roman liberty was a struggle against the kingship. When the rule of Tarquinius Superbus became intolerable, he was expelled from Rome, with his whole family (B.C. 510). But with the aid of the Etruscans and Latins he tried to regain his lost power; and the first days of the republic were, therefore, days full of strife and trouble. The stories of this period tell us of many deeds of Roman virtue and patriotism. In them we see the heroic efforts made by a liberty-loving people to rid themselves of a despotic king, and to form a freer government.

The Story of Brutus and Collatinus.—The legends first tell how the king was driven from Home. This was brought about by the efforts of two patriotic men, Brutus and Collatinus, who determined to avenge the dishonorable deeds of Tarquinius Superbus and his family. These patriots aroused the Roman people, and led them to pass a law to banish Tarquin and his corrupt household. The gates of the city were ordered to be closed against him. The soldiers saluted Brutus as the deliverer of their country. The people declared that the kingship should be abolished forever; and they elected Brutus and Collatinus to rule over them for a year.

The Conspiracy of Brutus's Sons.—The banished king then sent messengers to Rome to ask that his property be restored to him. While engaged on this mission, the messengers formed a plot to bring back the king to his throne; and the two sons of Brutus joined in the treacherous scheme. But a slave who happened to hear the plan of the conspirators exposed the whole affair. When Brutus found that his own sons were engaged in this act of treason, he did not allow his feelings as a father to prevent him from doing his duty as a patriot—but condemned them to death as traitors to their country.

The Attempts of the Etruscans to restore Tarquinius.—When the plot at Rome failed, Tarquinius appealed for help to the Etruscan cities of Veii and Tarquinii, which raised an army to assist him. In a fierce battle which followed, Brutus was slain by the king's son. The battle, which had been long in doubt, was decided by the god Sylvanus, whose voice was heard in the forest proclaiming that the Romans had won. Tarquinius next appealed to Lars Porsenna, king of Clusium, and the most powerful prince of Etruria. Collecting his army, Porsenna suddenly seized the Janiculum, the hill just across the Tiber, and Rome was saved only by the heroism of Horatius Cocles, who, with two companions, withstood the whole Etruscan army while the wooden bridge was destroyed. Porsenna was thus prevented from entering the city. After ravaging the surrounding country he soon made peace with the Romans and gave no further aid to the Tarquins.

The Attempt of the Latins.—The Tarquins then turned for aid to the Latins. The thirty Latin cities revolted and joined the cause of the banished king. The danger was so great that the Romans appointed a dictator to lead their armies into the field. Then was fought the noted battle of Lake Regillus, which, according to the old story, was decided by the aid of two gigantic youths, who rode upon snow-white horses in the Roman ranks, and whom the Romans recognized as the twin gods Castor and Pollux. A temple to these gods was built in the Forum in memory of this deliverance.

Significance of the Legends.—While we cannot believe everything contained in these romantic stories, we can yet see in them the record of a great historical event. We can see that the government of the kings was overthrown. We can also see that this change was not a peaceful change, but was attended by a severe struggle. We can see, finally, that the Romans honored the heroic virtues of courage and patriotism; and that they believed their destiny was in the hands of the gods.

II. THE NEW REPUBLICAN GOVERNMENT

The Two Consuls.—When the kingdom came to an end, the power of the kings was put into the hands of two consuls (at first called praetors), elected by the people. The consular power, though derived from the old kingly power, was yet different from it in many respects. In the first place, the power of the king had been a lifelong power; but the power of the consuls was limited to one year. Again, the royal power had been held by one person; but the consular power was held by two persons, so that each was a restraint upon the other. Moreover, the power of the king had been absolute, that is, it had extended to life and death over all citizens at all times; the power of the consuls, on the other hand, was limited, since they could not exercise the power of life and death, except outside of the city and over the army in the field. The consuls retained the old insignia of the king; but when in the city, the ax was withdrawn from the *fasces*. In this way the chief authority, which was placed in the hands of the consuls, was shorn of its worst features. It must also be noted that the priestly power of the king was not given to the consuls, but to a special officer, called king of the sacrifices (*rex sacrorum*); and the management of the finances was put in charge of two *quaestors* elected by the people.

The Dictatorship.—The Romans were wise enough to see that in times of great danger the power of the consuls might not be strong enough to protect the state. To meet such an emergency a dictator was appointed, who was a sort of temporary king. He had entire control of the city and the army. He was even given the power of life and death over citizens; and his lictors retained the ax in the *fasces*. But this extraordinary power could be held for only six months, after which time the consuls resumed their regular authority as chief magistrates. With the dictator there was generally appointed another officer, who was second in authority, called the master of horse; but over him, as over everyone else, the dictator was supreme.

The New Senators.—When the consuls were elected, it is said that one of their first acts was to fill up the senate to the number of three hundred members. The last king had practically ruled without the senate, and he had no reason to fill the vacancies when they occurred. But the new consuls wished the help of the senate, and therefore desired to keep its numbers complete. The new senators who were enrolled were called *conscripti*; and the whole body of senators became known as *patres conscripti*.

The Popular Assemblies.—With the establishment of the republic, the two assemblies with which we are already acquainted, the *comitia curiata* and the *comitia centuriata*, both remained. But the former lost a great deal of its old power, which became transferred to the latter. The assembly of the centuries was therefore the body in which the people generally expressed their will. Here they elected the officers, and passed the most important laws. It was this assembly which became the chief legislative body during the early republic.

The Laws of Valerius Poplicola.—It is said that after the death of Brutus, his colleague Valerius (who had succeeded Collatinus) did not call an assembly to elect another consul. This aroused the fear that Valerius wished to make himself king. But it was soon found that instead of aiming to be king, he was preparing a set of laws which would prevent any one from becoming king, and would also protect the people from the arbitrary power of their magistrates. One of these laws declared that any person who assumed the chief power without the people's consent should be condemned as a traitor. Another law granted to every citizen the right of an appeal to the people, in case he was condemned for a crime. These laws, known as the Valerian laws, may be called the "first charter of Roman liberty," because they protected the people from the exercise of arbitrary power. So highly honored was Valerius that he was surnamed Poplicola, or the People's Friend.

The Loss of Roman Territory.—We remember how extensive were the lands which were acquired by the Romans under the kings. But they had lost many of these lands during the struggles against the last Tarquin. They had lost their conquests in Etruria, and much of their land in Latium; and the thirty Latin cities had reasserted their independence. So that the authority of the new government was now reduced to a comparatively small strip of territory south of the Tiber, together with the Janiculum on the Etruscan side.

SELECTIONS FOR READING

Arnold, Hist., Ch. 7, "Banishing of King Tarquinius" (2).[1]

Shuckburgh, Ch. 6, "Expulsion of the Kings" (1).

Pelham, pp. 45-51, "Foundation of the Republic" (1).

Liddell, Ch. 6, "Decline of Roman Power" (1).

Mommsen, abridged, Ch. 6, "Change of the Constitution" (2).

Taylor, Ch. 2, "Foundation of the Republic" (1).

Plutarch, "Poplicola" (11).

Livy, Bk. II., Chs. 9-14, Wars of Lars Porsenna (4).

SPECIAL STUDY

THE OFFICE OF CONSUL.—Gow, p. 174 (8); How and Leigh, pp. 47-50 (1); Shuckburgh, pp. 203-205 (1); Ihne, Early Rome, pp. 117-122 (5); Mommsen, Vol. I., pp. 323-329 (2); Ramsay and Lanciani, pp. 166-174 (8); Harper's Dict. Antiqq., "Consules" (8).

[1] The figure in parenthesis refers to the number of the topic in the Appendix, where a fuller title of the book will be found.

CHAPTER VII

THE STRUGGLE FOR ECONOMIC RIGHTS

The Grievances of the Plebs, I.—The First Secession and Its Results, II.—Wars with the Volscians, Aequians, and Etruscans, III.

I. THE GRIEVANCES OF THE PLEBS

The Power of the Patricians.—The patricians and plebeians had united in their efforts to drive out the kings; but when the struggle against the kingship was ended, the chief fruits of the victory fell to the patricians. The plebeians could, it is true, still vote in the *comitia centuriata*; but they could not hold any of the new offices, nor could they sit in the senate. Rome became a republic, but it was an aristocratic, and not a democratic republic; that is, the chief power rested not in the whole people, but in a particular class. The plebeians might perhaps have submitted to the government of the patricians, if it had not been exercised in a selfish and oppressive manner. But the patrician rule proved to be as despotic as that of the kings; and a long and fierce struggle ensued between the two orders. As the patricians were generally more wealthy than the plebeians, the conflict became at first a struggle between the rich and the poor, a contest for a more equal distribution of wealth.

Poverty and Distress of the Plebeians.—The late wars had left the plebeians in a very dependent and deplorable condition. The wealthy patricians, for the most part, lived in the city; and their property was protected by the city walls. But the homes of the plebeians were generally in the country. Accordingly, when they were serving in the army, their little farms were neglected, or ravaged by the enemy, their families were driven away, and their property was destroyed. In this way, while serving their country, they were deprived of their houses and fields, and of the means of subsistence, and so were reduced to a condition of poverty and great distress.

The Unjust Law of Debt.—The sorest burden which now rested upon the plebeians was the harsh law of debt. Having lost their property by the misfortunes of war, they were obliged to borrow money of the rich patricians; and they were thus reduced to the condition of a debtor class. But a debtor in the early days of Rome was especially wretched. If he could not pay his debt, he was liable to be arrested, thrown into a dungeon, and made the slave of his creditor. His lot was chains, stripes, and slavery.

The law of debt was not only harsh in itself, but its effect was to keep the poor in a continual state of poverty, from which they could not easily escape.

The Unequal Division of the Public Land.—Another cause which kept the

39

plebeians in a state of poverty was the unjust distribution of the public land (*ager publicus*) which had been acquired in war. This land properly belonged to all the people, and might have been used to relieve the distress of the poor. But the government was in the hands of the patricians, and they disposed of this land for their own benefit; they allowed it to be "occupied," at a nominal rent, by members of their own order. As long as the land remained public, it could not be sold by the occupants; but the longer the rich patricians retained the occupation of this land, the more they would look upon it as their own property, and ignore the fact that it belonged to the whole Roman people. So that the common people were deprived of their just share of the land which they had helped to conquer.

II. THE FIRST SECESSION AND ITS RESULTS

First Secession of the Plebeians.—It was the hard law of debt which first drove the plebeians to revolt. As there was no legal way to redress their wrongs, they decided that they would no longer serve in the army, but leave the patricians to fight their own battles. They therefore deserted their general, marched in full array to a hill beyond the Anio, which they called the Sacred Mount (*Mons Sacer*), and proposed to form an independent city (B.C. 494). The patricians saw that the loss of the plebeian army would be the destruction of Rome. They were therefore compelled to make a solemn compact to the effect that the debts of all persons who were insolvent should be canceled; and that those who had been imprisoned on account of debt should be released.

The Tribunes of the People.—But the most important result of the first secession was the creation of a new office, that of tribune of the people. In order to protect the plebeians from any further oppressive acts on the part of the patrician magistrate, it was agreed to appoint two tribunes from among the plebeians themselves. These new officers were given the power to "veto"—that is, to forbid—the act of any magistrate which bore unjustly upon any citizen. In order that the tribunes might exercise their authority without hindrance, their persons were made "inviolable,"—which means that they could not be arrested, and that anyone who interfered with them in the exercise of their lawful duty could be put to death. The tribunes were assisted by two *aediles*, who were also chosen from the plebeian body.

The Plebeian Assembly.—The meetings which the plebeians had occasionally held before this time now assumed the character of a permanent assembly (*concilium plebis*). This assembly could be called together by the tribunes, who were permitted to address the people in regard to their interests; and no magistrate was allowed to interrupt them while speaking or to disperse this assembly (*lex Icilia*, B.C. 492). The assembly could also pass resolutions (*plebiscita*), which were binding upon the plebeians, but not as yet upon the whole people. It was not many years before the plebeian assembly was given the right to elect their own tribunes and aediles (*lex Publilia*, B.C. 472). In this way the plebeians acquired a position in the state which they had never before held.

The Agrarian Law of Spurius Cassius.—The second great cause of complaint was, as we have seen, the unjust distribution of the public land. To remove this injustice was the effort of the consul Spurius Cassius. This man was both a patriot and a statesman. He loved the people, and he labored to protect their interests. In order to strengthen Rome against her foreign enemies, he first of all made a new treaty with the Latin towns, and also a treaty with the neighboring tribe of the Hernicans.

But the most famous act of Sp. Cassius was the proposal of the first "agrarian law," that is, a law intended to reform the division of the public land (B.C. 486). It was not his purpose to take away any private land which legally belonged to the patricians; but to make a more just distribution of the land which properly belonged to the whole state. When this law was brought forward, the patricians used their influence to prevent its passage. After his year of office had expired, Sp. Cassius was charged with treason and with the attempt to make himself king. He was tried, condemned, scourged, and beheaded; and thus one of Rome's greatest patriots suffered the doom of a traitor. But the people remembered Sp. Cassius, and his name was inscribed upon a tablet and placed in the Forum, where it remained for many generations.

III. WARS WITH THE VOLSCIANS, AEQUIANS, AND ETRUSCANS

The Foreign Enemies of Rome.—While these struggles were going on to relieve the distress of the poor plebeians, the frontiers were continually threatened by foreign enemies. The chief enemies of Rome at this time were the Volscians, the Aequians, and the Etruscans. The Volscians occupied the southern plains of Latium, near the seacoast. The Aequians held the slopes of the Apennines on the northeast. The Etruscans held all their original territory on the right bank of the Tiber, except the hill Janiculum. On every side Rome was beset by foes; and for many years her armies fought in defense of their homes, and almost within sight of the city. By the treaties which Sp. Cassius had formed, the Romans, the Latins, and the Hernicans made common cause in repelling these attacks. There is no continuous history of these frequent wars, but the Roman historians have preserved the memory of them in certain legends, which were sacred to the Romans themselves, and which we should not forget if we would understand the character and spirit of the Roman people.

Coriolanus and the Volscians.—The Volscian wars have left us the story of

Coriolanus, which tells us that this young patrician opposed the distribution of grain among the plebeians; that he was threatened by the common people and fled to the Volscians, and led an army against his native city; that his mother and his wife went to the Volscian camp and pleaded with him to cease his wars upon Rome; that Rome was thus saved, and a temple was built to commemorate the patriotism of the Roman women.

Cincinnatus and the Aequians.—The memory of the Aequian wars is preserved in the story of the Roman patriot Cincinnatus, who was called from his country home to rescue the Roman army, which was surrounded by the Aequians, and threatened with destruction in a narrow defile in Mt. Algidus, near the Alban hills (see map, page 46); and who with great speed and skill defeated the Aequian army, compelling it to "pass under the yoke" as a sign of submission, and then returned the next evening to Rome in triumph. The "yoke" consisted of a spear supported in a horizontal position by two spears fixed upright in the ground.

The Fabii and the Etruscans.—With the Etruscan wars is linked the story of the Fabian gens, which was one of the greatest patrician houses of Rome; and which, having volunteered to carry on the war against the Etruscans at its own expense, was, with the exception of one person, utterly destroyed by the enemy. The Fabian gens was therefore honored for having sacrificed itself in the defense of Rome.

These stories should be read, not as an accurate narration of facts, but because they show the kind of virtues that the early Romans most admired.

SELECTIONS FOR READING

How and Leigh, Ch. 6, "First Struggle of the Plebeians" (1).[1]

Shuckburgh, Ch. 8, "Constitutional History from B.C. 509 to 390" (1).

Mommsen, abridged, pp. 50-58, "Tribunate of the Plebs" (2).

Ihne, Early Rome, Ch. 13, "Tribunes of the People" (5).

Arnold, Hist., Ch. 9, "Spurius Cassius" (2).

Plutarch, "Coriolanus" (11).

Livy, Bk. II., Chs. 27-33, First Secession of the Plebs (4).

SPECIAL STUDY

THE PUBLIC LAND, *ager publicus*.—Leighton, pp. 60-62 (1); Liddell, p.96 (1); How and Leigh, pp. 56-58 (1); Merivale, Gen. Hist., pp. 70-72 (1); Ihne, Early Rome, Ch. 14 (5); Ihne, Hist., Vol. I., Bk. 2, Ch. 7 (2); Mommsen, Vol. I., pp. 347-350 (2); Harper's Dict. Antiqq., "Agrariae Leges" (8); Niebuhr, Hist., Vol. II., p. 65 *et seq.* (2).

[1] The figure in parenthesis refers to the number of the topic in the Appendix, where a fuller title of the book will be found.

CHAPTER VIII

THE STRUGGLE FOR EQUAL LAWS

The Demand for Written Laws, I.—Decemvirs and the XII. Tables, II.—Second Secession and Its Results, III.

I. THE DEMAND FOR WRITTEN LAWS

Proposals of Terentilius Harsa (B.C. 462).—The conflict between the two orders had been going on for nearly fifty years; and yet no real solution had been found for their difficulties. The plebeians were at a great disadvantage during all this time, because the law was administered solely by the patricians, who kept the knowledge of it to themselves, and who regarded it as a precious legacy from their ancestors, too sacred to be shared with the lowborn plebeians. The laws had never been written down or published. The patricians could therefore administer them as they saw fit. This was a great injustice to the lower classes. It was clear that there was not much hope for the plebeians until they were made equal before the law. It was also clear that they could not be equal before the law as long as they themselves had no knowledge of what the law was. Accordingly one of the tribunes, Gaius Terentilius Harsa, proposed that a commission be appointed to gather up the law, and to publish it to the whole people. This proposal, though both fair and just, was bitterly opposed by the patricians, and was followed by ten years of strife and dissension.

Concessions to the Plebeians.—To rescue the city from these troubles, the senate tried to conciliate the plebeians by making certain concessions to them. For example, the number of tribunes was increased from two to five, and then to ten. This was supposed to give them greater protection than they had had before. Then it was decided to give up to them the public land on the Aventine hill, and thus to atone for not carrying out the agrarian law of Sp. Cassius. Finally, the amount of fine which any magistrate could impose was limited to two sheep and thirty oxen. It was thought that such concessions would appease the discontented people and divert their minds from the main point of the controversy.

Compromise between the Orders.—But these concessions did not satisfy the plebeians, who still clung to their demand for equal rights before the law. The struggle over the proposal of Terentilius, which lasted for nearly ten years, was ended only by a compromise. It was finally agreed that a commission of ten men, called decemvirs, should be appointed to draw up the law, and that this law should be published and be binding upon patricians and plebeians alike. It was also agreed that the commissioners should all be patricians; and that they should have entire control of the government while compiling the laws. The patricians were thus to give up their consuls and quaestors; and the plebeians were to give up their tribunes and aediles. Both parties were to cease their quarreling, and await the work of the decemvirs.

II. DECEMVIRS AND THE XII. TABLES

The Commission to Greece.—It is said that a commission of three men was sent to Greece, to consult the laws of Solon and other Greek codes. However true this story may be, it is not likely that the Romans intended to borrow the laws of another country by which to govern their own. The complaint of the plebeians was not that they did not have any laws, but that the laws which they had were unwritten and known only to the patricians. What they wanted was that the unwritten laws should be published; so that they could know what they were, and whether they were properly administered or not.

Formation of the XII. Tables (B.C. 450).—The first body of commissioners, or the First Decemvirate, entered upon the work assigned to it, gathered together the law which had hitherto been kept secret, and inscribed it on ten tables of brass. These tables were erected in the Forum, where they could be seen by everyone, and were declared binding on all the people. At the close of the year, a Second Decemvirate was appointed to complete the code, and two more tables were added. This whole body of law was called the Twelve Tables, and formed the basis of the most remarkable system of law that the world has ever seen. There was nothing strange, however, in the XII. Tables themselves. They contained nothing especially new. The old law of debt remained as it was, and the distinction between patricians and plebeians was not destroyed. The XII. Tables were important, because they put the law before the eyes of the people; and plebeians, as well as patricians, could know what were their rights. So highly valued was this code that it formed a part of Roman education, and the boys in school were obliged to commit it to memory.

Tyranny of the Second Decemvirate.—Although the second body of decemvirs had the honor of completing the XII. Tables, the way in which they exercised their power brought them into dishonor. With all their professed love of equal laws, they still hated the plebeians and used their authority in an oppressive manner. They appeared in the Forum each with twelve lictors, carrying the axes in the *fasces* as a sign that they claimed the power of life and death over every citizen. At the close of their year of office, they refused to resign, and continued their oppressive rule under the leadership of Appius Claudius. The story goes—whether true or not—that Appius Claudius attempted to gain possession of Virginia, who was the beautiful daughter of a plebeian soldier, and who was killed by her own father to save her from dishonor.

The repeated acts of tyranny committed by the second body of decemvirs at last made their rule intolerable.

III. SECOND SECESSION AND ITS RESULTS

Second Secession of the Plebs.—The tragic death of Virginia, it is said, aroused the people to vengeance. With his bloody knife in hand, Virginius rushed to the camp outside of the city and called upon the soldiers to resist the infamous power of the decemvirs. With the memory of the Sacred Mount still in mind, the army once more seceded from the city, and, followed by a multitude of citizens, took up their station again on this hill, determined no longer to fight in defense of tyranny. The Roman state seemed again on the point of ruin, and the decemvirs were forced to resign. The old government was restored. Two new consuls were elected, both of whom were friendly to the plebeians. These were Valerius and Horatius, names which the Roman people ever delighted to honor.

The Valerio-Horatian Laws (B.C. 448).—The second secession of the plebeians resulted in the overthrow of the decemvirate and the restoration of the consulship; but it also resulted in making the plebeians more respected than they had been before. The patricians were becoming more and more convinced that the plebeians were not only brave in fighting the enemies of Rome, but were also determined to defend their own liberties. The new consuls, Valerius and Horatius, came forward as their champions. Two of the rights of the people had been continually disregarded, namely, the right of appeal to the people, and the right of the tribunes to be sacredly protected in the exercise of their duties. These two rights were now solemnly reaffirmed. But what was quite as important, the assembly of the plebeians (*concilium plebis*) was now given power to make laws binding upon the whole people. It is supposed that this assembly had by this time been reorganized and based upon the tribal districts so as to include the patricians as well as the plebeians. This newly organized assembly came to be known as the *comitia tributa*, and we shall see it grow in influence and dignity, until it becomes the most important assembly of the republic. These laws of Valerius and Horatius we may call the "second charter of Roman liberty."

The Right of Intermarriage.—The patricians and plebeians had long lived side by side; but they had been kept socially distinct because it was not legal for them to intermarry. This prejudice was now passing away, as the plebeians were showing a spirit worthy of the patricians themselves. A great step toward equalizing the classes was now taken by the passage of a law (*lex Canuleia*, B.C. 445) which granted the right of intermarriage between the two orders. This insured their social and civil equality, and paved the way for their political equality, and finally their union into a harmonious people.

SELECTIONS FOR READING

Arnold, Hist., Ch. 13, "The Terentilian Law" (2).[1]

Ihne, Early Rome, Ch. 18, "Decemvirs and the XII. Tables" (5).

Mommsen, abridged, pp. 58-61, "The Decemvirate" (2).

Merivale, Gen. Hist., Ch. 8, "Efforts to obtain Equal Laws" (1).

Livy, Bk. III., Chs. 36-38, Tyranny of the Second Decemvirate (4).

SPECIAL STUDY

THE TWELVE TABLES.—How and Leigh, p. 70 (1); Shuckburgh, pp. 101-104 (1); Mommsen, Vol. I., pp. 363-368 (2); Liddell, Ch. 11 (1); Harper's Dict. Antiqq., "Twelve Tables" (8); Morey, Roman Law, pp. 25-43 (15).

[1] The figure in parenthesis refers to the number of the topic in the Appendix, where a fuller title of the book will be found.

CHAPTER IX

THE STRUGGLE FOR POLITICAL EQUALITY

The Contest for the Consulship, I.—Wars with Veii and the Gauls, II.—The Equalization of the Orders, III.

I. THE CONTEST FOR THE CONSULSHIP

Successes of the Plebeians.—Never before had the cause of the plebeians seemed so hopeful as it did at this time. The tyranny of the decemvirs had brought to their aid the better class of patricians. And the passage of the recent laws led them to look forward to still greater victories. They had already gained great successes, but there was still something else for them to obtain, in order to have full equality in the state. We may, perhaps, better understand just what the plebeians had gained, and what was still to be gained, if we look at the following table, which contains a list of the various rights possessed by a full Roman citizen:

The plebeians already possessed the lowest right, the *commercium*; they could hold property and carry on trade just like any other Roman citizens. They had just now obtained the *conubium*, or the right of contracting a legal marriage with a patrician. They had also the *suffragium*, or the right of voting, in the assemblies of the centuries and of the tribes. As regards the *honores*, or the right of holding office, they could be elected to the lower offices, that is, could be chosen tribunes of the people and aediles; but could not be elected to the higher offices, that is, could not be chosen consuls and quaestors. What the plebeians now wanted was a share in the higher offices, especially in the consulship.

The Military Tribunes, with Consular Power (B.C. 444).—Instead of allowing the plebeians a direct share in the consulship, the patricians agreed to the appointment of certain new officers, something like the consuls, who could be elected from either the patricians or the plebeians. These new officers were called "military tribunes with consular power," and were to be elected in the *comitia centuriata*, where the plebeians as well as the patricians were allowed to vote. But it was also provided that consuls might still be elected instead of the new military tribunes, if the senate thought such a course was best for the state. We can easily see how this plan would work. The patricians, who had control of the senate, could decide at any time that consuls were needed; or else they might control the election and choose the military tribunes from their own number. As a matter of fact, the senate, for some years after this, decided that consuls should be elected. But later the election of military tribunes became the rule, and the plebeians gradually grew in political influence and power.

The Censorship and the New Quaestors.—As the patricians saw that the plebeians were growing stronger, they resorted to a new plan to keep as much power as possible in their own hands. To do this, they created another new office, the censorship (B.C. 443), and transferred to the two censors some of the most important powers hitherto exercised by the consuls. The censors were to draw up the census, that is, to make an estimate of every man's property, to assign each man to a proper class in the centuries, whether he belonged to the *equites* or the *pedites*, and to designate who was entitled to sit in the senate. The new censors were to be elected every five years, from the patrician class. But to offset this advantage, the patricians agreed that there should be two new quaestors (B.C. 421), to be elected from the plebeians. So it was that the period following the decemvirate was a period full of adroit schemes and compromises; but the plebeians were steadily gaining new rights and privileges.

The Fate of Spurius Maelius.—That the patricians were not entirely reconciled to the growing influence of the plebeians, is shown by the story told of Sp. Maelius. While a severe famine was raging in Rome, and many poor citizens sought relief in suicide, Sp. Maelius, a wealthy plebeian, purchased grain at his own expense and distributed it to the suffering poor. His generosity so won the hearts of the people, that the patricians felt alarmed at his popularity, and charged him with the design of making himself king. It was claimed that secret meetings were held at his house, and that the republic was in danger. Hence a dictator was demanded. The aged Cincinnatus, who had rescued the beleaguered army at Mt. Algidus, was selected; and Servilius Ahala was appointed his second in command, or master of horse. Maelius was then summoned to appear before the dictator, to answer the charge of treason. But foreseeing his danger, he implored the protection of the people; whereupon Servilius Ahala drew a dagger and stabbed him to the heart. The fate of Maelius at first terrified the people, but they were Soon excited to vengeance, and Servilius was driven into exile. The name of Sp. Maelius was thus associated with that of Sp. Cassius, the author of the first agrarian law. These men were accused of aiming to be king; and both suffered death as the reward of their generous deeds.

II. WARS WITH VEII AND THE GAULS

Recovery of Roman Territory.—The reforms which had been carried on since the fall of the decemvirs gave fresh hope to the plebeians, and inspired the whole Roman people with new life and vigor. The armies in the field also began to be successful, and Rome recovered much of her lost ground in Latium. The triple league formed by Spurius Cassius between the Romans, Latins, and Hernicans, had resulted in checking the Volscians and Aequians. The Romans now felt encouraged to attack the Etruscans in the hope of recovering the territory which they had lost years before, when the Tarquins were expelled. Fidenae, the Etruscan city a few miles north of Rome, was captured, and the way was opened to attack Veii, the strongest city of Etruria.

Siege and Capture of Veii (B.C. 405-396).—The people of Veii were not disposed to meet the Romans in the open field, but retreated within their walls. It therefore became necessary to lay siege to the city. The great Etruscan walls were too strong to be taken by assault; and the Roman armies stationed themselves around the city for the purpose of starving the people into submission. The Roman soldiers were not permitted to return home and cultivate their farms, as they were wont to do; and so, for the first time, they were given regular pay for their services. For ten years the siege continued, when it was brought to a close by Camillus, who was appointed dictator. Veii was deprived of its inhabitants, and its walls inclosed a vacant city. The capture of Veii was the greatest victory which the Romans had yet achieved, and Camillus was given a splendid triumph, when he returned to Rome. The lands of southern Etruria also fell into the hands of the Romans; and four new rural tribes were added to the Roman domain.

Destruction of Rome by the Gauls (B.C. 390).—If the capture of Veii was the greatest victory which the Romans had ever achieved, we now approach one of the greatest disasters which they ever suffered. One reason why Rome was able to capture Veii was the fact that the great body of the Etruscans were obliged to face a new enemy on the northern frontier, an enemy whom they feared more than the Romans on the south. This enemy was the Gauls, the barbarous nation which held the valley of the Po, and which now swept south across the Apennines like a hurricane. News of this invasion reached Rome, and it was resolved to aid the Etruscans in repelling the common foe. The Roman army met the Gauls near the little river Allia, about eleven miles north of Rome, and suffered a terrible defeat. The Gauls pressed on to Rome. They entered, plundered, and burned the city. Only the Capitol remained. This was besieged for seven months, and, according to the legend, was at one time saved by M. Manlius, who was aroused by the cackling of the sacred geese just in time to resist a night assault. At last the Gauls, sated with plunder, and induced by a large bribe, retreated unmolested or, as one legend says, were driven from the city by Camillus, the hero of the Veientine war. The destruction of Rome by the Gauls was a great disaster, not only to Rome, but to all the world; because in it the records of the ancient city perished, leaving many things in the early history of ancient Rome dark and obscure.

The Restoration of Rome.—Such a disastrous event as the Gallic invasion would have disheartened almost any other people; but Rome bent before the storm and soon recovered after the tempest was past. Many of the people desired to abandon the city of ashes, and transfer their homes to the vacant town of Veii. But it was decided that Rome was the place for Romans. The city rose so quickly from its ruins that little care was taken in the work of rebuilding, so that the new streets were often narrow and irregular.

The Romans seemed to be in haste to resume the work of extending their power, which had been so favorably begun with the conquest of Veii, but which had been interrupted by the defeat on the Allia. Rome raised new armies and quickly defeated her old enemies, the Volscians, Aequians, and Etruscans, who tried to take advantage of her present distress. The hero Camillus added fresh laurels to his fame. The southern part of Etruria was recovered, and its towns garrisoned by military colonies. Many towns of Latium also were brought into subjection, and they afforded homes for the poor people. Rome seemed almost ready to enter upon a career of conquest; but the recurrence of poverty and distress demanded the attention of the government, and showed the need of further reforms.

III. THE EQUALIZATION OF THE ORDERS

Desire for Union.—It became more and more evident that the power of Rome depended upon the union of her people; that harmony, and not discord, was the source of her strength. The two orders had begun to feel that their interests were one and the same. There had been of late little severity in the application of the law of debt; there had been a disposition even to give the plebeians some right in the conquered land; and some progress had been made in opening to them the public offices. But the great loss of property and the devastation resulting from the Gallic invasion were sorely felt by the poorer classes, and led once more to a general state of poverty and distress. The old grievances were revived, and a new set of reformers appeared.

The Attempt of M. Manlius.—The first attempt to relieve the distress of the poor was that of Marcus Manlius, the defender of the Capitol. It is said that he rescued more than four hundred of his fellow-citizens from imprisonment by lending them money without interest. He sold his estates and devoted the proceeds to the relief of debtors. But from being a philanthropist, Manlius soon became a social agitator, and by his harangues sought to inflame the people against the government. The patricians therefore sought to crush him. He was charged with conspiracy against the state, and was finally condemned to death. Although his motives and methods were not above reproach, his admirers placed him by the side of Sp. Cassius and Sp. Maelius as a friend of the people who was unjustly condemned on the charge of aspiring to be king.

The Licinian Laws (B.C. 367).—The continuation of distress among the lower classes showed how useless it was to try to abolish poverty by mere acts of charity, or by exciting the populace. A more thorough mode of reform was adopted under the able leadership of the two tribunes, C. Licinius Stolo and L. Sextius.1 These men were able and broad-minded statesmen. It was not mere relief, but reformation, which they sought.

In the first place, they saw that some relief must be given to the helpless debtor class. But instead of confiscating all debts, they proposed that the interest already paid upon debts should be deducted from the principal; and that for the payment of the rest of the principal three years' time should be allowed.

In the next place, they saw that some definite regulation should be made in the distribution of the public land, which by right belonged to the plebeians as well as to the patricians. They therefore provided that the occupation of the public land should be thrown open equally to all classes; that no person should receive and hold more than five hundred iugera (about three hundred acres); and that the number of slaves employed on estates should be limited, thus giving an opportunity for the poor freemen to earn something for themselves.

Finally, they saw that the plebeians could not receive full justice until they were admitted to the highest offices of the state. They provided that the new "military tribunate" (p. 64) should be done away with, and that consuls should hereafter always be elected, one of whom must be a plebeian.

It was natural that such an important scheme of legislation as this should meet with much opposition, but after a few years of strife, these proposals became laws. This noble body of law may be called the "third charter of Roman liberty."

The Praetor and Curule Aediles.—The patricians were yet loath to lose everything; and so the judicial power was taken away from the consuls and given to a new officer, called the praetor (B.C. 367), who must still be a patrician; also it was provided that there should be two patrician aediles (called curule aediles), to police the city, and to offset the plebeian aediles. Although complete equality was not even yet reached, the struggle was practically ended; and the great Camillus, who had been appointed dictator and had done much to reconcile the people, consecrated a temple to Concord.

Final Equality of the Orders.—After the passage of the Licinian laws, there were a few offices which still remained in the possession of the patricians. These were the dictatorship, the censorship, the praetorship, and the curule aedileship. But it was not many years before these offices also were open to the plebeians,2 and the last barrier between the two orders was thus broken down. There was then no longer any civil or political distinction between the patrician and the plebeian. The old Roman aristocracy, which depended upon family relationship, passed away with the Licinian legislation and the laws which soon followed it. The union of patricians and plebeians into one compact body of citizens was a triumph for Rome greater than the conquest of Veii, or any other foreign victory. By it she conquered herself. She destroyed for a time the elements of discord within her own borders, and prepared herself to become the ruler of the world.

SELECTIONS FOR READING

Pelham, pp. 52-67, "Struggle between the Orders" (1).[3]

Ihne, Early Rome, Ch. 21, "Invasion of the Gauls" (5).

How and Leigh, Ch. 12, "The Licinian Laws" (1).

Abbott, Ch. 4, "The Struggle between the Orders" (13).

Mommsen, Vol. I., Bk. II., Ch. 3, "Equalization of the Orders" (2).

Taylor, Chs. 3-5, "Struggle between the Orders" (1).

Plutarch, "Camillus" (11).

Livy, Bk. V., Chs. 20-22, Capture of Veii (4).

SPECIAL STUDY

TABLE OF THE REPUBLICAN MAGISTRATES, giving their names, when created, mode of election, and powers.—Gow, pp. 172-184 (8); Shuckburgh, Ch. 16 (1); Ramsay and Lanciani, Ch. 5 (8); Eschenburg, pp. 248-252 (8); Harper's Dict. Antiqq., "Consules," "Tribunus," etc. (8).

[1] The abbreviations for the most common Latin proper names are the following: C. for Gaius; Cn. for Gnaeus; L. for Lucius; M. for Marcus; P. for Publius; Q. for Quintus; Sp. for Spurius; T. for Titus.

[2] The distinction between the plebeian and the curule aedileship gradually passed away. The dictatorship was opened to the plebeians in B.C. 356; the censorship by the law of Publilius Philo, in B.C. 351; and the praetorship in B.C. 337. The legislative power of the *comitia tributa* was confirmed by the Hortensian law in B.C. 286.

[3] The figure in parenthesis refers to the number of the topic in the Appendix, where a fuller title of the book will be found.

CHAPTER X

I. BEGINNING OF THE ROMAN CONQUEST

Character of the New Period.—The next period of Roman history is that in which Rome began her great career of conquest, in which she extended her dominion from the banks of the Tiber to the shores of the Italian peninsula. We are now to see how Rome became the great conquering nation of the world. The years which lie before us are therefore years which are filled with the clash of arms and the stories of battles. But they are also years in which Rome learned new lessons of government and law; and in which she came into contact with more civilized peoples, and became herself more civilized.

Roman Territory about the Tiber.—To understand the course of the Roman conquests, we should first keep in mind the extent of her territory at the beginning of this period. Much of the land about the Tiber, which she had lost with the expulsion of the kings, she had gradually recovered. So that now her territory included lands not only in Latium, but also in Etruria toward the north, and in the Volscian country toward the south. The Roman territory at the beginning of this period was not large, but it was compact and well organized into twenty-seven local tribes-twenty-three in the country and four in the city. The most formidable and dangerous neighbors of Rome at this time were the Etruscans on the north and the Samnites on the south.

The First Samnite War in Campania (B.C. 343-341).—In extending their territory, the Romans first came into contact with the Samnites, the most warlike people of central Italy. But the first Samnite war was, as we shall see, scarcely more than a prelude to the great Latin war and the conquest of Latium. The people of Samnium had from their mountain home spread to the southwest into the plains of Campania. They had already taken Capua from the Etruscans, and Cumae from the Greeks. Enamored with the soft climate of the plains and the refined manners of the Greeks, the Samnites in Campania had lost their primitive valor, and had become estranged from the old Samnite stock. In a quarrel which broke out between the old Samnites of the mountains and the Campanians, the latter appealed to Rome for help, and promised to become loyal Roman subjects. Although Rome had previously made a treaty with the Samnites, she did not hesitate to break this treaty, professing that she was under greater obligations to her new subjects than to her old allies. In this way began the first contest between Rome and Samnium for supremacy in central Italy—a contest which took place on the plains of Campania.

Battles of Mt. Gaurus and Suessula.—Very little is known of the details of this war. According to a tradition, which is not very trustworthy, two Roman armies were sent into the field—the one for the protection of Campania, and the other for the invasion of Samnium. The first army, it is said, met the Samnites at Mt. Gaurus, near Cumae, and gained a decisive victory. The Samnites retreated toward the mountains, and rallied at Suessula, where they were again defeated by the two Roman armies, which had united against them. So brilliant was the success of the Romans that the Carthaginians, it is said, sent to them a congratulatory message and a golden crown. Although these stories may not be entirely true, it is quite certain that the Romans obtained control of the northern part of Campania.

Mutiny of the Roman Legions.—This success, however, was marred by a mutiny of the Roman soldiers, who were stationed at Capua for the winter, and who threatened to take possession of the city as a reward for their services. They submitted only on the passage of a solemn law declaring that every soldier should have a just share in the fruits of war, regular pay, and a part of the booty; and that no soldier should be discharged against his will.

Rome withdraws from the War.—The discontent of the soldiers in the field soon spread to the Latin allies. The Latins had assisted the Romans and had taken a prominent part in the war; and while the Roman army was in a state of mutiny, they were the chief defenders of Campania against the Samnites. The Campanians, therefore, began to look to the Latins instead of the Romans, for protection; and they too shared in the general defection against Rome. Under these circumstances, Rome saw the need of subduing her own allies before undertaking a war with a foreign enemy. She therefore made a treaty with the Samnites, withdrew from the war, and prepared for the conquest of Latium.

II. THE GREAT LATIN WAR (B.C. 340-338)

The Demands of the Latins.—The relations between Rome and the Latin cities had been different at different times. In very early times, we remember, Rome was at the head of the Latin confederacy. Later she was united to the Latin league by a treaty of equal alliance, formed by Sp. Cassius. This treaty had been dissolved, and was afterward renewed. But the Latins believed that Rome wished to resume her old position as head of Latium; and this they were not willing to permit. They therefore decided that the time had now come to demand absolute equality with Rome; and if this were refused, to declare their independence. They at first sent an embassy to

Rome, demanding that Romans and Latins should be united in one republic, on terms of perfect equality, and that one consul and half of the senate be chosen from the Latins. This proposal was scornfully rejected. One senator, Manlius, declared that he would stab the first Latin who was admitted to the senate. Meeting with such a rebuff, the Latins renounced their allegiance to the "Roman Jupiter" and commenced their war for independence.

The Parties to the War.—When Rome withdrew from the first Samnite war, and formed a treaty with Samnium, the Latins continued to fight in behalf of the Campanians. The Latins and Campanians, therefore, continued their friendly relations, and became the common enemies of Rome and Samnium. By such a curious turn of fortune, Rome was able to fight her previous allies, the Latins, with the aid of her previous enemy, the Samnites.

Battle of Mt. Vesuvius and the Defeat of the Latins.—As Latium was now a hostile country, the Roman armies, under Manlius Torquatus and Decius Mus, were obliged to march around the northeastern boundaries of Latium, to join the Samnite forces. When they had formed a union in Samnium, they invaded Campania. They soon gained a decisive victory near Mt. Vesuvius. Driven from Campania, the Latins continued the war with resolute courage, but without avail. Tibur, Praeneste, Aricia, Lanuvium, Velitrae, and Antium were conquered in succession; and in the third year the last city, Pedum, also surrendered, and the Latin revolt was at an end. (For these cities see map, p. 46.)

Stories of Manlius and Decius.—There are two famous stories which are told in connection with this war, and which illustrate two traits of the Roman character— stern authority and patriotic devotion. The first story is told of Titus Manlius, the son of the consul commanding the army. The young Manlius, contrary to his father's orders, left the ranks to fight a single combat with one of the enemy's champions. The enemy was slain, and Manlius carried the spoils in triumph to his father. But the father, instead of congratulating his son on his success, condemned him to death for disobedience of orders. From this time the "Manlian orders" became a synonym for the severest discipline. The other story is told of Decius Mus, the consul, who, in response to a miraculous vision, sacrificed his own life that the Roman army might prevail.

III. THE PACIFICATION OF LATIUM

Rome's Policy of Pacification.—The chief result of the great Latin war was the breaking up of the Latin confederacy, and the adoption of a more efficient method of governing the Latin towns. The repeated revolts of the Latins had shown the danger of dealing with a number of towns united in a league, or confederacy. The only safety seemed to lie in destroying the league and dealing with each city by itself. This was the Roman policy of *isolation*. It was also evident that all the cities were not equally fit to exercise the right of Roman citizenship; and upon this was based the distinction between perfect and imperfect citizenship. The subject towns of Latium and those of Campania were thus treated in various ways.

Towns fully Incorporated.—In the first place, many of the towns of Latium were fully adopted into the Roman state. Their inhabitants became full Roman citizens, with all the private and public rights, comprising the right to trade and intermarry with Romans, the right to vote in the assemblies at Rome, and the right to hold any public office. Their lands became a part of the Roman domain. The new territory was organized into two new tribes, making now the total number twenty-nine.

Towns partly Incorporated.—But most of the towns of Latium. received only a part of the rights of citizenship. To their inhabitants were given the right to trade and the right to intermarry with Roman citizens, but not the right to vote or to hold office. This imperfect, or qualified, citizenship (which had before been given to the town of Caere) now became known as the "Latin right."

Latin and Roman Colonies.—In order to keep in subjection a refractory town, or to form an outpost on the frontier, it was customary to send out a body of citizen soldiers, who occupied the town. These were known as military, or Latin, colonies, and were made up of persons who possessed the Latin right. At the same time Rome established on the seacoast maritime, or Roman, colonies, as they were called, composed entirely of full Roman citizens.

Dependent Allies.—There were certain other towns which were not incorporated with Rome at all. They were allowed to retain their local government, but were compelled to make a treaty, by which they were obliged to cede their public lands to Rome, and to lend their support in time of war.

This wise method of treating the various subject communities cemented more closely the Latin cities to Rome; and was the beginning of an important policy, which was more fully carried out in the subsequent organization of Italy and of the Mediterranean world.

SELECTIONS FOR READING

Arnold, Hist., Ch. 29, "The Great Latin War" (2).[1]

How and Leigh, Ch. 13, "Subjugation of Latium" (1).

Liddell, Ch. 20, "Great Latin War" (1).

Ihne, Hist., Bk. III., Ch. 6, "Great War with the Latins" (2).

Mommsen, Vol. I., Bk. II., Ch. 5, "Subjugation of the Latins" (2).

SPECIAL STUDY

MAP OF LATIUM AND CAMPANIA after the Latin conquest, locating the chief towns, and distinguishing between (*a*) towns fully incorporated, (*b*) towns partly incorporated, (*c*) subject allies, (*d*) Latin colonies, and (*e*) Roman colonies.—How and Leigh, p. 103, also map between pp. 402 and 403 (1); Shuckburgh, maps on pp. 30 and 128 (1); Liddell, p. 193 (1); Pelham, pp. 81, 82 (1).

[1] The figure in parenthesis refers to the number of the topic in the Appendix, where a fuller title of the book will be found.

CHAPTER XI

THE CONQUEST OF CENTRAL ITALY

The Second Samnite War (B.C. 326-304), I.—The Third Samnite War (B.C. 298-290), II.—Results of the Samnite Wars, III.

I. THE SECOND SAMNITE WAR (B.C. 326-304)

Renewal of the Struggle for Central Italy.—The question as to who should be supreme in central Italy, Rome or Samnium, was not yet decided. The first struggle had been interrupted by the Latin war; and a twelve years' peace followed. The Samnites saw that Rome was becoming stronger and stronger. But they could not prevent this, because they themselves were threatened in the south by a new enemy. Alexander of Epirus, the uncle of Alexander the Great, had invaded Italy to aid the people of Tarentum, and also with the hope of building up a new empire in the West. Rome also regarded Alexander as a possible enemy, and hastened to make a treaty with him against the Samnites. But the death of Alexander left the Tarentines to shift for themselves, and left the Samnites free to use their whole force against Rome in the decisive struggle now to come for the mastery of central Italy.

Cause of the War again in Campania.—The direct cause of the second Samnite war, like that of the first, grew out of troubles in Campania. Here were situated the twin cities of Palaepolis (the old city) and Neapolis (the new city), which were still in the hands of the Greeks, but under the protection of the Samnites. Many disputes arose between the people of these cities and the Roman settlers in Campania. Palaepolis appealed to the Samnites for help, and a strong garrison was given to it. The Romans demanded that this garrison should be withdrawn. The Samnites refused. The Romans then declared war and laid siege to Palaepolis, which was soon captured by Q. Publilius Philo.

Battle at the Caudine Forks (B.C. 321).—In the early part of the war the Romans were nearly everywhere successful. They formed alliances with the Apulians and Lucanians on the south, and they also took the strong city of Luceria in Apulia; so that the Samnites were surrounded by the Roman army and their allies. But in spite of these successes, the great Samnite general, Pontius, inflicted upon the Romans one of the most humiliating defeats that they ever suffered. The Roman consuls in Campania, deceived by the false report that Luceria was besieged by the whole Samnite force, decided to hasten to its relief by going directly through the heart of the Samnite territory. In passing through a defile in the mountains near Caudium, called the

"Caudine Forks," the whole Roman force was entrapped by Pontius and obliged to surrender. The army was compelled to pass under the yoke; and the consuls were forced to make a treaty, yielding up all the territory conquered from the Samnites. But the Roman senate refused to ratify this treaty, and delivered up the offending consuls to the Samnites. Pontius, however, refused to accept the consuls as a compensation for the broken treaty; and demanded that the treaty should be kept, or else that the whole Roman army should be returned to the Caudine Forks, where they had surrendered. Rome refused to do either, and the war was continued.

Uprising of the Etruscans.—After breaking this treaty and recovering her army, Rome looked forward to immediate success. But in this she was disappointed. Everything seemed now turning against her. The cities in Campania revolted, the Samnites conquered Luceria in Apulia and Fregellae on the Liris, and gained an important victory in the south of Latium near Anxur. To add to her troubles, the Etruscans came to the aid of the Samnites and attacked the Roman garrison at Sutrium. The hostile attitude of the Etruscans aroused Rome to new vigor. Under the leadership of Q. Fabius Maximus Rullianus, the tide was turned in her favor. Many victories were gained over the Etruscans, closing with the decisive battle at Lake Vadimonis, and the submission of Etruria to Rome.

Capture of Bovianum and End of the War.—Rome now made desperate efforts to recover her losses in the south. Under the consul L. Papirius Cursor, who was afterward appointed dictator, the Romans recaptured Luceria and Fregellae. The Samnites were defeated at Capua and driven out of Campania. The war was then carried into Samnium, and her chief city, Bovianum, was captured. This destroyed the last hope of the Samnites. They sued for peace and were obliged to give up all their conquests and to enter into an alliance with Rome.

II. THE THIRD SAMNITE WAR (B.C. 298-290)

The Italian Coalition against Rome.—Although Rome was successful in the previous war, it required one more conflict to secure her supremacy in central Italy. This war is known as the third Samnite war, but it was in fact a war between Rome and the principal nations of Italy—the Samnites, the Umbrians, the Etruscans, and the Gauls. The Italians saw that either Rome must be subdued, or else all Italy would be ruled by the city on the Tiber. This was really a war for Italian independence.

Cause of the War in Lucania.—Rome and Samnium both saw the need of strengthening themselves for the coming conflict. Rome could depend upon the Latins, the Volscians, and the Campanians in the south. She also brought under her power the Aequians and the Marsians on the east. So that all her forces were compact and well in hand. The Samnites, on the contrary, were obliged to depend upon forces which were scattered from one end of the peninsula to the other. They determined first to win over to their side the Lucanians, who were their nearest neighbors on the south, but who had been the allies of Rome in the previous war. This attempt of the Samnites to get control of Lucania led to the declaration of war by Rome.

The War carried into Etruria.—The Samnites now made the most heroic efforts to destroy their hated rival. Three armies were placed in the field, one to defend Samnium, one to invade Campania, and the third to march into Etruria. This last army was expected to join the Umbrians, the Etruscans, and the Gauls, and to attack Rome from the north. This was a bold plan, and alarmed the city. Business was stopped, and all Roman citizens were called to arms. The Roman forces moved into Etruria under the consuls Q. Fabius Rullianus and Decius Mus, the son of the hero who sacrificed himself in the battle at Mt. Vesuvius. The hostile armies were soon scattered, and the Samnites and Gauls retreated across the Apennines to Sentinum (map, p. 81).

Battle of Sentinum (B.C. 295).—Upon the famous field of Sentinum was decided the fate of Italy. Fabius was opposed to the Samnites on the right wing; and Decius Mus was opposed to the Gauls on the left. Fabius held his ground; but the Roman left wing under Decius was driven back by the terrible charge of the Gallic war chariots. Decius, remembering his father's example, devoted himself to death, and the Roman line was restored. The battle was finally decided in favor of the Romans; and the hope of a united Italy under the leadership of Samnium was destroyed.

End of the Italian Coalition.—After the great battle of Sentinum, the Gauls dispersed; Umbria ceased its resistance; and the Etruscans made their peace in the following year. But the Samnites continued the hopeless struggle in their own land. They were at last compelled to submit to Curius Dentatus, and to make peace with Rome. Another attempt to form a coalition against Rome, led by the Lucanians, failed; and Rome was left to organize her new possessions.

III. RESULTS OF THE SAMNITE WARS

Rome's Position in Central Italy.—The great result of the Samnite wars was to give Rome the controlling position in central Italy. The Samnites were allowed to retain their own territory and their political independence. But they were compelled to give up all disputed land, and to become the subject allies of Rome. The Samnites were a brave people and fought many desperate battles; but they lacked the organizing skill and resources of the Romans. In this great struggle for supremacy Rome succeeded on account of her persistence and her great fortitude in times of danger and disaster; but more than all else, on account of her wonderful ability to unite the forces under her control.

Increase of the Roman Territory.—As a result of these wars, the Roman territory was extended in two directions. On the west side of the peninsula, the greater part of Campania was brought into the Roman domain; and the Lucanians became the subject allies of Rome. On the east side the Sabines were incorporated with Rome, receiving the partial right of citizenship, which in a few years was extended to full citizenship. Umbria was also subdued. The Roman domain now stretched across the Italian peninsula from sea to sea. The inhabitants of Picenum and Apulia also became subject allies.

The New Colonies.—In accordance with her usual policy, Rome secured herself by the establishment of new colonies. Two of these were established on the west side— one at Minturnae at the month of the Liris River, and the other at Sinuessa in Campania (map, p. 80). In the south a colony was placed at Venusia, which was the most powerful garrison that Rome had ever established, up to this time. It was made up of twenty thousand Latin citizens, and was so situated as to cut off the connection between Samnium and Tarentum.

SELECTIONS FOR READING

Pelham, Bk. II., Ch. 2, "Conquest of Italy" (1).[1]

Michelet, Bk. II., Ch. 2, "Conquest of Central Italy" (6).

How and Leigh, Ch. 15, "Conquest of the Italians" (1).

Arnold, Hist., Ch. 33, "Third Samnite War" (2).

Mommsen, Vol. I., Bk. II., "Struggle of the Italians against Rome" (2).

SPECIAL STUDY

ROMAN ROADS.—How and Leigh, p. 555 (1); Leighton, p. 111 (1); Ramsay and Lanciani, pp. 76-78 (8); Guhl and Koner, pp. 341-344 (16); Harper's Dict. Antiqq., "Via" (8).

[1] The figure in parenthesis refers to the number of the topic in the Appendix, where a fuller title of the book will be found.

CHAPTER XII

THE CONQUEST OF SOUTHERN ITALY

Rupture between Rome and Tarentum, I.—War with Pyrrhus (B.C. 280-275), II.—Final Reduction of Italy, III.

I. RUPTURE BETWEEN ROME AND TARENTUM

Greek Cities in Southern Italy.—All the peninsular portion of Italy was now under the practical dominion of Rome, except the Greek cities in the south. These cities were the centers of Greek art and culture. Situated upon the coast, they had engaged in commerce, and on account of their wealth they were subject to the depredations of their less civilized neighbors, the Lucanians and Bruttians. With no great capacity for organization, they were accustomed, when assailed, to appeal to some stronger power for help. They had sometimes looked to Greek princes, as in the case of Alexander of Epirus. But now, when Thurii was threatened by the Lucanians, this city threw itself upon the mercy of Rome. Rome promptly interfered, and placed garrisons not only in Thurii, but also in other cities along the coast, as Croton, Locri, and Rhegium (see map, p. 88).

Rome and Tarentum.—The most important of the Greek cities of Italy was Tarentum. This city was now alarmed at the rapid advances made by Rome on the southern coast. Hemmed in on all sides by the Roman outposts, Tarentum found it necessary to decide whether she should open her gates to Rome, or maintain her independence with the aid of some Greek ally. She had already a commercial treaty with Rome, which prevented the ships of the latter power from passing the Lacinian promontory. But this treaty would not prevent the Roman armies from threatening the city by land.

Cause of the Rupture.—While this question was yet undecided, a Roman war fleet, on its way to the coast of Umbria, anchored in the harbor of Tarentum. The people were angered by this breach of the treaty, and immediately attacked the fleet. Five of the Roman vessels were captured, and the crews were either put to death or sold into slavery. A Roman embassy which was sent to Tarentum to demand reparation was grossly insulted. The Romans thereupon declared war, and sent an army to subdue the insolent city.

Tarentum calls upon Pyrrhus.—There was now but one course open to the people of Tarentum, and that was to appeal to Greece for protection. Pyrrhus was at this time king of Epirus. He was a brilliant and ambitious leader, and aspired to found an empire in the West. When Tarentum appealed to him for help, he was ready not only to aid this city, but to rescue all the Greek cities of Italy from Rome, and also all the cities of Sicily from the power of Carthage. The war which the Romans began against Tarentum was thus turned into a war against Pyrrhus, who was the ablest general of his time.

II. WAR WITH PYRRHUS (B.C. 280-275)

Pyrrhus lands in Italy.—Pyrrhus landed in Italy, bringing with him a mercenary army raised in different parts of Greece, consisting of twenty-five thousand men and twenty elephants. Tarentum was placed under the strictest military discipline. Rome, on her part, made the greatest preparations to meet the invader. Her garrisons were strengthened. One army was sent into Etruria, to prevent an uprising in the north; and the main army, under the consul Valerius Laevinus, was sent to southern Italy.

Battle of Heraclea (B. C. 280).—The first battle between the Italian and Greek soldiers occurred at Heraclea, not far from Tarentum. It was here that the Roman legion first came into contact with the Macedonian phalanx. The legion was drawn up in three separate lines, in open order; and the soldiers, after hurling the javelins, fought at close quarters with the sword. The phalanx, on the other hand, was a solid mass of soldiers in close order, with their shields touching, and twenty or thirty ranks deep. Its weapon was a long spear, so long that the points of the first five ranks all projected in front of the first rank. Pyrrhus selected his ground on the open plain. Seven times the Roman legions charged against his unbroken phalanxes. After the Roman attack was exhausted, Pyrrhus turned his elephants upon the Roman cavalry, which fled in confusion, followed by the rest of the Roman army. The Romans, though defeated in this battle, displayed wonderful courage and discipline, so that Pyrrhus exclaimed, "With such an army I could conquer the world!"

Embassy of Cineas.—The great losses which Pyrrhus suffered convinced him that the Romans could not be conquered with the forces which he had under his command; and that he had better turn his attention to the Carthaginians in Sicily. He therefore resolved to use his victory as a means of obtaining an honorable peace with the Romans. His most trusted minister, Cineas, who is said to have conquered more nations with his tongue than Pyrrhus had with his sword, was sent to Rome with the proposal to make peace, on condition that the Romans should relinquish their conquests in southern Italy. So persuasive were the words of Cineas, that the Roman senate seemed ready to consider his offer. But the charm of his speech was broken by the stern eloquence of Appius Claudius, the blind old censor, who called upon the senate never to make peace with an enemy on Roman soil. Failing in his mission, Cineas returned to his master with the report that the Roman senate was "an assembly of kings." To give force to the claims of Cineas, Pyrrhus had pushed his army into Campania, and even into Latium; but finding the cities loyal to Rome, he withdrew again to Tarentum.

Battle of Asculum (B.C. 279).—In southern Italy, Pyrrhus received the support of the Greek cities, of the Bruttians, the Lucanians, and even the Samnites. In the next year he marched into Apulia, in the direction of the Roman stronghold Luceria. The hostile armies met at Asculum, a few miles south of Luceria. The battle of Asculum was a repetition of Heraclea. The Roman legions charged in vain against the Greek phalanxes; and were then routed by the elephants, which they could not withstand. But again, although the Romans were defeated, the great losses of Pyrrhus prevented him from following up his victory.

Pyrrhus in Sicily (B.C. 278-276).—Pyrrhus resolved to turn his back upon Italy, where his victories had been so barren, and go to the rescue of the Greek cities in Sicily, which were subject to Carthage. Leaving his general, Milo, at Tarentum, he crossed over to Syracuse, and gained many victories over the Carthaginians. He drove them to their stronghold in Lilybaeum, at the western extremity of the island; but this city he failed to capture. He then called upon the people of Sicily to build a fleet, but they murmured at his severe command. Believing that such a people was unworthy of his aid, he returned to Tarentum. In the meantime the Romans had recovered nearly all their lost ground in southern Italy.

Battle of Beneventum and Departure of Pyrrhus (B.C. 275).—Before abandoning Italy, Pyrrhus determined once more to try the fortunes of war. One of the consular armies, under Curius Dentatus, lay in a strong position near Beneventum in the hilly regions of Samnium. Pyrrhus resolved to attack this army before it could be reënforced. He stormed the Roman position, and was repulsed. The Roman consul then pursued him to the plains and gained a complete victory. Baffled and disappointed, Pyrrhus retreated to Tarentum; and leaving a garrison in that city under his lieutenant, Milo, he led the remnants of his army back to Greece.

III. FINAL REDUCTION OF ITALY

Fall of Tarentum (B.C. 272).—After the departure of Pyrrhus, Rome had no real rival left in Italy. The complete reduction of the peninsula speedily followed. Tarentum was besieged, and after a stubborn resistance of four years, Milo agreed to surrender, on condition of being allowed to withdraw his garrison to Epirus (B.C. 272). The city was allowed to retain its local government, but was obliged to pay an annual tribute to Rome.

The Lucanians, Bruttians, and Samnites.—Some of the people in the south of

Italy were still loath to accept the supremacy of Rome, and kept up a kind of guerrilla warfare for some time. But the Lucanians and Bruttians were soon obliged to submit, and all the cities on the coast finally came under the Roman power. A temporary revolt of the Samnites was also crushed. The Roman power in the south was secured by strong colonies, planted at Paestum in Lucania (B.C. 273) and at Beneventum in Samnium (B.C. 268).

Picenum and Umbria.—With the south pacified, Rome soon brought into submission the Italian remnants on the eastern coast. The chief city of Picenum, Ancona (see map, p. 81), was taken by storm (B.C. 268), and the whole country was reduced. Farther to the north, the chief city of Umbria, Ariminum, was also taken (B.C. 266), and the territory yielded to Rome.

Reduction of Etruria.—A spirit of defection still existed in some parts of Etruria. The most haughty of the Etruscan cities was Volsinii, which was selected as an example. Its walls were razed to the ground, and its works of art were transferred to Rome. After the fall of this city, all the other towns not already allied to Rome were willing to submit; and Rome ruled supreme from the Rubicon and Macra to the Sicilian strait.

SELECTIONS FOR READING

Liddell, Ch, 26, "Pyrrhus in Italy" (1).[1]

How and Leigh, Ch. 16, "War with Tarentum and Pyrrhus" (1).

Shuckburgh, Ch. 15, "Rome and Tarentum" (1).

Mommsen, Vol. I., Bk. II., Ch. 7, "Struggle between Pyrrhus and Rome" (2).

SPECIAL STUDY

THE ROMAN ARMY.—How and Leigh, pp. 135-141 (1); Leighton, Ch. 29 (1); Liddell, pp. 187-189 (1); Shuckburgh, pp. 214-218 (1); Beesly, Ch. 6 (6); Ramsay and Lanciani, Ch. 12 (8); Eschenburg, pp. 270-285 (8); Guhl and Koner, pp. 567-591 (16); Harper's Dict. Antiqq., "Legio," "Exercitus" (8).

[1] The figure in parenthesis refers to the number of the topic in the Appendix, where a fuller title of the book will be found.

CHAPTER XIII

The Sovereign Roman State, I.—The Subject Communities, II.—The Military System, III.

I. THE SOVEREIGN ROMAN STATE

The Sovereign and Subject Communities.—To understand properly the history of Rome, we must study not only the way in which she conquered her territory, but also the way in which she organized and governed it. The study of her wars and battles is less important than the study of her policy. Rome was always learning lessons in the art of government. As she grew in power, she also grew in political wisdom. With every extension of her territory, she was obliged to extend her authority as a sovereign power. If we would comprehend the political system which grew up in Italy, we must keep clearly in mind the distinction between the people who made up the sovereign body of the state, and the people who made up the subject communities of Italy. Just as in early times we saw two distinct bodies, the patrician body, which ruled the state, and the plebeian body, which was subject to the state; so now we shall see, on the one hand, a ruling body of citizens, who lived in and outside the city upon the Roman domain (*ager Romanus*), and on the other hand, a subject body of people, living in towns and cities throughout the rest of Italy. In other words, we shall see a part of the territory and people incorporated into the state, and another part unincorporated—the one a sovereign community, and the other comprising a number of subject communities.

Extent of the Roman Domain.—The Roman domain proper, or the *ager Romanus*, was that part of the territory in which the people became incorporated into the state, and were admitted to the rights of citizenship. It was the sovereign domain of the Roman people. This domain land, or incorporated territory, had been gradually growing while the conquest of Italy was going on. It now included, speaking generally, the most of Latium, northern Campania, southern Etruria, the Sabine country, Picenum, and a part of Umbria. There were a few towns within this area, like Tibur and Praeneste, which were not incorporated, and hence not a part of the domain land, but retained the position of subject allies.

The Thirty-three Tribes.—Within the Roman domain were the local tribes, which had now increased in number to thirty-three. They included four urban tribes, that is, the wards of the city, and twenty-nine rural tribes, which were like townships in the country. All the persons who lived in these tribal districts and were enrolled, formed a part of the sovereign body of the Roman people, that is, they had a share in the government, in making the laws, and in electing the magistrates.

The Roman Colonies.—The colonies of citizens sent out by Rome were allowed to retain all their rights of citizenship, being permitted even to come to Rome at any time to vote and help make the laws. These colonies of Roman citizens thus formed a part of the sovereign state; and their territory, wherever it might be situated, was regarded as a part of the *ager Romanus*. Such were the colonies along the seacoast, the most important of which were situated on the shores of Latium and of adjoining lands.

The Roman Municipia.—Rome incorporated into her territory some of the conquered towns under the name of *municipia*, which possessed all the burdens and some of the rights of citizenship. At first, such towns (like Caere) received the private but not the public rights (*civitas sine suffragio*),—see page 64,—and the towns might govern themselves or be governed by a prefect sent from Rome. In time, however, the municipia obtained not only local self-government but also full Roman citizenship; and this arrangement was the basis of the Roman municipal system of later times.

II. THE SUBJECT COMMUNITIES

The Subject Territory.—Over against this sovereign body of citizens living upon the *ager Romanus*, were the subject communities scattered throughout the length and breadth of the peninsula. The inhabitants of this territory had no share in the Roman government. Neither could they declare war, make peace, form alliances, or coin money, without the consent of Rome. Although they might have many privileges given to them, and might govern themselves in their own cities, they formed no part of the sovereign body of the Roman people.

The Latin Colonies.—One part of the subject communities of Italy comprised the Latin colonies. These were the military garrisons which Rome sent out to hold in subjection a conquered city or territory. They were generally made up of veteran soldiers, or sometimes of poor Roman citizens, who were placed upon the conquered land and who ruled the conquered people. But such garrisons did not retain the full rights of citizens. They lost the political rights, and generally the *conubium* (p. 64), but retained the *commercium*. These colonies, scattered as they were throughout Italy, carried with them the Latin language and the Roman spirit, and thus aided in extending the influence of Rome.

The Italian Allies.—The largest part of the subject communities were the Italian cities which were conquered and left free to govern themselves, but which were bound to Rome by a special treaty. They were obliged to recognize the sovereign power of Rome. They were not subject to the land tax which fell upon Roman citizens, but were obliged to furnish troops for the Roman army in times of war. These cities of Italy, thus held in subjection to Rome by a special treaty, were known as federated cities (*civitates foederatae*), or simply as allies (*socii*); they formed the most important part of the Italian population not incorporated into the Roman state.

This method of governing Italy was, in some respects, based upon the policy which had formerly been adopted for the government of Latium (see p. 77). The important distinction between Romans, Latins, and Italians continued until the "social war" (consult map, p. 167).

III. THE MILITARY SYSTEM

The Roman Army.—The conquest of Italy was due, in great measure, to the efficiency of the Roman army. The strength of the Roman government, too, depended upon the army, which was the real support of the civil power. By their conquests the Romans became a nation of warriors. Every citizen between the ages of seventeen and forty-five was obliged to serve in the army, when the public service required it. In early times the wars lasted only for a short period, and consisted in ravaging the fields of the enemy; and the soldier's reward was the booty which he was able to capture. But after the siege of Veii, the term of service became longer, and it became necessary to give to the soldiers regular pay. This pay, with the prospect of plunder and of a share in the allotment of conquered land; furnished a strong motive to render faithful service.

Divisions of the Army.—In case of war it was customary to raise four legions, two for each consul. Each legion was composed of thirty maniples, or companies, of heavy-armed troops,—twenty maniples consisting of one hundred and twenty men each, and ten maniples of sixty men each,—making in all three thousand heavy-armed troops. There were also twelve hundred light-armed troops, not organized in maniples. The whole number of men in a legion was therefore forty-two hundred. To each legion was usually joined a body of cavalry, numbering three hundred men. After the reduction of Latium and Italy, the allied cities were also obliged to furnish a certain number of men, according to the terms of the treaty.

Order of Battle.—In ancient times the Romans fought in the manner of the Greek phalanx, in a solid square. This arrangement was well suited to withstand an attack on a level plain, but it was not adapted to aggressive warfare. About the time of Camillus, the Romans introduced the more open order of "maniples." When drawn up in order of battle, the legion was arranged in three lines: first, the *hastati*, made up of young men; second, the *principes*, composed of the more experienced soldiers; and third, the *triarii*, which comprised the veterans, capable of supporting the other two lines. Each line was composed of ten maniples, those of the first two lines consisting of one hundred and twenty men each, and those of the third line consisting of sixty men each; the maniples, or companies, in each line were so arranged that they were opposite the spaces in the next line, as follows:

1. *Hastati* – – – – – – – – – –
2.
Principes – – – – – – – – – –
3. *Triarii* – – – – – – – – – –

This arrangement enabled the companies in front to retreat into the spaces in the rear, or the companies in the rear to advance to the spaces in front. Behind the third line usually fought the light-armed and less experienced soldiers (*rorarii* and *accensi*). Each maniple carried its own ensign; and the legion carried a standard surmounted with a silver eagle.

Armor and Weapons.—The defensive armor of all the three lines was alike—a coat of mail for the breast, a brass helmet for the head, greaves for the legs, and a large oblong shield carried upon the left arm. For offensive weapons, each man carried a short sword, which could be used for cutting or thrusting. The soldiers in the first two lines each had also two javelins, to be hurled at the enemy before coming into close quarters; and those of the third line each had a long lance, which could be used for piercing. It was with such arms as these that the Roman soldiers conquered Italy.

Military Rewards and Honors.—The Romans encouraged the soldiers with rewards for their bravery. These were bestowed by the general in the presence of the whole army. The highest individual reward was the "civic crown," made of oak leaves, given to him who had saved the life of a fellow-citizen on the battlefield. Other suitable rewards, such as golden crowns, banners of different colors, and ornaments, were bestowed for singular bravery. When a general slew the general of the enemy, the captured spoils (*spolia opima*) were hung up in the temple of Jupiter Feretrius. The highest military honor which the Roman state could bestow was a triumph,—a solemn procession, decreed by the senate, in which the victorious general, with his army, marched through the city to the Capitol, bearing in his train the trophies of war.

Military Roads.—An important part of the military system of Rome was the network of military roads by which her armies and munitions of war could be sent into every part of Italy. The first military road was the Appian Way (*via Appia*), built by Appius Claudius during the Samnite wars. It connected Rome with Capua, and was afterward extended to Beneventum and Venusia, and finally as far as Brundisium. This furnished a model for the roads which were subsequently laid out to other points in Italy. The Latin Way (*via Latina*) ran south into the Samnite country and connected with the Appian Way near Capua and at Beneventum. The Flaminian Way (*via Flaminia*) ran north through eastern Etruria and Umbria to Ariminum. From this last-mentioned place, the Aemilian Way (*via Aemilia*) extended into Cisalpine Gaul as far as Placentia on the river Po. Another important road, the Cassian Way (*via Cassia*) ran through central Etruria to Arretium, and connected with the Aemilian Way in Cisalpine Gaul. Along the western coast of Etruria ran the Aurelian Way (*via Aurelia*). These were the chief military roads constructed during the time of the republic. So durable were these highways that their remains exist to the present day (see "special study," p. 85).

SELECTIONS FOR READING

Merivale, Gen. Hist., Ch. 16, "Survey of Roman Institutions" (1)[1]

Mommsen, Vol. I., Bk. II., Ch. 7, "Union of Italy" (2).

Liddell, Ch. 27, "Settlement of Italy" (1).

Pelham, pp. 97-107, "Rome as Mistress of Italy" (1).

Leighton, Ch. 19, "Roman Supremacy in Italy" (1).

Taylor, Ch. 6, "Rome and Italy" (1).

Duruy, Vol. I., Ch. 17, "Organization of Italy" (2).

SPECIAL STUDY

ROMAN AND LATIN COLONIES.—Shuckburgh, p. 164, note 2 (1); Liddell, pp. 254-257 (1); Arnold, Hist., Ch. 41 (2); Ramsay and Lanciani, pp. 118-120 (8); Harper's Dict. Antiqq., "Colonia" (8); Niebuhr, Vol. III., pp. 240-252 (2).

[1] The figure in parenthesis refers to the number of the topic in the Appendix, where a fuller title of the book will be found.

CHAPTER XIV

THE FIRST PUNIC WAR (B.C. 264-241)

Carthage and Rome, I.—Operations of the First Punic War, II.—Events Following the War (B.C. 241-218), III.

I. CARTHAGE AND ROME

Beginning of Foreign Conquests.—The ambition and the resources of Rome were not exhausted with the conquest of Italy. It was but a step from the Greek cities of Italy to the Greek cities of Sicily. But when Rome ventured to cross the Sicilian Strait, she was drawn into a struggle which was not ended until she was mistress of the Mediterranean. In passing beyond the limits of her own peninsula, she became one of the great world powers. The strength which she had acquired in her wars with the Latins and Etruscans and Samnites, she was now to use in the greater conflicts with Carthage and Macedonia and Syria.

The Origin of Carthage.—The first foreign power with which Rome came in contact, outside of Italy, was Carthage. This city was originally a colony of Tyre, and had come to be the capital of a great commercial empire on the northern coast of Africa. The origin of Carthage, like that of Rome, is almost lost in the clouds of tradition. An old story tells us how Queen Dido was driven from Tyre and landed in Africa, as Aeneas did in Italy, with a band of fugitives. It is said that Dido purchased from the African princes as much land as an oxhide would cover; and cunningly cut the hide into thin strips and encircled enough land, upon which to found a city. Vergil has told us the romantic story of Dido and Aeneas, and the death of the queen. But all we really know of the origin of this city is that it was settled by Phoenicians from Tyre, and early acquired dominion over the native races of Africa, the Lydians and the Numidians.

Government of Carthage.—When Carthage came into conflict with Rome, it had in some respects the same kind of government as the Roman republic. It had two chief magistrates (called *suffetes*), corresponding to the Roman consuls. It had a council of elders, called the "hundred," which we might compare to the Roman senate. It had also an assembly something like the Roman *comitia*. But while the Carthaginian government had some outward similarity to the Roman, it was in its spirit very different. The real power was exercised by a few wealthy and prominent families. The Carthaginians, moreover, did not understand the Roman method of incorporating their subjects into the state; and hence did not possess a great body of loyal citizens, as did Rome. But one great advantage of the Carthaginian government was the fact that it placed the command of the army in the hands of a permanent able leader, and not in the hands of its civil magistrates, who were constantly changing as were the consuls at Rome.

The Civilization of Carthage.—Carthage brought into the western Mediterranean the ideas and civilization which the Phoenicians had developed in the East. Her power was based upon trade and commercial supremacy. She had brought under her control the trading colonies of northern Africa and many of the Greek cities of Sicily. She was, in fact, the great merchant of the Mediterranean. She had grown wealthy and strong by buying and selling the products of the East and the West—the purple of Tyre, the frankincense of Arabia, the linen of Egypt, the gold of Spain, the silver of the Balearic Isles, the tin of Britain, and the iron of Elba. She had formed commercial treaties with the chief countries of the world. She coveted not only the Greek cities of Sicily, but the Greek cities of Italy as well. We can thus see how Rome and Carthage became rivals for the possession of the countries bordering upon the western Mediterranean Sea.

Rome and Carthage Compared.—In comparing these two great rivals of the West, we might say that they were nearly equal in strength and resources. Carthage had greater wealth, but Rome had a better organization. Carthage had a more powerful navy, but Rome had a more efficient army. Carthage had more brilliant leaders, while Rome had a more steadfast body of citizens. The main strength of Carthage rested in her wealth and commercial resources, while that of Rome depended upon the character of her people and her well-organized political system. The greatness of the Carthaginians was shown in their successes, while the greatness of the Romans was most fully revealed in the dark hours of disaster and trial.

II. OPERATIONS OF THE FIRST PUNIC WAR

Outbreak of the War in Sicily (B.C. 264).—The first conflict between Rome and Carthage, which is known as the first Punic1 war, began in Sicily; and really came to be a contest for the possession of that island. Sicily was at this time divided between three powers. (1) Carthage held all the western part of the island, with the important cities of Agrigentum on the south, Panormus on the north, and Lilybaeum at the extreme point. (2) The southeastern part of the island was under the control of the king of Syracuse, who ruled not only this city, but also some of the neighboring towns. (3) The northeastern corner of the island was in the possession of a body of Campanian soldiers, who had been in the service of the king of Syracuse, and who, on returning home, had treacherously seized the city of Messana.

These Campanian mercenaries, who called themselves Mamertines, or Sons of

79

Mars, murdered the inhabitants and ravaged the surrounding country. The king of Syracuse attacked them, laid siege to their city, and reduced them to such an extremity that they felt obliged to look for help. The choice lay between Rome and Carthage. They finally decided to call upon Rome for help. The Roman senate hesitated to help these robbers against Syracuse, which was a friendly power. But when the question was left to the assembly, the people fearing that Carthage would be called upon if they refused, it was decided to help the Mamertines, and thus prevent the Carthaginians from getting possession of this part of Sicily. In this way began the first Punic war.

Capture of Messana and Agrigentum.—A Roman army, under Appius Claudius, was dispatched to Sicily, and gained a foothold upon the island. But the Mamertines, during the delay of the Romans, had already admitted a Carthaginian garrison into the city. This seemed to the Roman general to be a breach of faith. He accordingly invited the Carthaginian commander, Hanno, to a friendly conference, and then treacherously ordered him to be seized. Whereupon the latter, in order to regain his liberty, agreed to give up the city. Thus the Romans got possession of Messana. The king of Syracuse then formed an alliance with the Carthaginians to drive the Romans out of the island; but both their armies were defeated. When the Romans had thus shown their superiority, the king of Syracuse changed his policy and formed an alliance with the Romans to drive the Carthaginians out of the island. Town after town fell before the Roman army; and in the second year of the war, the important city of Agrigentum was captured, after a siege of seven months (B.C. 262).

Rome becomes a Naval Power.—The Romans now learned that Carthage, to be overcome, must be met upon the sea, as well as upon the land. When the Carthaginian fleet first appeared, it recovered most of the coast cities which had been lost to the Romans. It ravaged the coasts of Italy, and by its command of the sea made it difficult for Rome to send fresh troops to Sicily. The Romans had, it is true, a few ships; but these were triremes, or ships with only three banks of oars, and were unable to cope with the great Carthaginian vessels, which were quinquiremes, or ships with five banks of oars. The Romans saw that they must either give up the war, or else build a fleet equal to that of the Carthaginians. Taking as a model a Carthaginian vessel which had been wrecked on the Italian shore, they constructed, it is said, a hundred vessels like it in sixty days. In the meantime their soldiers were trained into sailors by practicing the art of rowing upon rude benches built upon the land and arranged like the banks of a real vessel. The Romans knew that their soldiers were better than the Carthaginians in a hand-to-hand encounter. To maintain this advantage, they provided their ships with drawbridges which could be used in boarding the enemy's vessels.

Thus equipped with a fleet, Rome ventured upon the sea as a rival of the first naval power of the world.

Victory of Duilius at Mylae (B.C. 260).—The new Roman fleet was put under the command of the consul Duilius. The Carthaginians were now plundering the northern coast of Sicily near Mylae. Without delay Duilius sailed to meet them. As the fleets came together, the Romans dropped their drawbridges upon the enemy's ships and quickly boarded them. In the hand-to-hand encounter, the Romans proved their superiority. The Carthaginians were routed; and fifty of their vessels were either sunk or captured. This was a most decisive victory. The Romans had fought and gained their first great battle upon the sea. Duilius was given a magnificent triumph, and to commemorate the victory, a column was erected in the Forum, adorned with the beaks of the captured vessels (*Columna Rostrata*).

Invasion, of Africa by Regulus, (B.C. 256).—Elated by this success, the Romans felt prepared to carry the war into Africa. With a still larger fleet, they defeated the Carthaginian squadron which attempted to bar their way on the southern coast of Sicily, off the promontory of Ecnomus. Two legions, under L. Manlius Vulso and Regulus, landed on the coast of Africa east of Carthage, and laid waste the country. So easily was this accomplished that the Romans decided that one consul, with his army, would be enough to finish the work in Africa. Vulso was therefore recalled, and Regulus remained. The Carthaginians attempted in vain to make peace; and in despair, it is said, even threw some of their children into the flames to propitiate their god Moloch. They then placed their army in the hands of a Spartan soldier named Xanthippus. This general defeated the Roman legions with great slaughter, and made Regulus a prisoner. A fleet was then sent from Italy to rescue the survivors, but this fleet on its return was wrecked in a storm. Thus ingloriously closed the war in Africa.

The War Confined to Sicily (B.C. 255-241).—For several years after this, the war languished in Sicily. The long series of Roman disasters was relieved by the capture of Panormus on the northern coast, which was soon followed by a second victory over the Carthaginians at the same place. It is said that the Carthaginians, after this second defeat, desired an exchange of prisoners, and sent Regulus to the Roman senate to advocate their cause, under the promise that he would return if unsuccessful. But Regulus, it is said, persuaded the senate not to accept the offer of the Carthaginians; and then, in spite of the tears and entreaties of his friends, went back to Carthage. Whether this story is true or not, it illustrates the honor and patriotism of the true Roman.

After the Roman victories at Panormus, the Carthaginians were pushed into the extreme western part of the island. The Romans then laid siege to Lilybaeum, the stronghold of the Carthaginian power. Failing to capture this place, the Roman consul, P. Claudius, determined to destroy the enemy's fleet lying near Drepanum; but he was defeated with the loss of over ninety ships. The superstitious Romans believed that this defeat was due to the fact that Claudius had impiously disregarded the auguries; when the sacred chickens had refused to eat, he had in a fit of passion thrown them into the sea. The consul was recalled by the senate, and a dictator was appointed in his place. After the loss of other fleets by storms, and after fruitless campaigns against the great Carthaginian soldier, Hamilcar Barca, the Roman cause seemed a failure.

Victory at the Aegates Islands (B.C. 241).—It is in the midst of such discouraging times as these that we are able to see the strong elements of the Roman character—patriotism, fortitude, and steadfast perseverance. With a loss of one sixth of their population and a vast amount of treasure, they still persisted in the attempt to conquer Sicily. Wealthy citizens advanced their money to build a new fleet. In this way two hundred ships were built and placed under the consul C. Lutatius Catulus. A decisive victory was gained at the Aegates Islands, off the western extremity of Sicily. The Carthaginians were unprepared for the terrible defeat which they suffered, and were obliged to sue for peace. They were obliged to give up Sicily; release all the Roman prisoners without ransom; and pay to the Romans 3,200 talents (about $4,000,000), within ten years. Thus ended the first Punic war, which had lasted for twenty-three years. During this time Rome had shown her ability to fight upon the sea and had fairly entered the lists as one of the great powers of the world. But this first contest with Carthage, severe as it was, was merely a preparation for the more terrible struggle which was yet to-come.

III. EVENTS FOLLOWING THE WAR (B.C. 241-218)

Sicily becomes the First Roman Province.—In the interval between the first and second Punic wars, both Rome and Carthage sought to strengthen and consolidate their power. They knew that the question of supremacy was not yet decided, and sooner or later another contest must come. Rome found herself in possession of a new territory outside of Italy, which must be organized. She had already three kinds of territory: (1) the Roman domain (*ager Romanus*), where all were, generally speaking, full citizens; (2) the Latin colonies, in which the people had a part of the rights of citizens; and (3) the Italian land, in which the people were not citizens, but were half independent, having their own governments, but bound to Rome as allies in war. In Sicily a new system was introduced. The people were made neither citizens nor allies, but subjects. The land was generally confiscated, and the inhabitants were obliged to pay a heavy tribute. The whole island—except Syracuse, which remained independent—was governed by a praetor sent from Rome. By this arrangement Sicily became a "province"—which is another name for a conquered territory outside of Italy.

Annexation of Sardinia and Corsica.—Besides Sicily, there were in the Mediterranean two other islands which seemed by nature to belong to Italy. These were Sardinia and Corsica. While Carthage was engaged in suppressing a revolt of her own soldiers, which is known as the "mercenary war" in Africa, Rome saw a favorable opportunity to get possession of Sardinia. Carthage protested against such an act; and Rome replied by demanding the cession of the island, and also the payment of a fine of 1200 talents (about $1,500,000). Carthage was obliged to submit to this unjust demand; but she determined to avenge herself in the future. As Sardinia came to her so easily, Rome proceeded to take Corsica also, and the two islands were erected into a second Roman province. Rome thus obtained possession of the three great islands of the western Mediterranean.

Suppression of the Illyrian Pirates.—The attention of Rome was soon directed to the eastern coast of the Adriatic Sea. An appeal came from the Greek cities for protection against the pirates of the Adriatic. These pirates were the people of Illyricum, who made their living by plundering the ships and ravaging the coasts of their Greek neighbors. With a fleet of two hundred ships, Rome cleared the Adriatic Sea of these pirates. She then took the Greek cities under her protection; Rome thus obtained a foothold upon the eastern coast of the Adriatic, which brought her into friendly relations with Greece, and afterward into hostile relations with Macedonia.

Conquest of Cisalpine Gaul.—As Rome began to be drawn into foreign wars, she became aware that her position at home could not be secure so long as the northern part of Italy remained unconquered. The Alps formed the natural boundary of Italy; and to this boundary she felt obliged to extend her power. She planted colonies upon the Gallic frontier, and in these towns made a large assignment of lands to her own citizens. The Gauls resented this as an encroachment upon their territory; they appealed to arms, invaded Etruria, and threatened Rome. The invaders were defeated and driven back, and the war was continued in the valley of the Po until the whole of Cisalpine Gaul was finally subdued. The conquered territory was secured by new colonies, and Rome was practically supreme to the Alps. Her people were made more devoted to her by the share which they received in the new land. Her dominions were now so well organized, and her authority so secure, that she felt prepared for another contest with Carthage.

SELECTIONS FOR READING

Pelham, Bk. III., Ch. 1, "Rome and Carthage" (1).[2]

Liddell, Ch. 28, "Events leading to the First Punic War" (1).

Arnold, Hist., Ch. 39, "Constitution and Power of Carthage" (2).

Mommsen, Vol. II., Bk. III., Ch. 1, "Carthage"; Ch. 2, "War concerning Sicily" (2).

Mommsen, abridged, Ch. 12, "Carthage"; Ch. 13, "First Punic War" (2).

Shuckburgh, Ch. 17, "Rome and Carthage" (1).

How and Leigh, Ch. 18, "First Punic War" (1).

SPECIAL STUDY

THE ROMAN NAVY.—Arnold, Hist., p. 428 (2); How and Leigh, pp. 141-143, 152 (1); Shuckburgh, pp. 237, 241 (1); Eschenburgh, p. 282 (8); Ramsay and Lanciani, pp. 453-458 (8); Guhl and Koner, pp. 253-264 (16); Harper's Dict. Antiqq., "Navis" (8).

[1] So called because the Latin word for Carthaginian is *Punicus*.

[2] The figure in parenthesis refers to the number of the topic in the Appendix, where a fuller title of the book will be found.

CHAPTER XV

THE SECOND PUNIC WAR (B.C. 218-201)

From Saguntum to Cannae (B.C. 218-216), I.—From Cannae to the Metaurus (B.C. 216-207), II.—From the Metaurus to Zama (B.C. 207-201), III.

I. FROM SAGUNTUM TO CANNAE (B.C. 218-216)

Beginning of the War in Spain.—The second Punic war, which now followed, was to decide the fate of Rome, and perhaps of Europe. Its real cause was the growing rivalry between the two great powers that were now struggling for supremacy in the western Mediterranean. But it was directly brought about by the rapid growth of the Carthaginian dominion in Spain. While Rome was adding to her strength by the conquest of Cisalpine Gaul and the reduction of the islands in the sea, Carthage was building up a great empire in the Spanish peninsula. Here she expected to raise new armies, with which to invade Italy. This was the policy of Hamilcar Barca, her greatest citizen and soldier. The work was begun by Hamilcar himself, and then continued by his son-in-law, Hasdrubal, who founded the city of New Carthage as the capital of the new province.

Rome began to be alarmed, as she saw the territory of her rival extending toward the north. She induced Carthage to make a treaty not to extend her conquests beyond the river Iberus (Ebro), in the northern part of Spain. Rome also formed a treaty of alliance with the Greek city of Saguntum, which, though south of the Iberus, was up to this time free and independent. Carthage continued the work of conquering the southern part of Spain, without infringing upon the rights of Rome, until Hasdrubal died. Then Hannibal, the young son of the great Hamilcar, and the idol of the army, was chosen as commander. This young Carthaginian, who had in his boyhood sworn an eternal hostility to Rome, now felt that his mission was come. He marched from New Carthage and proceeded to attack Saguntum, the ally of Rome; and after a siege of eight months, captured it. The Romans sent an embassy to Carthage to demand the surrender of Hannibal. The story is told that Quintus Fabius, the chief Roman envoy, lifted up a fold of his toga and said to the Carthaginian senate, "Here we bring you peace and war; which do you choose?" "Give us either," was the reply. "Then I offer you war," said Fabius. "And this we accept," shouted the Carthaginians. Thus was begun the most memorable war of ancient times.

Hannibal and Rome.—Rome was now at war, not only with Carthage, but with Hannibal. The first Punic war had been a struggle with the greatest naval power of the

Mediterranean, but the second Punic war was to be a conflict with one of the greatest soldiers that the world has ever seen. As a military genius, no Roman could compare with him. If the Romans could have known what ruin and desolation were to follow in the train of this young man of Carthage, they might have hesitated to enter upon this war. But no one could know the future. While Carthage placed her cause in the hands of a brilliant captain, Rome felt that she was supported by a courageous and steadfast people. It will be interesting for us to follow this contest between a great man and a great nation.

Hannibal's Invasion of Italy.—Even at the beginning of the war Hannibal showed his great genius as a soldier. The Romans formed an excellent plan to send two armies into the enemy's country—one into Africa under Sempronius, and the other into Spain under P. Cornelius Scipio (*sip'i-o*). But Hannibal, with the instinct of a true soldier, saw that Carthage would be safe if Italy were invaded and Rome threatened. Leaving his brother Hasdrubal to protect Spain, he crossed the Pyrenees with fifty thousand infantry, nine thousand cavalry, and a number of elephants. Without delay he pushed on to the river Rhone; outflanked the barbarians, who were trying to oppose his passage; and crossed the river above, just as the Roman army (which had expected to meet him in Spain) had reached Massilia (Marseilles). When the Roman commander, P. Cornelius Scipio, found that he had been outgeneraled by Hannibal, he sent his brother Cn. Scipio on to Spain with the main army, and returned himself to Cisalpine Gaul, expecting to destroy the Carthaginian if he should venture to come into Italy. Hannibal in the meantime pressed on; and in spite of innumerable difficulties and dangers crossed the Alps. He finally reached the valley of the Po, with only twenty thousand foot and six thousand horse. Here he recruited his ranks from the Gauls, who eagerly joined his cause against the Romans.

Hannibal's Early Victories.—When the Romans were aware that Hannibal was really in Italy, they made preparations to meet and to destroy him. Sempronius was recalled with the army originally intended for Africa; and Scipio, who had returned from Massilia, gathered together the scattered forces in northern Italy and took up his station at Placentia on the Po. The cavalry of the two armies first met in a skirmish on the north side of the Po, near the little stream Ticinus. The Romans were defeated, and Scipio himself was severely wounded. Hannibal then crossed to the south of the Po. To prevent his advance, Scipio took up a strong position on the bank of the river Trebia. Scipio was soon joined by his colleague Sempronius, who came to him from Ariminum on the Adriatic coast. The two hostile armies were now separated by the river Trebia. Here again Hannibal showed his great skill as a general. By a feigned

87

attack he drew the Romans over to his own side of the river. He then attacked them in front, upon the flank, and in the rear; and the Roman army was nearly annihilated. The remnant of the army fled to Placentia. This great disaster did not discourage the Romans. They soon raised new armies with which to resist the invaders.

Battle of Lake Trasumenus (B.C. 217).—In the following spring, the new consul, Flaminius, placed his own army at Arretium, in Etruria, and his colleague's army at Ariminum, to guard the only roads upon which it seemed possible that Hannibal could move, in order to reach Rome. But Hannibal, instead of going by either of these roads on which he was expected to go, crossed the Apennines and pushed on toward Rome through the marshy regions of Etruria. He thus got between the Roman armies and the Roman capital. He knew that Flaminius would be obliged to hasten to Rome to protect the city. He also knew by what road Flaminius must go, and he determined to destroy the Roman army on its way. He posted his army on the heights near the northern shore of Lake Trasumenus (Trasimene), overlooking a defile through which the Roman army must pass. The Romans approached this defile and entered it, not suspecting the terrible fate which awaited them. At a given signal, the soldiers of Hannibal rushed to the attack. The Romans were overwhelmed on every side, and those who escaped the fierce Gauls and the dreaded cavalry of Numidia were buried in the waters of the lake. Fifteen thousand Romans and Italians fell on that fatal field, with Flaminius, their leader. The Roman army was practically destroyed. Northern Italy was now at the mercy of Hannibal, and Rome seemed an easy prey to the victorious Carthaginian.

Fabius Maximus, Dictator.—"We have lost a great battle, our army is destroyed, Flaminius is killed!" was the simple announcement which the praetor made, after the frightful disaster at Lake Trasumenus. But this simple announcement brought consternation to the Roman people. They recalled the days of the Gauls and the battle on the Allia. But they were still determined to defend their country. The times seemed to demand a dictator, and Q. Fabius Maximus was appointed. He was a member of that Fabian gens which had before proved its devotion to the country; and he was also that ambassador who had offered to Carthage the choice between peace and war. He ordered new armies to be raised, and the city to be put in a state of defense.

Hannibal did not see fit to attack Rome; but, turning to the east, he moved through Umbria and Picenum into Apulia, plundering the country as he went. He hoped to draw to his standard the allies of Rome in southern Italy, by showing that they were safe only under his protection. He also wished to provoke Fabius to a pitched battle. But Fabius had learned some lessons from the war; and he adopted the safe policy of harassing the army of Hannibal and of avoiding a general engagement. On account of this cautious strategy he was called Fabius Cunctator, or the Delayer. In order to irritate him to a conflict, Hannibal marched through Samnium into the rich fields of Campania. Fabius then tried to shut Hannibal up in this little territory by holding the mountain passes. But when Hannibal was ready to go, he opened his way by a stratagem. He ordered his light-armed troops in the night to drive up the mountain side a herd of cattle, with lighted fagots tied to their horns. The Romans who guarded the way, deceived or panic-stricken by this unusual demonstration, abandoned their post. Hannibal marched through the unguarded pass, and was free again to plunder the countries of southern Italy. He moved eastward through Samnium, and then descended into the region of Apulia. During all this time the allied cities of Italy had remained faithful to Rome.

Battle of Cannae (B.C. 216).—The cautious strategy of Fabius soon became unpopular; and the escape of Hannibal from Campania especially excited the dissatisfaction of the people. Two new consuls were therefore chosen, who were expected to pursue a more vigorous policy. These were Terentius Varro and Aemilius Paullus. Hannibal's army was now in Apulia, near the little town of Cannae on the Aufidus River. To this place the consuls led their new forces, consisting of eighty thousand infantry and six thousand cavalry,—the largest army that the Romans had, up to that time, ever gathered on a single battlefield; Hannibal's army consisted of forty thousand infantry and ten thousand cavalry. But the brain of Hannibal was more than a match for the forty thousand extra Romans, under the command of less able generals. The Roman consuls took command on alternate days. Paullus was cautious; but Varro was impetuous and determined to fight Hannibal at the first opportunity. As this was Hannibal's greatest battle, we may learn something of his wonderful skill by looking at, its plan.

The Romans drew up their heavy infantry in solid columns, facing to the south, to attack the center of Hannibal's line. In front of the heavy-armed troops were the light-armed soldiers, to act as skirmishers. On the Roman right, near the river, were two thousand of the Roman cavalry, and on the left wing were four thousand cavalry of the allies. With their army thus arranged, the Romans hoped to defeat Hannibal. But Hannibal laid his plan not simply to defeat the Roman army, but to draw it into such a position that it could be entirely destroyed. He therefore placed his weakest troops, the Spanish and Gallic infantry, in the center opposite the heavy infantry of the Romans, and pushed them forward in the form of a crescent, with the expectation that they would be driven back and pursued by the Romans. On either flank he placed an invincible body of African troops, his best and most trusted soldiers, drawn back in long, solid columns, so that they could fall upon the Romans when the center had been driven in. On his left wing, next to the river, were placed four thousand Spanish and Gallic cavalry, and on the right wing his superb body of six thousand Numidian cavalry, which was to swing around and attack the Roman army in the rear, when it had become engaged with the African troops upon the right and left.

The description of this plan is almost a description of the battle itself. When the Romans had pressed back the weak center of Hannibal's line, they found themselves ingulfed in the midst of the Carthaginian forces. Attacked on all sides, the Roman army became a confused mass of struggling men, and the battle became a butchery. The army was annihilated; seventy thousand Roman soldiers are said to have been slain, among whom were eighty senators and the consul Aemilius. The small remnant of survivors fled to the neighboring towns, and Varro, with seventy horsemen, took refuge in the city of Venusia. This was the most terrible day that Rome had seen since the destruction of the city by the Gauls, nearly two centuries before. Every house in Rome was in mourning.

II. FROM CANNAE TO THE METAURUS (B.C. 216-207)

Hannibal's New Allies.—The battle of Cannae convinced the Italian allies that it would be better to have the help, rather than the hostility, of such a man as Hannibal. The Apulians, the Lucanians, the Samnites, the Bruttians, revolted and put themselves under his protection. But the Latin colonies and the Greek cities generally remained loyal to Rome. Capua, however, the most important city in Italy, after Rome, opened her gates to Hannibal; and Tarentum, which held a Roman garrison, was betrayed into his hands. The influence of Hannibal's victory was also apparent outside of Italy. Syracuse transferred her allegiance from Rome to Carthage, and many other cities in Sicily threatened to revolt. Philip V., the king of Macedonia, also made an alliance with Hannibal, and threatened to invade Italy to assist him. Hannibal at this time was at the height of his power.

Dismay and Fortitude of the Romans.—During the period which followed the battle of Cannae, the Roman character was put to its severest test. The people feared the worst. Everything seemed turning against them. They were in dismay; but they did not despair. The popular excitement was soon allayed by the firmness of the senate. Under the wise counsels of Fabius Maximus, new plans were made for the recovery of Italy. But the problem now seemed greater than ever before. The war must be carried on, not only in Italy, to recover the revolted allies and to meet the continued attacks of Hannibal; but also in Spain, to prevent reënforcements coming from Hasdrubal; and in Sicily, to prevent the cities of that province from following the example of Syracuse;

and finally in Greece, to prevent the king of Macedonia from interfering in the affairs of Italy. In the face of all discouragements, the Roman people, supported by the faithful Latin towns and colonies, remained firm; and with fixed resolution determined to prosecute the war with greater vigor than ever before.

The Turning of the Tide.—It was at this point that the fortunes of war began to turn in favor of the Romans. The first ray of hope came from Spain, where it was learned that Hasdrubal had been defeated by the Scipios. Then Hannibal's army met its first repulse in Campania. The Romans also, by forming a league with the Aetolian cities of Greece and sending them a few troops, were able to prevent Macedonia from giving any aid to Hannibal. Soon Syracuse was captured after a siege by the Roman praetor Marcellus. Moreover, Hannibal's forces were weakened by the need of protecting his new allies, scattered in various parts of southern Italy.

Recovery of Capua.—The Romans were greatly incensed by the revolt of Capua, and determined to punish its citizens. Regular siege was laid to the city, and two Roman armies surrounded its walls. Hannibal marched to the relief of the beleaguered city and attempted to raise the siege; but could not draw the Roman army from its intrenchments. As a last resort, he marched directly to Rome, hoping to compel the Romans to withdraw their armies from Capua for the defense of the capital. Although he plundered the towns and ravaged the fields of Latium, and rode about the walls of Rome, the fact that "Hannibal was at the gates," did not entice the Roman army away from Capua. Rome was well defended, and Hannibal, having no means of besieging the city, withdrew again into the southern part of Italy. Capua was soon taken by the Romans; its chief citizens were put to death for their treason, many of the inhabitants were reduced to slavery, and the city itself was put under the control of a prefect. It was apparent that Hannibal could not protect his Italian allies; and his cause seemed doomed to failure, unless he could receive help from his brother Hasdrubal, who was still in Spain.

The Scipios in Spain (B.C. 218-212); Battle of the Metaurus (B.C. 207).—Hasdrubal had been kept in Spain by the vigorous campaign which the Romans had conducted in that peninsula under the two Scipios. Upon the death of these generals, the young Publius Cornelius Scipio was sent to Spain and earned a great name by his victories. But Hasdrubal was determined to go to the rescue of his brother in Italy. He followed Hannibal's path over the Alps into the valley of the Po. Hannibal had moved northward into Apulia, and was awaiting news from Hasdrubal. There were now two enemies in Italy, instead of one. One Roman army under Claudius Nero was, therefore, sent to oppose Hannibal in Apulia; and another army under Livius Salinator was sent to meet Hasdrubal, who had just crossed the river Metaurus, in Umbria.

It was necessary that Hasdrubal should be crushed before Hannibal was informed of his arrival in Italy. The consul Claudius Nero therefore left his main army in Apulia, and with eight thousand picked soldiers hurried to the aid of his colleague in Umbria. The battle which took place at the Metaurus was decisive; and really determined the issue of the second Punic war. The army of Hasdrubal was entirely destroyed, and he himself was slain. The first news which Hannibal received of this disaster was from the lifeless lips of his own brother, whose head was thrown by the Romans into the Carthaginian camp. Hannibal saw that the death of his brother was the doom of Carthage; and he sadly exclaimed, "O Carthage, I see thy fate!" Hannibal retired into Bruttium; and the Roman consuls received the first triumph that had been given since the beginning of this disastrous war.

III. FROM THE METAURUS TO ZAMA (B.C. 207-201)

Publius Scipio Africanus.—Of all the men produced by Rome during the Punic wars, Publius Cornelius Scipio (afterward called Africanus) came the nearest to being a military genius. From boyhood he had, like Hannibal, served in the army. At the death of his father and uncle, he had been intrusted with the conduct of the war in Spain. With great ability he had defeated the armies which opposed him, and had regained the entire peninsula, after it had been almost lost. With his conquest of New Carthage and Gades (see map, p. 112), Spain was brought under the Roman power. On his return to Rome, Scipio was unanimously elected to the consulship. He then proposed his scheme for closing the war. This plan was to keep Hannibal shut up in the Bruttian peninsula, and to carry the war into Africa. Although this scheme seemed to the aged Fabius Maximus as rash, the people had entire confidence in the young Scipio, and supported him. From this time Scipio was the chief figure in the war, and the senate kept him in command until its close.

The War carried into Africa.—Scipio now organized his new army, which was made up largely of volunteers, and equipped by patriotic contributions. He embarked from Sicily and landed in Africa. He was assisted by the Numidian king, Masinissa, whom he had previously met in Spain; and whose royal title was now disputed by a rival named Syphax, an ally of Carthage. The title to the kingship of Numidia thus became mixed up with the war with Carthage. Scipio and Masinissa soon defeated the Carthaginian armies in Africa, and the fate of Carthage was sealed.

Recall of Hannibal.—While the war was progressing in Africa, Hannibal still held his place in Bruttium like a lion at bay. In the midst of misfortune, he was still a hero. He kept control of his devoted army, and was faithful to his duty when all was lost.

Carthage was convinced that her only hope was in recalling Hannibal to defend his native city. Hannibal left Italy, the field of his brilliant exploits, and landed in Africa. Thus Rome was relieved of her dreaded foe, who had brought her so near to the brink of ruin.

Battle of Zama and End of the War (B.C. 201).—The two greatest generals then living were now face to face upon the soil of Africa. The final battle of the war was fought (B.C. 202) near Zama (see map, p. 112). Hannibal fought at a great disadvantage. His own veterans were reduced greatly in number, and the new armies of Carthage could not be depended upon. Scipio changed the order of the legions, leaving spaces in his line, through which the elephants of Hannibal might pass without being opposed. In this battle Hannibal was defeated, and the Carthaginian army was annihilated. It is said that twenty thousand men were slain, and as many more taken prisoners. The great war was now ended, and Scipio imposed the terms of peace (B.C. 201). These terms were as follows: (1) Carthage was to give up the whole of Spain and all the islands between Africa and Italy; (2) Masinissa was recognized as the king of Numidia and the ally of Rome; (3) Carthage was to pay an annual tribute of 200 talents (about $250,000) for fifty years; (4) Carthage agreed not to wage any war without the consent of Rome.

Rome was thus recognized as the mistress of the western Mediterranean. Carthage, although not reduced to a province, became a dependent state. Syracuse was added to the province of Sicily, and the territory of Spain was divided into two provinces, Hither and Farther Spain. Rome had, moreover, been brought into hostile relations with Macedonia, which paved the way for her conquests in the East.

SELECTIONS FOR READING

Mommsen, Vol. II., Bk. III., Ch. 4, "Hamilcar and Hannibal" (2).[1]

Mommsen, abridged, Ch. 14, "Second Punic War" (2).

Arnold, Hist., p. 478, "Hannibal's Passage of the Alps" (2).

Shuckburgh, p. 314, "Battle of Trasimene" (1).

How and Leigh, p. 229, "Battle of Zama" (1).

Plutarch, "Marcellus," "Fabius" (11).

Livy, Bk. XXI., Chs. 7-15, Siege of Saguntum (4).

    See also Appendix (25) "Hannibal."

SPECIAL STUDY

BATTLE OF CANNAE.—Liddell, pp. 311-315 (1); Shuckburgh, pp. 323-328 (1); How and Leigh, pp. 194-198 (1); Arnold, Hist., pp. 496-500 (2); Mommsen, Vol. II., pp. 154-158 (2); Livy, Bk. XXII., Chs. 44-52 (4); Appian, Bk. VIII., Ch. 4 (4);

Polybius, Bk. III., sects. 112-118 (4).

CHAPTER XVI

THE CONQUESTS IN THE EAST (B.C. 200-133)

The Condition of the East, I.—The First and Second Macedonian Wars, II.—War with Antiochus of Syria (B.C. 192-189), III.—The Third Macedonian War (B.C. 171-168), IV.

I. THE CONDITION OF THE EAST

The Divisions of the Empire of Alexander.—At the time of the second Punic war, the countries about the Mediterranean may be considered as forming two distinct worlds: the Western world, in which Rome and Carthage were struggling for mastery; and the Eastern world, which was divided among the successors of Alexander the Great. It was more than a century before this time that Alexander had built up a great empire, extending from Greece to the middle of Asia. By his conquests the ideals of Greek art and literature and philosophy had been spread into the eastern countries. But Alexander had none of the genius for organization which the Romans possessed, and so at his death his empire fell to pieces. The fragments were seized by his different generals, and became new and distinct kingdoms. At this time there were three of these kingdoms which were quite extensive and powerful. These were: (1) the kingdom of Egypt under the Ptolemies, in Africa; (2) the kingdom of Syria under the Seleucidae, in Asia; and (3) the kingdom of Macedonia under the direct successors of Alexander, in southeastern Europe (see map, p. 124).

Egypt under the Ptolemies.—Under the reign of the Ptolemies, Egypt had attained a remarkable degree of prosperity. Her territory not only included the valley of the Nile, but extended into Asia, taking in Palestine, Phoenicia, and the southern part of Syria (Coele-Syria), besides Cyprus and some other islands. Its capital, Alexandria, was perhaps the most cultivated city of the world, where the learned men of all countries found their home. So devoted was Egypt to the arts of peace, that she kept aloof, as far as possible, from the great wars of this period. But she was an object of envy to the kings of Syria and Macedonia; and toward the close of the second Punic war, in order to protect herself, she had formed an alliance with Rome. The friendly relations between Rome and Egypt were preserved, while Rome carried on war with the other great powers of the East.

Syria under Antiochus III.—The most important fragment of Alexander's empire in Asia was Syria, or the kingdom of the Seleucidae—so called from the name of its founder, Seleucus the Conqueror. It covered a large part of western Asia, comprising the valley of the Euphrates, upper Syria, and portions of Asia Minor. Its rulers

96

included four kings by the name of Seleucus, and eight by the name of Antiochus. These names also appear in the capital cities of the Syrian empire, Seleucia on the Tigris and Antioch in upper Syria. The most powerful of these kings was Antiochus III., surnamed the Great. He did much to enlarge and strengthen the empire. But he incurred the hostility of Rome by giving asylum to Rome's great enemy, Hannibal, and also by attempting to make conquests in Europe. There were a few small states in Asia Minor, like Pergamum, Bithynia, Pontus, and the island republic of Rhodes, which were not included in the kingdom of Syria and which were inclined to look to Rome for protection.

Macedonia and the Greek Cities.—The third great fragment of Alexander's empire was Macedonia, which aspired to be supreme in eastern Europe. A part of Greece fell under its authority. But many of the Greek cities remained free; and they united into leagues or confederations, in order to maintain their independence. One of these was the Achaean league, made up of the cities of southern Greece, or the Peloponnesus; and another was the Aetolian league, including a large number of cities in central Greece. When Philip V. came to the throne of Macedonia, his kingdom was in a flourishing condition. The young ruler was ambitious to extend his power; and came into hostile relations with Rome, which espoused the cause of the Greek cities.

II. THE FIRST AND SECOND MACEDONIAN WARS

The First Macedonian War (B.C. 215-206).—It was the indiscreet alliance of Philip of Macedonia with Hannibal, during the second Punic war, which we have already noticed, that brought about the first conflict between Rome and Macedonia. But Rome was then so fully occupied with her struggle with Carthage that all she desired to do was simply to prevent Philip from making his threatened invasion of Italy. Rome therefore sent a small force across the Adriatic, made friends with the Aetolians, and kept Philip occupied at home. The Macedonian king was thus prevented from sending any force into Italy. The Aetolians, not satisfied with the support given to them by Rome, soon made peace with Philip; and the Romans themselves, who were about to invade Africa, were also willing to conclude a treaty of peace with him. Thus closed what is generally called the first Macedonian war, which was really nothing more than a diversion to prevent Philip from giving aid to Hannibal after the battle of Cannae.

Beginning of the Second Macedonian War (B.C. 200-197).—When the second Punic war was fairly ended, Rome felt free to deal with Philip of Macedonia, and to take a firm hand in settling the affairs of the East. Philip had annoyed her, not only by making an alliance with Hannibal, but afterward by sending a force to assist him at the battle of Zama. And now the ambitious schemes of Philip were not at all to the liking of Rome. For instance, he made an agreement with Antiochus of Syria to cut up the possessions of Egypt, a country which was friendly to Rome. He was also overrunning the coasts of the Aegean Sea, and was threatening the little kingdom of Pergamum in Asia Minor, and the little republic of Rhodes, as well as the cities of Greece. When appeal came to Rome for protection, she espoused the cause of the small states, and declared war against Macedonia.

Battle of Cynoscephalae (B.C. 197).—The great hero of this war was T. Quinctius Flamininus; and the decisive battle was fought near a hill in Thessaly called Cynoscephalae (Dog's Heads). Here Philip was completely defeated, and his army was destroyed. Although Macedonia was not reduced to the condition of a province, it became practically subject to Rome. Macedonia was thus humbled, and there was no other power in Europe to dispute the supremacy of Rome.

The Liberation of Greece (B.C. 196).—To complete her work in eastern Europe, and to justify her position as defender of the Greek cities, Rome withdrew her garrisons and announced the independence of Greece. This was proclaimed by Flamininus at the Isthmian games, amid wild enthusiasm and unbounded expressions of gratitude. Rome was hailed as "the nation which, at its own expense, with its own labor, and at its own risk, waged war for the liberty of others, and which had crossed the sea that justice, right, and law should everywhere have sovereign sway" (Livy, xxxiii, 33).

III. WAR WITH ANTIOCHUS OF SYRIA (B.C. 192-189)

Beginning of the War; the Aetolians.—There was now left in the world only one great power which could claim to be a rival of Rome. That power was Syria, under its ambitious ruler, Antiochus III. A number of things led to the conflict between Rome and this great power in Asia. But the direct cause of the war grew out of the intrigues of the Aetolians in Greece. This restless people stirred up a discord among the Greek cities, and finally called upon Antiochus to espouse their cause, and to aid them in driving the Romans out of the country. Antiochus accepted this invitation, crossed the Hellespont, and landed in Greece with an army of 10,000 men (B.C. 192).

Battles of Thermopylae and Magnesia.—Rome now appeared as the protector of Europe against Asia. She was supported by her previous enemy, Philip of Macedonia; and she was also aided by the kingdom of Pergamum and the republic of Rhodes. The career of Antiochus in Greece was short. He was defeated by Marcus Porcius Cato in the famous pass of Thermopylae (B.C. 191), and was driven back across the sea into Asia Minor. The next year the Romans followed him, and fought their first battle upon the continent of Asia. The Roman army was nominally under the command of the new consul, L. Cornelius Scipio, but really under the command of his famous brother, Scipio Africanus, who accompanied him. The decisive battle was fought at Magnesia (B.C. 190), not far from Sardis in western Asia Minor. Forty thousand of the enemy were slain, with a comparatively small loss to the Romans. Scipio imposed the terms of peace, which required Antiochus (1) to give up all his possessions in Asia Minor— the most of which were added to the kingdom of Pergamum, with some territory to the republic of Rhodes; (2) to give up his fleet and not to interfere in European affairs; (3) to pay the sum of 15,000 talents (nearly $20,000,000) within twelve years; and (4) to surrender Hannibal, who had taken an active part in the war.

Subjection of the Aetolians.—After the great victory of Magnesia, Rome turned her arms against the Aetolians, who were so foolish as to continue the struggle. Their chief city, Ambracia, was taken; and they were soon forced to submit. Macedonia and all Greece, with the exception of the Achaean league, were now brought into subjection to the Roman authority.

The Fate of Hannibal.—To the Romans it seemed an act of treachery that Hannibal, who had been conquered in a fair field at Zama, should continue his hostility by fighting on the side of their enemies. But Hannibal never forgot the oath of eternal enmity to Rome, the oath which he had sworn at his father's knee. When Antiochus agreed to surrender him, Hannibal fled to Crete, and afterward took refuge with the king of Bithynia. Here he continued his hostility to Rome by aiding this ruler in a war against Rome's ally, the king of Pergamum. The Romans still pursued him, and sent Flamininus to demand his surrender. But Hannibal again fled, and, hunted from the face of the earth, this great soldier, who had been the most terrible foe that Rome had ever encountered, took his own life by drinking poison. It is said that the year of his death was the same year (B.C. 183) in which died his great and victorious antagonist, Scipio Africanus.

IV. THE THIRD MACEDONIAN WAR (B.C. 171-168)

Roman Policy in the East.—By the great battles of Cynoscephalae and Magnesia, Rome had reason to believe that she had broken the power of her rivals in the East. But she had not yet adopted in that part of the world the policy which she had previously employed in the case of Sicily and Spain, namely, of reducing the territory to the condition of provinces. She had left the countries of the East nominally free and independent; and had placed them in the condition of subject allies, or of tributary states. She had compelled them to reduce their armies, to give her an annual tribute, and to promise not to make a war without her consent. In this way she believed that

Macedonia and Syria would be obliged to keep the peace. Over the weaker powers, like the Greek cities, the kingdom of Pergamum, and the republic of Rhodes, she had assumed the position of a friendly protector. But in spite of this generous policy, a spirit of discontent gradually grew up in the various countries, and Rome was soon obliged, as we shall see, to adopt a new and more severe policy, in order to maintain peace and order throughout her growing empire.

Beginning of the Third Macedonian War.—Philip of Macedonia had been a faithful ally of Rome during the late war with Antiochus; but at its close he felt that he had not been sufficiently rewarded for his fidelity. He saw that the little states of Pergamum and Rhodes had received considerable accessions to their territories, while he himself was apparently forgotten. On account of this seeming neglect, he began to think of regaining his old power. When he died, he was succeeded by his son, Perseus, who continued the design of making Macedonia free from the dictation of Rome. Perseus did what he could to develop the resources of his kingdom, and to organize and strengthen his army. He even began to be looked upon by the Greek cities as their champion against the encroachments of Rome. But the time soon came when he was obliged to answer for his arrogant conduct. The Romans became convinced of the ambitious scheme of Perseus, and entered upon a new war against Macedonia.

Battle of Pydna (B.C. 168).—After three unsuccessful campaigns, the Romans finally placed in command of their army an able general, Aemilius Paullus, the son of the consul who was slain at Cannae. The two armies met near Pydna, (see map, p. 128), and Perseus suffered a crushing defeat. Here the Macedonian phalanx fought its last great battle, and the Roman legions gave a new evidence of their superior strength. Twenty thousand Macedonians were slain, and eleven thousand were captured. It is said that the spoils of this battle were so great that the citizens of Rome were henceforth relieved from the payment of taxes. Paullus received at Rome the most magnificent triumph that had ever been seen. For three days the gorgeous procession marched through the streets of Rome, bearing the trophies of the East. Through the concourse of exultant people was driven the chariot of the defeated king of Macedonia, followed by the victorious army adorned with laurels, and its successful commander decked with the insignia of Jupiter Capitolinus, with a laurel branch in his hand.

The Settlement of Macedonia.—The question now arose as to what should be done with Macedonia, which had so many times resisted the Roman power. The Romans were not yet ready to reduce the country to a province, and were not willing to have it remain independent. It was therefore split up into four distinct republics, which were to be entirely separated from one another, but which were to be dependent upon Rome. With a show of generosity, Rome compelled the people to pay as tribute only half of what had been previously paid to the Macedonian king. But the republics could have no relations with one another, either by way of commerce or intermarriage. All the chief men of Greece who had given any aid to the Macedonian king were transported to Italy, where they could not stir up a revolt in their native country. Among these Achaean captives was the famous historian, Polybius, who during this time gathered the materials of his great work on Roman history.

SELECTIONS FOR READING

Pelham, Bk. III., Ch. 2, "Rome and the East" (1).[1]

Arnold, Hist., Ch. 35, "State of the East" (2).

How and Leigh, Ch. 25, "Eastern States and Second Macedonian War" (1).

Liddell, Ch. 39, "Settlement of Greece" (1).

Mommsen, Vol. II., Bk. III., Ch. 8, "The Eastern States" (2).

Mommsen, abridged, Ch. 17, "War with Antiochus" (2).

Merivale, Gen. Hist., Ch. 25, "Deaths of Three Great Men" (1).

Plutarch, "Aemilius Paullus," "Flamininus" (11).

Livy, Bk. XXXIII., Chs. 32, 33, The Liberation of Greece (4).

SPECIAL STUDY

ACHAEAN AND AETOLIAN LEAGUES.—Liddell, pp. 416-417 (1); Shuckburgh, pp. 413-415 (1); How and Leigh, pp. 257-259 (1); Mommsen, Vol. II., pp. 262-265 (2).

[1] The figure in parenthesis refers to the number of the topic in the Appendix, where a fuller title of the book will be found.

CHAPTER XVII

REDUCTION OF THE ROMAN CONQUESTS
Reduction of Macedonia and Greece, I.—Third Punic War and Reduction of Africa (B.C. 149-146), II.—Pacification of the Provinces, III.

I. REDUCTION OF MACEDONIA AND GREECE

Change of the Roman Policy.—We sometimes think that Rome started out upon her great career of conquest with a definite purpose to subdue the world, and with clear ideas as to how it should be governed. But nothing could be farther from the truth. She had been drawn on from one war to another, often against her own will. When she first crossed the narrow strait into Sicily at the beginning of the first Punic war, she little thought that in a hundred years her armies would be fighting in Asia; and when in early times she was compelled to find some way of keeping peace and order in Latium, she could not have known that she would, sooner or later, be compelled to devise a way to preserve the peace and order of the world. But Rome was ever growing and ever learning. She learned how to conquer before she learned how to govern. It was after the third Macedonian war that Rome became convinced that her method of governing the conquered lands was not strong enough to preserve peace and maintain her own authority. She had heretofore left the conquered states to a certain extent free and independent. But now, either excited by jealousy or irritated by the intrigues and disturbances of the conquered people, she was determined to reduce them to a more complete state of submission.

New Disturbances in Macedonia.—She was especially convinced of the need of a new policy by the continued troubles in Macedonia. The experiment which she had tried, of cutting up the kingdom into four separate states, had not been entirely successful. To add to the disturbances there appeared a man who called himself Philip, and who pretended to be the son of Perseus. He incited the people to revolt, and even defeated the Romans in a battle; but he was himself soon defeated and made a prisoner.

Revolt of the Achaean Cities.—The spirit of revolt, excited by the false Philip, spread into Greece. The people once more began to feel that the freedom of Rome was worse than slavery. It is true that Rome had liberated the Achaean captives who had been transported to Italy after the third Macedonian war; but these men, who had spent so much of their lives in captivity, carried back to Greece the bitter spirit which they still cherished. The Greek cities became not only unfriendly to Rome, but were also at strife with one another. Sparta desired to withdraw from the Achaean league, and appealed to Rome for help. Rome sent commissioners to Greece to settle the difficulty; but the Achaean came together in their assembly at Corinth and insulted the Roman commissioners, and were then rash enough to declare war against Rome herself.

Destruction of Corinth (B.C. 146).—The war which now followed, for the subjugation of Greece, was at first conducted by Metellus; and afterward by Mummius, an able general but a boorish man, who hated the Greeks and cared little for their culture. Corinth, the chief city of the Achaean league, was captured; the art treasures, pictures and statues, the splendid products of Greek genius, were sent to Rome. The inhabitants were sold as slaves. And by the cruel command of the senate, the city itself was reduced to ashes. This was a barbarous act of war, such an act as no civilized nation has ever approved. That the Romans were not yet fully civilized, and knew little of the meaning of art, is shown by the story told of Mummius. This rude consul warned the sailors who carried the pictures and statues of Corinth to Rome, that "if they lost or damaged any of them, they must replace them with others of equal value."

Macedonia reduced to a Province.—The time had now come for Rome to adopt her new policy in respect to Macedonia. The old divisions into which the kingdom had been divided were abolished, and each city or community was made directly responsible to the governor sent from Rome. By this new arrangement, Macedonia became a province. The cities of Greece were allowed to remain nominally free, but the political confederacies were broken up, and each city came into direct relation with Rome through the governor of Macedonia. Greece was afterward organized as a separate province, under the name of Achaia.

II. THIRD PUNIC WAR AND REDUCTION OF AFRICA (B.C. 149-146)

Revival of Carthage.—The new policy which Rome applied to Macedonia she also adopted with respect to Carthage. Since the close of the second Punic war, Carthage had faithfully observed the terms of the treaty which Rome had imposed. She had abandoned war and devoted herself to the arts of peace. Her commerce had revived; her ships were again plying the waters of the Mediterranean; and she seemed destined to become once more a rich and prosperous city. But her prosperity was the cause of her ruin. The jealousy of Rome was aroused by the recovery of her former rival. The story is often told, that Cato (the Censor) was sent to Carthage on an embassy; that he was astonished at the wealth and prosperity which everywhere met his gaze; that he pictured the possibility of another struggle with that queen of the seas; and that he closed every speech in the senate with the words, "Carthage must be destroyed."

Beginning of the Third Punic War.—Whether Rome was really alarmed at the growth of Carthage or only jealous of its commercial prosperity, the words of Cato became the policy of the senate. The Romans only waited for an opportunity to put this policy into effect. This they soon found in the quarrels between Carthage and Numidia, whose king, Masinissa, was an ally of Rome. After appealing in vain to the senate to protect their rights against Masinissa, the Carthaginians were bold enough to take up arms to protect their own rights. But to Rome it was a deadly offense to take up arms against her ally. As a guaranty to keep the peace, the Carthaginians were commanded to give up three hundred of their noblest youths as hostages. The hostages were accordingly given up. The Carthaginians were then informed that, as they were then under the protection of Rome, they would not need to go to war; and that they must surrender all their arms and munitions. This hard demand was also complied with, and Carthage became defenseless. The demand was now made that, as the city was fortified, it too must be given up, and the inhabitants must remove to a point ten miles from the coast; in other words, that "Carthage must be destroyed." To such a revolting and infamous command the Carthaginians could not yield, and they resolved upon a desperate resistance.

Siege and Destruction of Carthage (B.C. 146).—Never was there a more heroic defense than that made by Carthage in this, her last struggle. She was without arms, without war ships, without allies. To make new weapons, the temples were turned into workshops; and it is said that the women cut off their long hair to be twisted into bowstrings. Supplies were collected for a long siege; the city became a camp. For three long years the brave Carthaginians resisted every attempt to take the city. They repelled the assault upon their walls. They were then cut off from all communication with the outside world by land—and they sought an egress by the sea. Their communication by water was then cut off by a great mole, or breakwater, built by the Romans—and they cut a new outlet to the sea. They then secretly built fifty war ships, and attacked the Roman fleet. But all these heroic efforts simply put off the day of doom. At last, under Scipio Aemilianus, the Romans forced their way through the wall, and the city was taken street by street, and house by house. Carthage became the prey of the Roman soldiers. Its temples were plundered; its inhabitants were carried away as captives; and by the command of the senate, the city itself was consigned to flames. The destruction of Carthage took place in the same year (B.C. 146) in which Corinth was destroyed. The terrible punishment inflicted upon these two cities in Greece and Africa was an evidence of Rome's grim policy to be absolutely supreme everywhere.

Africa reduced to a Province.—Like Macedonia, Africa was now reduced to the form of a province. It comprised all the land which had hitherto been subject to Carthage. Utica was made the new capital city, where the Roman governor was to reside. All the cities which had favored Carthage were punished by the loss of their land, or the payment of tribute. The cities which had favored Rome were allowed to remain free. Numidia, on account of its fidelity to Rome, was continued as an independent ally. In this way the condition of every city and people was dependent upon the extent of its loyalty to Rome. After Africa was made a province, it soon became a Romanized country. Its commerce passed into the hands of Roman merchants; the Roman manners and customs were introduced; and the Latin language became the language of the people.

III. PACIFICATION OF THE PROVINCES

Condition of Spain.—While the Romans were thus engaged in creating the new provinces of Macedonia and Africa, they were called upon to maintain their authority in the old provinces of Spain and Sicily. We remember that, after the second Punic war, Spain was divided into two provinces, each under a Roman governor. But the Roman authority was not well established in Spain, except upon the eastern coast. The tribes in the interior and on the western coast were nearly always in a state of revolt. The most rebellious of these tribes were the Lusitanians in the west, in what is now Portugal; and the Celtiberians (see map, p. 112) in the interior, south of the Iberus River. In their efforts to subdue these barbarous peoples, the Romans were themselves too often led to adopt the barbarous methods of deceit and treachery.

War with the Lusitanians.—How perfidious a Roman general could be, we may learn from the way in which Sulpicius Galba waged war with the Lusitanians. After one Roman army had been defeated, Galba persuaded this tribe to submit and promised to settle them upon fertile lands. When the Lusitanians came to him unarmed to receive their expected reward, they were surrounded and murdered by the troops of Galba. But it is to the credit of Rome that Galba was denounced for this treacherous act. Among the few men who escaped from the massacre of Galba was a young shepherd by the name of Viriathus. Under his brave leadership, the Lusitanians continued the war for nine years. Finally, Viriathus was murdered by his own soldiers, who were bribed to do this treacherous act by the Roman general. With their leader lost, the Lusitanians were obliged to submit (B.C. 138).

The Numantine War.—The other troublesome tribe in Spain was the Celtiberians, who were even more warlike than the Lusitanians. At one time the Roman general was defeated and obliged to sign a treaty of peace, acknowledging the independence of the Spanish tribe. But the senate—repeating what it had done many years before, after the battle of the Caudine Forks—refused to ratify this treaty, and surrendered the Roman commander to the enemy. The "fiery war," as it was called, still continued and became at last centered about Numantia, the chief town of the Celtiberians. The defense of Numantia, like that of Carthage, was heroic and desperate. Its fate was also like that of Carthage. It was compelled to surrender (B.C. 133) to the same Scipio Aemilianus. Its people were sold into slavery, and the town itself was blotted from the earth.

The Servile War in Sicily.—While Spain was being pacified, a more terrible war broke out in the province of Sicily. This was an insurrection of the slaves of the island. One of the worst results of the Roman conquest was the growth of the slave system. Immense numbers of the captives taken in war were thrown upon the market. One hundred and fifty thousand slaves had been sold by Aemilius Paullus; fifty thousand captives had been sent home from Carthage. Italy and Sicily swarmed with a servile population. It was in Sicily that this system bore its first terrible fruit. Maltreated by their masters, the slaves rose in rebellion under a leader, called Eunus, who defied the Roman power for three years. Nearly two hundred thousand insurgents gathered about his standard. Four Roman armies were defeated, and Rome herself was thrown into consternation. After the most desperate resistance, the rebellion was finally quelled and the island was pacified (B.C. 132).

Bequest of Pergamum; Province of Asia.—This long period of war and conquest, by which Rome finally obtained the proud position of mistress of the Mediterranean, was closed by the almost peaceful acquisition of a new province. The little kingdom of Pergamum, in Asia Minor, had maintained, for the most part, a friendly relation to Rome. When the last king, Attalus III., died (B.C. 133), having no legal heirs, he bequeathed his kingdom to the Roman people. This newly acquired territory was organized as a province under the name of "Asia." The smaller states of Asia Minor, and Egypt, Libya, and Numidia, retained a subordinate relation as dependencies. The supreme authority of Rome, at home and abroad, was now firmly established.

SELECTIONS FOR READING

Merivale, Gen. Hist., Chs. 26, 27, "Rome after the Conquests" (1).[1]
Pelham, Bk. III , Ch. 3, "The Roman State and People" (1).
Liddell, Chs. 49, 50, "Rome at the Close of the Conquests" (1).
How and Leigh, Ch. 32, "Foreign and Provincial Affairs" (1).
Mommsen, Vol. II., Bk. III., Ch. 11, "The Government and the Governed" (2).

Arnold, Prov. Admin., Ch. 2, "Period of the Republic" (19).

Harper's Dict. Antiqq., "Provincia" (8).

SPECIAL STUDY

TAXATION OF THE PROVINCES.—Pelham, pp. 185-187 (1); Liddell, pp. 389-393 (1); Mommsen, abridged, pp. 496-498 (2); Arnold, Prov. Admin., pp. 179-187 (19); Ihne, Hist., Vol. IV., Bk. VI., Ch. 7 (2); Ramsay and Lanciani, Ch. 8 (8); Harper's Dict. Antiqq., "Stipendium," "Publicani," "Vectigalia," (8).

[1] The figure in parenthesis refers to the number of the topic in the Appendix, where a fuller title of the book will be found.

CHAPTER XVIII

ROME AS A WORLD POWER

I. THE ROMAN GOVERNMENT

Effects of the Conquests.—We have thus followed the career of Rome during the most heroic period of her history. We have traced the path of her armies from the time they crossed the Sicilian Strait until they were finally victorious in Africa, in Spain, in Greece, and in Asia Minor. We have seen new provinces brought under her authority, until she had become the greatest power of the world. We may well wonder what would be the effect of these conquests upon the character of the Roman people, upon their government, and upon their civilization. Many of these effects were no doubt very bad. By their conquests the Romans came to be ambitious, to love power for its own sake, and to be oppressive to their conquered subjects. By plundering foreign countries, they also came to be avaricious, to love wealth more than honor, to indulge in luxury, and to despise the simplicity of their fathers. But still it was the conquests that made Rome the great power that she was. By bringing foreign nations under her sway, she was obliged to control them, and to create a system of law by which they could be governed. In spite of all its faults, her government was the most successful that had ever existed up to this time. It was the way in which Rome secured her conquests that showed the real character of the Roman people. The chief effect of the conquests was to transform Rome from the greatest *conquering* people of the world, to the greatest *governing* people of the world.

The New Nobility.—The oldest Roman government was, we remember, based upon the patrician class. We have already seen how the separation between the patricians and the plebeians was gradually broken down. The old patrician aristocracy had passed away, and Rome had become, in theory, a democratic republic. Everyone who was enrolled in the thirty-five tribes was a full Roman citizen, and had a share in the government. But we must remember that not all the persons who were under the Roman authority were full Roman citizens. The inhabitants of the Latin colonies were not full Roman citizens. They could not hold office, and only under certain conditions could they vote. The Italian allies were not citizens at all, and could neither vote nor hold office. And now the conquests had added millions of people to those who were not citizens. The Roman world was, in fact, governed by the comparatively few people who lived in and about the city of Rome. But even within this class of citizens at Rome, there had gradually grown up a smaller body of persons, who became the real holders of political power. This small body formed a new nobility—the *optimates*. All who had held the office of consul, praetor, or curule aedile—that is, a "curule office"—were regarded as nobles (*nobiles*), and their families were distinguished by the right of setting up the ancestral images in their homes (*ius imaginis*). Any citizen might, it is true, be elected to the curule offices; but the noble families were able, by their wealth, to influence the elections, so as practically to retain these offices in their own hands.

The Greatness of the Senate.—The new nobility sought to govern the world through the senate. The senators were chosen by the censor, who was obliged to place upon his list, first of all, those who had held a curule office. On this account, the nobles had the first claim to a seat in the senate; and, consequently, they came to form the great body of its members. When a person was once chosen senator he remained a senator for life, unless disgraced for gross misconduct. In this way the nobles gained possession of the senate, which became, in fact, the most permanent and powerful branch of the Roman government. Although it was an aristocratic and exclusive body, it was made up of some of the most able men of Rome. Its members were men of distinction, of wealth, and generally of great political ability. Though often inspired by motives which were selfish, ambitious, and avaricious, it was still the greatest body of rulers that ever existed in the ancient world. It managed the finances of the state; controlled the erection of public works; directed the foreign policy; administered the provinces; determined largely the character of legislation, and was, in fact, the real sovereign of the Roman state.

The Weakness of the Assemblies.—We should naturally infer that with the increase of the power of the senate, the power of the popular assemblies would decline. The old patrician assembly of the curies (*comitia curiata*) had long since been reduced to a mere shadow. But the other two assemblies—that of the centuries and that of the tribes—still held an important place as legislative bodies. But there were two reasons why they declined in influence. The first reason was their unwieldy character. As they grew in size and could only say *Yes* or *No* to the questions submitted to them, they were made subject to the influence of demagogues, and lost their independent position. The second reason for their decline was the growing custom of first submitting to the senate the proposals which were to be passed upon by them. So that, as long as the senate was so influential in the state, the popular assemblies were weak and inefficient.

II. ROME AND THE PROVINCES

The Organization of the Provinces.—The most important feature of the new Roman government was the organization of the provinces. There were now eight of these provinces: (1) Sicily, acquired as the result of the first Punic war; (2) Sardinia and Corsica, obtained during the interval between the first and second Punic wars; (3) Hither Spain and (4) Farther Spain, acquired in the second Punic war; (5) Illyricum, reduced after the third Macedonian war; (6) Macedonia (to which Achaia was attached), reduced after the destruction of Corinth; (7) Africa, organized after the third Punic war; and (8) Asia, bequeathed by Attalus III., the last king of Pergamum.

The method of organizing these provinces was in some respects similar to that which had been adopted for governing the cities in Italy. Rome saw clearly that to control these newly conquered cities and communities, they must, like the cities of Italy, be isolated, that is, separated entirely from one another, so that they could not combine in any effort to resist her authority. Every city was made directly responsible to Rome. The great difference between the Italian and the provincial towns was the fact that the chief burden of the Italian town was to furnish military aid—soldiers and ships; while that of the provincial town was to furnish tribute—money and grain. Another difference was that Italian land was generally free from taxes, while provincial land was subject to tribute.

The Provincial Governor.—A province might be defined as a group of conquered cities, outside of Italy, under the control of a governor sent from Rome. At first these governors were praetors, who were elected by the people. Afterward they were propraetors or proconsuls—that is, persons who had already served as praetors or consuls at Rome. The governor held his office for one year; and during this time was the supreme military and civil ruler of the province. He was commander in chief of the army, and was expected to preserve his territory from internal disorder and from foreign invasion. He controlled the collection of the taxes, with the aid of the quaestor, who kept the accounts. He also administered justice between the provincials. Although the governor was responsible to the senate, the welfare or misery of the provincials depended largely upon his own disposition and will.

The Towns of the Province.—All the towns of the province were subject to Rome; but it was Rome's policy not to treat them all in exactly the same way. Like the cities of Italy, they were graded according to their merit. Some were favored, like Gades and Athens, and were treated as allied towns (*civitates foederatae*); others, like Utica, were free from tribute (*immunes*); but the great majority of them were considered as tributary (*stipendiariae*). But all these towns alike possessed local self-government, so far as this was consistent with the supremacy of Rome; that is, they retained their own laws, assemblies, and magistrates.

The Administration of Justice.—In civil matters, the citizens of every town were judged by their own magistrates. But when a dispute arose between citizens of different towns, it was the duty of the governor to judge between them. At the beginning of his term of office, he generally issued an edict, setting forth the rules upon which he would decide their differences. Each succeeding governor reissued the rules of his predecessor, with the changes which he saw fit to make. In this way justice was administered with great fairness throughout the provinces; and there grew up a great body of legal principles, called the "law of nations" (*ius gentium*), which formed an important part of the Roman law.

The Collection of Taxes.—The Roman revenue was mainly derived from the new provinces. But instead of raising these taxes directly through her own officers, Rome let out the business of collecting the revenue to a set of money dealers, called *publicani*. These persons agreed to pay into the treasury a certain sum for the right of collecting taxes in a certain province. Whatever they collected above this sum, they appropriated to themselves. This rude mode of collecting taxes, called "farming" the revenues, was unworthy of a great state like Rome, and was the chief cause of the oppression of the provincials. The governors, it is true, had the power of protecting the people from being plundered. But as they themselves received no pay for their services, except what they could get out of the provinces, they were too busy in making their own fortunes to watch closely the methods of the tax-gatherers. Like every other conquering nation, the Romans were tempted to benefit themselves at the expense of their subjects.

III. THE NEW CIVILIZATION

Foreign Influences; Hellenism at Rome.—When we think of the conquests of Rome, we usually think of the armies which she defeated, and the lands which she subdued. But these were not the only conquests which she made. She appropriated not only foreign lands, but also foreign ideas. While she was plundering foreign temples, she was obtaining new ideas of religion and art. The educated and civilized people whom she captured in war and of whom she made slaves, often became the teachers of her children and the writers of her books. In such ways as these Rome came under the influence of foreign ideas. The most powerful of these foreign influences was that of Greece. We might say that when Greece was conquered by Rome, Rome was civilized by Greece. These foreign influences were seen in her new ideas of religion and philosophy, in her literature, her art, and her manners.

The Roman Religion.—As Rome came into contact with other people, we can see how her religion was affected by foreign influences. The worship of the family remained much the same; but the religion of the state became considerably changed. It is said that the entire Greek Olympus was introduced into Italy. The Romans adopted the Greek ideas and stories regarding the gods; and their worship became more showy and elaborate. Even some of the superstitious and fantastic rites of Asia found their way into Rome. These changes did not improve the religion. On the contrary, they made it more corrupt. The Roman religion, by absorbing the various ideas of other people, became a world-wide and composite form of paganism. One of the redeeming features of the Roman religion was the worship of exalted qualities, like Honor and Virtue; for example, alongside of the temple to Juno, temples were also erected to Loyalty and Hope.

Roman Philosophy.—The more educated Romans lost their interest in religion, and betook themselves to the study of Greek philosophy. They studied the nature of the gods and the moral duties of men. In this way the Greek ideas of philosophy found their way into Rome. Some of these ideas, like those of the Stoics, were elevating, and tended to preserve the simplicity and strength of the old Roman character. But other ideas, like those of the Epicureans, seemed to justify a life of pleasure and luxury.

Roman Literature.—Before the Romans came into contact with the Greeks, they cannot be said to have had anything which can properly be called a literature. They had certain crude verses and ballads; but it was the Greeks who first taught them how to write. It was not until the close of the first Punic war, when the Greek influence became strong, that we begin to find the names of any Latin authors. The first author, Andronicus, who is said to have been a Greek slave, wrote a Latin poem in imitation of Homer. Then came Naevius, who combined a Greek taste with a Roman spirit, and who wrote a poem on the first Punic war; and after him, Ennius, who taught Greek to the Romans, and wrote a great poem on the history of Rome, called the "Annals." The Greek influence is also seen in Plautus and Terence, the greatest writers of Roman comedy; and in Fabius Pictor, who wrote a history of Rome, in the Greek language.

Roman Art.—As the Romans were a practical people, their earliest art was shown in their buildings. From the Etruscans they had learned to use the arch and to build strong and massive structures. But the more refined features of art they obtained from the Greeks. While the Romans could never hope to acquire the pure aesthetic spirit of the Greeks, they were inspired with a passion for collecting Greek works of art, and for adorning their buildings with Greek ornaments. They imitated the Greek models and professed to admire the Greek taste; so that they came to be, in fact, the preservers of Greek art.

Roman Manners and Morals.—It is difficult for us to think of a nation of warriors as a nation of refined people. The brutalities of war seem inconsistent with the finer arts of living. But as the Romans obtained wealth from their wars, they affected the refinement of their more cultivated neighbors. Some men, like Scipio Africanus, looked with favor upon the introduction of Greek ideas and manners; but others, like Cato the Censor, were bitterly opposed to it. When the Romans lost the simplicity of the earlier times, they came to indulge in luxuries and to be lovers of pomp and show. They loaded their tables with rich services of plate; they ransacked the land and the sea for delicacies with which to please their palates. Roman culture was often more artificial than real. The survival of the barbarous spirit of the Romans in the midst of their professed refinement is seen in their amusements, especially the gladiatorial shows, in which men were forced to fight with wild beasts and with one another to entertain the people.

In conclusion, we may say that by their conquests the Romans became a great and, in a certain sense, a civilized people, who appropriated and preserved many of the best elements of the ancient world; but who were yet selfish, ambitious, and avaricious, and who lacked the genuine taste and generous spirit which belong to the highest type of human culture.

SELECTIONS FOR READING

Mommsen, Vol. II., Bk. III., Ch. 10, "Third Macedonian War" (2).[1]

Michelet, Bk. II., Ch. 8, "Reduction of Spain and the Greek States" (6).

How and Leigh, Ch. 27, "Fall of Macedonia and Greece" (1).

Pelham, Bk. III., Ch. 3, "The Roman State and People" (1).

Granrud, Third Period, "The Supremacy of the Senate" (13).

Abbott, Ch. 5, "The Supremacy of the Nobilitas" (13).

SPECIAL STUDY

CATO THE CENSOR AND THE GREEK INFLUENCE.—Liddell, pp. 450-455 (1); How and Leigh, pp. 302-305, see also index "Hellenism" (1); Shuckburgh, pp. 405, 406, 518-521 (1); Cruttwell, pp. 91-98 (17); Pelham, pp. 192-198 (1); Mommsen, Vol. II., pp. 413-423, 557-567 (2); Plutarch, "Cato the Censor" (11).

[1] The figure in parenthesis refers to the number of the topic in the Appendix, where a fuller title of the book will be found.

CHAPTER XIX

THE TIMES OF THE GRACCHI

The Causes of Civil Strife, I.—The Reforms of Tiberius Gracchus, II.—The Reforms of Gaius Gracchus, III.

I. THE CAUSES OF CIVIL STRIFE

Character of the New Period.—If the period which we have just considered is the most heroic in Roman history, that which we are about to consider is one of the saddest, and yet one of the most interesting. It is one of the saddest, because it was a time when the Roman state was torn asunder by civil strifes, and the arms of the conquerors were turned against themselves. It is one of the most interesting, because it shows to us some of the greatest men that Rome ever produced, men whose names are a part of the world's history. Our attention will now be directed not so much to foreign wars as to political questions, to the struggle of parties, and the rivalry of party leaders. And as a result of it all, we shall see the republic gradually passing away, and giving place to the empire.

Divisions of the Roman People.—If we would understand this period of conflict, we should at the outset get a clear idea of the various classes of people in the Roman world. Let us briefly review these different grades of society.

First, there was the *senatorial order,*—men who kept control of the higher offices, who furnished the members of the senate, and who really ruled the state. Next was the *equestrian order,*—men who were called equites, or knights, on account of their great wealth, who formed the moneyed class, the capitalists of Rome, and who made their fortunes by all sorts of speculation, especially by gathering the taxes in the provinces. These two orders formed the aristocratic classes.

Below these was the great mass of the *city population*—the poor artisans and paupers, who formed a rabble and the materials of a mob, and who lived upon public charity and the bribes of office-seekers, and were amused by public shows given by the state or by rich citizens. Then came the poor *country farmers* living upon the Roman domain—the peasants, many of whom had been deprived of their lands by rich creditors or by the avaricious policy of the government. These two classes formed the mass of the poorer citizens of Rome.

Outside of the Roman domain proper (*ager Romanus*) were the *Latin colonists*, who were settled upon conquered lands in Italy, who had practically no political rights, and who were very much in the same social condition as the Roman peasants. Besides these were the *Italian allies*, who had been subdued by Rome in early times, and had

117

been given none of the rights of citizenship. These two classes formed the subject population of Italy.

Now if we go outside of Italy we find the great body of *provincials*, some of them favored by being left free from taxation, but the mass of them subject to the Roman tribute; and all of them excluded from the rights and privileges of citizens.

Finally, if we go to the very bottom of the Roman population, we find the *slaves*, having none of the rights of citizens or of men. A part of them, the house slaves, were treated with some consideration; but the field slaves were treated wretchedly, chained in gangs by day and confined in dungeons by night.

Thus we have an aristocratic class, made up of the senators and equites; a poor citizen class, made up of the city rabble and the country farmers about Rome; and then a disfranchised class, made up of the Latins, the Italians, and the provincials, besides the slaves.

Defects of the Roman Government.—When we look over these various classes of the Roman people, we must conclude that there were some radical defects in the Roman system of government. The great mass of the population were excluded from all political rights. The Latins, the Italians, the provincials, and the slaves, as we have seen, had no share in the government. This seems quite contrary to the early policy of Rome. We remember that before she began her great conquests, Rome had started out with the policy of *incorporation*. She had taken in the Sabines on the Quirinal hill, the Luceres on the Caelian, the plebeians of the city, and the rural tribes about Rome. But after that time she had abandoned this policy, and no longer brought her conquered subjects within the state. This was the first defect of the Roman system.

But even those people who were given the rights of citizens were not able to exercise these rights in an efficient way. Wherever a Roman citizen might be, he must go to Rome to vote or to take part in the making of the laws. But when the citizens of Rome met together in the Forum, or on the Campus Martius, they made a large and unwieldy body, which could not do any important political business. Rome never learned that a democratic government in a large state is impossible without *representation*; that is, the election by the people of a few leading men to protect their interests, and to make the laws for them. The giving up of the policy of incorporation and the absence of the principle of representation were the two great defects in the Roman political system.

The Decay of Patriotism.—We may not blame the Romans for not discovering the value of representation, since this system may be regarded as a modern invention. But we must blame those who were the rulers of the state for their selfishness and their lack of true patriotism. There were, no doubt, some patriotic citizens at Rome who were devoted to the public welfare; but the majority of the men who governed the state were men devoted to their own interests more than to the interests of the country at large. The aristocratic classes sought to enrich themselves by the spoils of war and the spoils of office; while the rights and the welfare of the common citizens, the Italians, and the provincials were too often forgotten or ignored.

The Growth of Large Estates.—One of the causes which led to the civil strife was the distress and misery of the people in different parts of Italy, resulting from the growth of large landed estates. Years before, the people had possessed their little farms, and were able to make a respectable living from them. Laws had been passed—especially the Licinian laws (seep. 70)—to keep the public lands distributed in such a way as to benefit the poorer people. But it was more than two hundred years since the Licinian laws were passed; and they were now a dead letter. Many of the small farms had become absorbed into large estates held by rich landlords; and the class of small farmers had well-nigh disappeared. This change benefited one class of the people at the expense of the other. The Roman writer Pliny afterward saw the disastrous effects of this system, and said that it was the large estates which destroyed Italy.

The Evils of Slave Labor.—But this was not all. If the poor farmers, who had been deprived of their own fields, could have received good wages by working upon the estates of the rich landlords, they might still have had some means of living. But they were even deprived of this; because the estates were everywhere worked by slaves. So that slavery, as well as large estates, was a cause which helped to bring Italy to the brink of ruin.

II. THE REFORMS OF TIBERIUS GRACCHUS

Character of Tiberius Gracchus.—The first serious attempt to remedy the existing evils was made by Tiberius Sempronius Gracchus. He was the elder of two brothers who sacrificed their lives in efforts to benefit their fellow-citizens. Their mother was the noble-minded Cornelia, the daughter of the great Scipio Africanus, the type of the perfect mother, who regarded her boys as "jewels" more precious than gold, and who taught them to love truth, justice, and their country. Tiberius when a young man had served in the Spanish army under Scipio Aemilianus, the distinguished Roman who conquered Carthage and Numantia. It is said that when Tiberius Gracchus passed through Etruria, on his way to and from Spain, he was shocked to see the fertile fields cultivated by gangs of slaves, while thousands of free citizens were living in idleness and poverty. He was a man of refined nature and a deep sense of justice, and he determined to do what he could to remedy these evils.

His Agrarian Laws.—Tiberius Gracchus was elected tribune and began his work of reform (B.C. 133). He believed that the wretched condition of the Roman people was due chiefly to the unequal division of the public land, and especially to the failure to enforce the Licinian laws. He therefore proposed to revive these laws; to limit the holding of public land to five hundred *iugera* (about three hundred acres) for each person; to pay the present holders for any improvements they had made; and then to rent the land thus taken up to the poorer class of citizens. This seemed fair enough; for the state was the real owner of the public land, and could do what it wished with its own. But the rich landlords; who had held possession of this land for so many years, looked upon the measure as the same thing as taking away their own property. When it was now proposed to redistribute this land, there immediately arose a fierce conflict between the old senatorial party and the followers of Tiberius.

His Illegal Action.—Tiberius determined to pass his law in spite of the senate. The senate, on the other hand, was equally determined that the law should not be passed. Accordingly, the senators induced one of the tribunes, whose name was M. Octavius, to put his "veto" upon the passage of the law. This act of Octavius was entirely legal, for he did what the law gave him the right to do. Tiberius, on the other hand, in order to outdo his opponent, had recourse to a highhanded measure. Instead of waiting a year for the election of new tribunes who might be devoted to the people's cause, he called upon the people to deprive Octavius of his office. This was an illegal act, because there was no law which authorized such a proceeding. But the people did as Tiberius desired, and Octavius was deposed. The law of Tiberius was then passed in the assembly of the tribes, and three commissioners were chosen to carry it into effect.

This of course roused the indignation of the senators, who determined to prosecute Tiberius when his term of office had expired. Tiberius knew that as long as he held the office of tribune his person would be sacred, and he could not be tried for his action; hence he announced himself as a candidate for re-election. This, too, was illegal, for the law forbade a reelection until after an interval of ten years.

Fall of Tiberius Gracchus.—The law of Tiberius and the method which he had used to pass it, increased the bitterness between the aristocratic party and the popular party who came to be known, respectively, as the *optimates* and the *populares*. The senators denounced Tiberius as a traitor; the people extolled him as a patriot. The day appointed for the election came. Two tribes had already voted for the re-election of Tiberius, when a band of senators appeared in the Forum, headed by Scipio Nasica, armed with sticks and clubs; and in the riot which ensued Tiberius Gracchus and three hundred of his followers were slain. This was the first blood shed in the civil wars of

Rome. The killing of a tribune by the senators was as much an illegal act as was the deposition of Octavius. Both parties had disregarded the law, and the revolution was begun.

III. THE REFORMS OF GAIUS GRACCHUS

The Rise of Gaius Gracchus.—After the death of Tiberius his law was for a time carried into execution. The commissioners proceeded with their work of re-dividing the land. But the people were for a time without a real leader. The cause of reform was then taken up by Gaius Gracchus, the brother of Tiberius, and the conflict was renewed. Gaius was in many respects an abler man than Tiberius. No more sincere and patriotic, he was yet a broader statesman and took a wider view of the situation. He did not confine his attention simply to relieving the poor citizens. He believed that to rescue Rome from her troubles, it was necessary to weaken the power of the senate, whose selfish and avaricious policy had brought on these troubles. He also believed that the Latins and the Italians should be protected, as well as the poor Roman citizens.

His Efforts to Benefit the People.—When Gaius Gracchus obtained the position of tribune (B.C. 123) his influence for a time was all-powerful. He was eloquent and persuasive, and practically had the control of the government. From his various laws we may select those which were the most important, and which best show his general policy. First of all, he tried to help the people by a law which was really the most mischievous of all his measures. This was his famous "corn law." It was intended to benefit the poor population in the city, which was at that time troublesome and not easy to control. The law provided that any Roman citizen could receive grain from the public storehouses for a certain price less than its cost. But the number of the poor in the city was not decreased; the paupers now flocked to Rome from all parts of Italy to be fed at the public crib. This corn law became a permanent institution of Rome. We may judge of its evil effect when it is said that not many years afterward there were three hundred and twenty thousand citizens who were dependent upon the government for their food. Gaius may not have known what evil effect this law was destined to produce. At any rate, it insured his popularity with the lower classes. He then renewed the agrarian laws of his brother; and also provided for sending out colonies of poor citizens into different parts of Italy, and even into the provinces.

His Efforts to Weaken the Senate.—But Gaius believed that such measures as these would afford only temporary relief, as long as the senate retained its great power. It was, of course, impossible to overthrow the senate. But it was possible to take from it some of the powers which it possessed. From the senators had hitherto been selected the jurors (*iudices*) before whom were tried cases of extortion and other crimes. By a law Gaius took away from the senate this right to furnish jurors in criminal cases, and gave it to the equites, that is, the wealthy class outside of the senate. This gave to the equites a more important political position, and drew them over to the support of Gaius, and thus tended to split the aristocratic classes in two. The senate was thus deprived not only of its right to furnish jurors, but also of the support of the wealthy men who had previously been friendly to it. This was a great triumph for the popular party; and Gaius looked forward to another victory.

His Effort to Enfranchise the Italians.—When he was reelected to the tribunate Gaius Gracchus came forward with his grand scheme of extending the Roman franchise to the people of Italy. This was the wisest of all his measures, but the one which cost him his popularity and influence. It aroused the jealousy of the poorer citizens, who did not wish to share their rights with foreigners. The senators took advantage of the unpopularity of Gaius, and now posed as the friends of the people. They induced one of the tribunes, by the name of Drusus, to play the part of the demagogue. Drusus proposed to found twelve new colonies at once, each with three thousand Roman citizens, and thus to put all the reforms of Gaius Gracchus into the shade. The people were deceived by this stratagem, and the attempt of Gaius to enfranchise the Italians was defeated.

His Failure and Death.—Gaius did not succeed, as he desired, in being elected tribune for the third time. A great part of the people soon abandoned him, and the ascendency of the senate was again restored. It was not long before a new law was passed which prevented any further distribution of the public land (*lex Thoria*). Gaius failed to bring about the reforms which he attempted; but he may be regarded as having accomplished three things which remained after his death: (1) the elevation of the equestrian order; (2) the establishment of the Roman poor law, or the system of grain largesses; and (3) the extension of the colonial system to the provinces. He lost his life in a tumult in which three thousand citizens were slain (B.C. 121).

Thus in a similar way the two Gracchi, who had attempted to rescue the Roman people from the evils of a corrupt government, perished. Their efforts at agrarian reform did not produce any lasting effect; but they pointed out the dangers of the state, and drew the issues upon which their successors continued the conflict. Their career forms the first phase in the great civil conflict at Rome.

SELECTIONS FOR READING
Pelham, Bk. IV., Ch. l, "From the Gracchi to Sulla" (1).[1]
Beesly, Ch. 1, "Antecedents of the Revolution" (6).

Merivale, Gen. Hist., Ch. 28, "Tiberius Gracchus" (1).

Taylor, Ch. 9, "The Reformers" (1).

Ihne, Hist., Bk. VII., Ch. 1, "Political and Economical Condition" (2).

Mommsen, Vol. II., Bk. III., Ch. 12, "Management of Land" (2).

Mommsen, abridged, Ch. 20, "Reforms of the Gracchi" (2).

Ramsay and Lanciani, Ch. 7, "Public Lands and Agrarian Laws" (8).

Harper's Dict. Antiqq., "Agrariae Leges" (8).

Plutarch, "Tiberius Gracchus," "Caius Gracchus" (11).

SPECIAL STUDY

THE ROMAN EQUITES.—Liddell, p. 504 (1); How and Leigh, p. 315 (1); Shuckburgh, p. 560 (1); Ramsay and Lanciani, p. 98 (8); Gow, see index "Equites" (8); Mommsen, Vol. II., pp. 377-380 (2); Harper's Dict. Antiqq., "Equites" (8).

[1] The figure in parenthesis refers to the number of the topic in the Appendix, where a fuller title of the book will be found.

CHAPTER XX

THE TIMES OF MARIUS AND SULLA

The Rise of Marius, I.—The Social War and the Rise of Sulla, II.—The Civil War between Marius and Sulla, III.—The Dictatorship of Sulla (B.C. 82-79), IV.

I. THE RISE OF MARIUS

New Phase of the Civil Strife.—The troubles under the Gracchi had grown out of the attempts of two patriotic men to reform the evils of the state. The shedding of Roman blood had been limited to riots in the city, and to fights between the factions of the different parties. We now come to the time when the political parties seek the aid of the army; when the civil strife becomes in reality a civil war, and the lives of citizens seem of small account compared with the success of this or that political leader. To understand this second phase of the revolution, we must consider what was the condition of Rome after the fall of the Gracchi; how Marius came to the front as the leader of the popular party; and how he was overthrown by Sulla as the leader of the aristocratic party.

Corrupt Rule of the Aristocracy.—After the fall of the Gracchi the rule of the aristocracy was restored, and the government became more corrupt than ever before. The senators were often incompetent, and they had no clearly defined policy. They seemed desirous only to retain power and to enrich themselves, while the real interests of the people were forgotten. The little farms which Tiberius Gracchus had tried to create were again swallowed up in large estates. The provincials were ground down with heavy taxes. The slaves were goaded into insurrection. The sea swarmed with pirates, and the frontiers were threatened by foreign enemies.

The Jugurthine War and Marius (B.C. 111-105).—The attention of the senate was first directed to a war in Africa. This war has no great interest for us, except that it shows how corrupt Rome was, and that it brought to the front a great soldier, who became for a time the leader of the people.

The war in Africa grew out of the attempt of Jugurtha to make himself king of Numidia, which kingdom we remember was an ally of Rome. The senate sent commissioners to Numidia in order to settle the trouble; but the commissioners sold themselves to Jugurtha as soon as they landed in Africa. The Roman people were incensed, and war was declared against Jugurtha. The conduct of the war was placed in the hands of the consul, L. Calpurnius Bestia, who on arriving in Africa accepted Jugurtha's gold and made peace. The people were again indignant, and summoned

Jugurtha to Rome to testify against the consul. When Jugurtha appeared before the assembly, and was about to make his statement, one of the tribunes, who had also been bought by African gold, put a veto upon the proceedings; so that by the bribery of a tribune it became impossible to punish the bribery of a consul. Jugurtha remained in Rome until he caused one of his rivals to be murdered, when he was banished from the city. He expressed his private opinion of Rome when he called it "a venal city, ready to perish whenever it could find a purchaser."

The war in Numidia was continued under the new consul, Q. Caecilius Metellus, who selected as his lieutenant Gaius Marius, a rough soldier who had risen from the ranks, but who had a real genius for war. So great was the success of Marius that he was elected consul, and superseded Metellus in the supreme command of the African army. Marius fulfilled all the expectations of the people; he defeated the enemy, and Jugurtha was made a prisoner. A triumph was given to the conqueror, in which the captive king was led in chains; and Marius became the people's hero.

Marius and the Cimbric War (B.C. 113-101).—But a greater glory now awaited Marius. While he had been absent in Africa, Rome was threatened by a deluge of barbarians from the north. The Cimbri and Teutones, fierce peoples from Germany, had pushed down into the southern part of Gaul, and had overrun the new province of Narbonensis (established B.C. 120). It seemed impossible to stay these savage invaders. Army after army was defeated. It is said that sixty thousand Romans perished in one battle at Arausio (B.C. 107) on the banks of the Rhone. The way seemed open to Italy, and all eyes turned to Marius as the only man who could save Rome. On the same day on which he received his triumph, Marius was reelected to the consulship, and assigned to his new command. This was contrary to law, to reelect an officer immediately after his first term; but the Romans had come to believe that "in the midst of arms, the laws are silent."

Marius set to work to reorganize the Roman army. The army became no longer a raw body of citizens arranged according to wealth; but a trained body of soldiers drawn from all classes of society, and devoted to their commander. With the discretion of a true soldier Marius determined to be fully prepared before meeting his formidable foe. The Cimbri turned aside for a time into Spain. Marius remained patiently on the Rhone, drilling his men and guarding the approaches to the Alps. As the time passed by, the people continued to trust him, and elected him as consul a third, and then a fourth time. At length the barbarians reappeared, ready for the invasion of Italy. One part, the Teutones, prepared to invade Italy from the west; while the other part, the Cimbri, prepared to cross the Alps into the northwestern corner of Italy. Against the Teutones Marius posted his own army; and to meet the Cimbri he dispatched his colleague, Q. Lutatius Catulus. In the battle of Aquae Sextiae he annihilated the host of the Teutones (B.C. 102); and the people elected him a fifth time to the consulship. Soon the Cimbri crossed the Alps and drove Catulus across the Po. Marius joined him, drove back the barbarians, and utterly routed them near Vercellae (B.C. 101). Italy was thus saved. For this twofold victory Rome gave to Marius a magnificent triumph, celebrated with double splendor. He was hailed as the savior of his Country, the second Camillus, and the third Romulus.

Marius as a Party Leader.—Marius was now at the height of his popularity. There had never before been a man in Rome who so far outshone his rivals. As he was a man of the common people, the leaders of the popular party saw that his great name would be a help to their cause.

The men who aspired to the leadership of the popular party since the death of the Gracchi were Saturninus and Glaucia. To these men Marius now allied himself, and was elected to the consulship for the sixth time. This alliance formed a sort of political "ring," which professed to rule the state in the interest of the people; but which aroused a storm of opposition on the part of the senators. As in the days of the Gracchi, tumults arose, and the streets of Rome again became stained with blood. The senate called upon Marius, as consul, to put down the insurrection. Marius reluctantly complied; and in the conflict that followed, his colleagues, Saturninus and Glaucia, were killed. Marius now fell into disrepute. Having at first allied himself to the popular leaders and afterward yielded to the senate, he lost the confidence of both parties. In spite of his greatness as a soldier, he proved his utter incapacity as a party leader. He soon retired from Rome in the hope of recovering his popularity, and of coming back when the tide should turn in his favor.

II. THE SOCIAL WAR AND THE RISE OF SULLA

Rome and the Italian Allies.—With the failure of Marius, and the death of his colleagues, the senate once more recovered the reins of government. But the troubles still continued. The Italian allies were now clamoring for their rights, and threatening war if their demands were not granted. We remember (see p. 94) that when Rome had conquered Italy, she did not give the Italian people the rights of citizenship. They were made subject allies, but received no share in the government. The Italian allies had furnished soldiers for the Roman armies, and had helped to make Rome the mistress of the Mediterranean. They believed, therefore, that they were entitled to all the rights of Roman citizens; and some of the patriotic leaders of Rome believed so too. But it seemed as difficult to break down the distinction between Romans and

Italians as it had been many years before to remove the barriers between the patricians and the plebeians.

Attempt and Failure of Drusus.—At this crisis there appeared it new reformer, the tribune M. Livius Drusus, son of the Drusus who opposed Gaius Gracchus. He was a well-disposed man, who seemed to believe that all the troubles of the state could be settled by a series of compromises. Of a noble nature, of pure motives, and of generous disposition, he tried to please everybody, and succeeded in pleasing nobody. First, to please the populace, he proposed to increase the largesses of grain; and to make payment easy by introducing a cheap copper coin which should pass for the same value as the previous silver one. Next, to reconcile the senators and the equites, he proposed to select the jurors (*iudices*) from both classes, thus dividing the power between them. Finally, to meet the demands of the Italians, he proposed to grant them what they asked for, the Roman franchise.

It was one thing to propose these laws; it was quite another thing to pass them. As the last law was the most offensive, he began by uniting the equites and the people for the purpose of passing the first two laws. These were passed against the will of the senate, and amid scenes of great violence. The senate declared the laws of Drusus null and void. Disregarding this act of the senate as having no legal force, he then proposed to submit to the assembly the law granting the franchise to the Italians. But this law was as offensive to the people as the others had been to the senate. Denounced by the senate as a traitor and abandoned by the people, this large-hearted and unpractical reformer was at last murdered by an unknown assassin; and all his efforts came to nothing.

Revolt of the Italian Allies (B.C. 90).—The death of Drusus drove the Italians to revolt. The war which followed is known in history as the "social war," or the war of the allies (*socii*). It was, in fact, a war of secession. The purpose of the allies was now, not to obtain the Roman franchise, but to create a new Italian nation, where all might be equal. They accordingly organized a new republic with the central government at Corfinium, a town in the Apennines. The new state was modeled after the government at Rome, with a senate of five hundred members, two consuls, and other magistrates. Nearly all the peoples of central and southern Italy joined in this revolt.

Rome was now threatened with destruction, not by a foreign enemy like the Cimbri and Teutones, but by her own subjects. The spirit of patriotism revived; and the parties ceased for a brief time from their quarrels. Even Marius returned to serve as a legate in the Roman army. A hundred thousand men took the field against an equal number raised by the allies. In the first year the war was unfavorable to Rome. In the second year (B.C. 89) new preparations were made and new commanders were appointed: Marius, on account of his age, was not continued in his command; while L. Cornelius Sulla, who was once a subordinate of Marius, was made chief commander in Campania. Marius felt deeply this slight, and began to be envious of his younger rival. The great credit of bringing this war to a close was due to Pompeius Strabo (the father of Pompey the Great) and Sulla. The first Italian capital, Corfinium, was taken by Pompeius; and the second capital, Bovianum, was captured by Sulla (B.C. 88). The social war was thus ended; but it had been a great affliction to Italy. It is roughly estimated that three hundred thousand men, Romans and Italians, lost their lives in this struggle. The compensation of this loss was the incorporation of Italy with Rome.

The Enfranchisement of Italy.—Although Rome was victorious in the field, the Italians obtained what they had demanded before the war began, that is, the rights of Roman citizenship. The Romans granted the franchise (1) to all Latins and Italians who had remained loyal during the war (*lex Iulia*, B.C. 90); and (2) to every Italian who should be enrolled by the praetor within sixty days of the passage of the law (*lex Plautia Papiria*, B.C. 89). Every person to whom these provisions applied was now a Roman citizen. The policy of incorporation, which had been discontinued for so long a time, was thus revived. The distinction between Romans, Latins, and Italians was now broken down, at least so far as the Italian peninsula was concerned. The greater part of Italy was joined to the *ager Romanus*, and Italy and Rome became practically one nation.

The Elevation of Sulla.—Another result of the social war, which had a great effect upon the destinies of Rome, was the rise of Sulla. War was not a new occupation for Sulla. In the campaign against Jugurtha he had served as a lieutenant of Marius. In the Cimbric war he had displayed great courage and ability. And now he had become the most conspicuous commander in the Italian war. As a result of his brilliant exploits, he was elected to the consulship. The senate also recognized him as the ablest general of the time, when it now appointed him to conduct the war in the East against the great enemy of Rome, Mithridates, king of Pontus.

III. THE CIVIL WAR BETWEEN MARIUS AND SULLA

The Jealousy of Marius.—Marius had watched with envy the growing fame of Sulla. Although old enough to retire from active life, he was mortified in not receiving the command of the Eastern army. When Sulla was now appointed to this command, Marius determined if possible to displace him, or to satisfy his revenge in some other way. From this time Marius, who once seemed to possess the elements of greatness, appears to us as a vindictive and foolish old man, deprived of reason and the sense of honor. To prove that he had not lost the vigor of youth, it is said that he used to appear in the Campus Martius and exercise with the young soldiers in wrestling and boxing. The chief motive which now seemed to influence him was the hatred of Sulla and the Sullan party.

Marius rejoins the Popular Party.—To regain his influence with the people Marius once more entered politics, and joined himself to the popular leaders. The most prominent of these leaders was now the tribune P. Sulpicius Rufus. With the aid of this politician, Marius hoped to win back the favor of the people, to weaken the influence of the senate, which had supported Sulla, and then to displace Sulla himself. This programme was set forth in what are called the "Sulpician laws" (B.C. 88). By the aid of an armed force these laws were passed, and two messengers were sent to Sulla to command him to turn over his army to Marius. To displace a commander legally appointed by the senate was an act unheard of, even in this period of revolution.

Sulla appeals to the Army.—If Marius and Sulpicius supposed that Sulla would calmly submit to such an outrage, they mistook his character. Sulla had not yet left Italy. His legions were still encamped in Campania. He appealed to them to support the honor and authority of their commander. They responded to his appeal, and Sulla at the head of his troops marched to Rome. For the first time the Roman legions fought in the streets of the capital, and a question of politics was settled by the army. Marius and Sulpicius were driven from the city, and Sulla for the time being was supreme. He called together the senate, and caused the leaders of the popular party to be declared outlaws. He then annulled the laws passed by Sulpicius, and gave the senate the power hereafter to approve or reject all laws before they should be submitted to the people. With the army at his back Sulla could do what he pleased. When he had placed the government securely in the hands of the senate, as he thought, he left Rome for the purpose of conducting the war against Mithridates in the East.

The Flight of Marius.—Marius was now an exile, a fugitive from the country which he had once saved. The pathetic story of his flight and wanderings is graphically told by Plutarch. He says that Marius set sail from Ostia, and was forced by a storm to land at Circeii (see map, p. 167), where he wandered about in hunger and great suffering; that his courage was kept up by remembering that when a boy he had found an eagle's nest with seven young in it, which a soothsayer had interpreted as meaning that he would be consul seven times; that he was again taken on board a vessel and landed at Minturnae, where he was captured and condemned to death; that the slave who was ordered to kill him dropped his sword as he heard the stern voice of his intended victim shouting, "Man, darest thou kill Gaius Marius?" that he was then released and wandered to Sicily, and then to Africa, where, a fallen hero, he sat amid the ruins of Carthage; that at last he found a safe retreat in a little island off the African coast, and waited for vengeance and the time of his seventh consulship.

Sulla and the Mithridatic War (B.C. 88-84).—While Marius was thus enduring the miseries of exile, Sulla was gathering fresh glories in the East. When Sulla landed in Greece he found the eastern provinces in a wretched state. Mithridates, the king of Pontus (see map, p. 142), had extended his power over a large part of Asia Minor. He had overrun the Roman province of Asia. He had induced the Greek cities on the coast, which had been brought under the Roman power, to revolt and join his cause. He had massacred over eighty thousand Italians living on the Asiatic coast. He had also sent his armies into Greece and Macedonia, and many of the cities there, including Athens, had declared in his favor. The Roman power in the East seemed well-nigh broken.

It was at this time that Sulla showed his greatest ability as a soldier. He drove back the armies of Mithridates, besieged Athens and reduced it. He destroyed an army at Chaeronea (B.C. 86, see map, p. 128), and another at Orchomenus (B.C. 85). Within four years he reëstablished the Roman power, and compelled Mithridates to sign a treaty of peace. The defeated king agreed to give up all his conquests; to surrender eighty war vessels; and to pay 3000 talents ($3,750,000). After imposing upon the disloyal cities of Asia Minor the immense fine of 20,000 talents ($25,000,000), Sulla returned to Italy to find his own party overthrown, and himself an outlaw.

Cinna and the Marian Massacres.—During the absence of Sulla, Rome had passed through a reign of terror. The time had now come when parties sought to support themselves by slaughtering their opponents. The two consuls who were left in power when Sulla left Rome, were Cn. Octavius, a friend of Sulla, and L. Cornelius Cinna, a friend of Marius. Cinna, who was an extreme partisan, proposed to rescind the laws of Sulla and reënact those of Sulpicius. But the senate was vehemently opposed to any such scheme. When the assembly of the tribes met in the Forum to vote upon this proposal of Cinna, Octavius carried the day in an armed conflict in which ten thousand citizens are said to have lost their lives. But the victory of Octavius was short. Cinna was, it is true, deprived of his office; but following the example of his enemy Sulla, he appealed to the army for support.

At the same time Marius returned from his exile to aid the cause of Cinna. Uniting their forces, Marius and Cinna then marched upon Rome. The city was taken. Marius saw that the time had now come to satisfy his vengeance for the wrongs which he thought had been done him. The gates of the city were closed, and the massacres began. The first victim was the consul Octavius, whose head was hung up in the Forum. Then followed the leaders of the senatorial part For five days Marius was furious, and revelled in blood. The friends of Sulla were everywhere cut down. The city was a scene of murder, plunder, and outrage. After this spasm of slaughter a reign of terror continued for several months. No man's life was safe if he was suspected by Marius. Marius and Cinna then declared themselves to be consuls. But Marius held this, his seventh consulship, but a few days, when he died—a great man who had crumbled into ruins.

After the death of Marius, Cinna, the professed leader of the popular party, ruled with the absolute power of a despot. He declared himself consul each year, and named his own colleague. But he seemed to have no definite purpose, except to wipe out the work of Sulla, and to keep himself supreme. At last, hearing of the approach of Sulla, he led an army to prevent him from landing in Italy; but was killed in a mutiny of his own soldiers.

Sulla's War with the Marian Party.—Sulla landed in Italy (B.C. 83) with a victorious army of forty thousand men. He had restored the power of Rome against her enemies abroad; he now set to work to restore her authority against her enemies at home. He looked upon the popular party as a revolutionary faction, ruling with no sanction of law or justice. Its leaders since the death of Cinna were Cn. Papirius Carbo, the younger Marius, and Q. Sertorius. The landing of Sulla in Italy without disbanding his army was the signal for civil war. Southern Italy declared in his favor, and many prominent men looked to him as the deliverer of Rome. The choicest of his new allies was the son of Pompeius Strabo, then a young man of twenty-three, but whose future fame, as Pompey the Great, was destined to equal that of Sulla himself. Sulla marched to Campania and routed the forces of one consul, while troops of the other consul deserted to him in a body. He then attacked the young Marius in Latium, defeated him, and shut him up in the town of Praeneste (see map, p.46). Northern Italy was at the same time held in check by Pompey. A desperate battle was fought at Clusium, in Etruria (see map, p. 81), in which Sulla and Pompey defeated the army of Carbo. At last an army of Samnites which had joined the Marian cause was cut to pieces at the Colline gate (see map, p. 38) under the very walls of Rome. Sulla showed what might be expected of him when he ordered six thousand Samnite prisoners to be massacred in cold blood.

The Sullan Proscriptions.—With Italy at his feet and a victorious army at his back,

Sulla, the champion of the senate, was now the supreme ruler of Rome. Before entering upon the work of reconstructing the government, he determined first of all to complete the work of destroying his enemies. It is sometimes said that Sulla was not a man of vindictive nature. Let us see what he did. He first outlawed all civil and military officers who had taken part in the revolution against him, and offered a reward of two talents (about $2500) to the murderer of any of these men. He then posted a list (*proscriptio*) containing the names of those citizens whom he wished to have killed. He placed eighty names on the first list, two hundred and twenty more on the second, as many more on the third, and so on until nearly five thousand citizens had been put to death in Rome.

But these despotic acts were not confined to Rome; they extended to every city of Italy. "Neither temple, nor hospitable hearth, nor father's house," says Plutarch, "was free from murder." Sulla went to Praeneste, and having no time to examine each individual, had all the people brought to one spot to the number of twelve thousand, and ordered them to be massacred. His sense of justice was not satisfied by punishing the living. The infamous Catiline had murdered his own brother before the war had closed, and he asked Sulla to proscribe him as though he were alive—which was done. The heads of the slain victims Sulla caused to be piled in the streets of Rome for public execration. The tomb of Marius himself was broken open and his ashes were scattered. Besides taking the lives of his fellow-citizens, Sulla confiscated the lands of Italy, swept away cities, and wasted whole districts. If the proscriptions of Sulla were not inspired by the mad fury of revenge which led to the Marian massacres, they were yet prompted by the merciless policy of a tyrant.

IV. THE DICTATORSHIP OF SULLA (B.C. 82-79)

The Office of Perpetual Dictator.—When Sulla had destroyed his enemies he turned to the work of reconstructing the government in the interests of the senate and the aristocracy. The first question with Sulla was, What office should he hold in order to accomplish all he wished to do? The Gracchi had exercised their great influence by being elected tribunes. Marius had risen to power through his successive consulships. But the office neither of tribune nor of consul was suited to the purposes of Sulla. He wished for absolute power—in fact, to hold the royal *imperium*. But since the fall of the Tarquins no man had ever dared assume the name of "king." Sulla was shrewd enough to see how he could exercise absolute power under another name than that of king. The dictator was, in fact, a sort of temporary king. To make this office perpetual would be practically to restore the royal power. Accordingly, Sulla had himself declared dictator to hold the office as long as he pleased. All his previous acts were then confirmed. He was given the full power of life and death, the power to confiscate property, to distribute lands, to create and destroy colonies, and to regulate the provinces. Military Support of Sulla's Power.—Sulla believed that a ruler to be strong must always be ready to draw the sword. He therefore did not mean to lose his hold upon his veteran soldiers. When his twenty-three legions were disbanded, they were not scattered, but were settled in Italy as military colonies. Each legion formed the body of citizens in a certain town, the lands being confiscated and assigned to the soldiers. The legionaries were thus bound in gratitude to Sulla, and formed a devoted body of militia upon which he felt that he could rely. By means of these colonies, Sulla placed his power upon a military basis.

Restoration of the Senate.—It was one of Sulla's chief purposes to restore the senate to its former position as the chief ruling body. In the first place, he filled it up with three hundred new members, elected by the *comitia tributa* from the equites. The senatorial list was no longer to be made out by the censor, but everyone who had been quaestor was now legally qualified to be a senator. In the next place, the jurors (*iudices*) in criminal trials were henceforth to be taken from the senate, and not from the equestrian order. But as the new senators were from this order, the two classes became reconciled; and Sulla succeeded in doing what Drusus had failed to accomplish. But more than all, no laws could hereafter be passed by the assembly of the tribes until first approved by the senate.

Weakening of the Assembly.—Sulla saw that the revolutionary acts of the last fifty years had been chiefly the work of the *comitia tributa* under the leadership of the tribunes. The other assembly—that of the centuries—had, it is true, equal power to make laws. But the assembly of the tribes was more democratic, and the making of laws had gradually passed into the hands of that body. Sulla took away from the tribes the legislative power, and gave to the senate the authority to propose all laws to be submitted to the centuries. The tendency of this change was to limit the assemblies to the mere business of electing the officers—the lower officers being elected by the tribes, and the higher officers by the centuries. To keep control of the elections Sulla enfranchised ten thousand slaves, and gave them the right to vote; these creatures of Sulla were known as "Cornelii," or Sulla's freedmen.

Changes in the Magistrates.—In Sulla's mind the most revolutionary and dangerous office in the government was that of the tribune. This officer hitherto could practically control the state. He had had the chief control of legislation; and also by his veto he could stop the wheels of government. Sulla changed all this. He limited the power of the tribune to simple "intercession," that is, the protection of a citizen from an act of official injustice. He also provided that no tribune could be elected to the curule offices. The other officers were also looked after. The consuls and praetors must henceforth devote themselves to their civil duties in the city; and then as proconsuls and propraetors they might afterward be assigned by the senate to the governorship of the provinces. Again, no one could be consul until he had been praetor, nor praetor until he had been quaestor; and the old law was enforced, that no one could hold the same office the second time until after an interval of ten years.

Reform of the Judicial System.—The most permanent part of Sulla's reforms was the creation of a regular system of criminal courts. He organized permanent commissions (*quaestiones perpetuae*) for the trial of different kinds of crimes. Every criminal case was thus tried before a regular court, composed of a presiding judge, or praetor, and a body of jurymen, called *iudices*. We must remember that whenever the word *iudices* is used in the political history of this period it refers to these jurors in criminal cases, who were first chosen from the senate, then from the equites, and now under Sulla from the senate again. The organization of regular criminal courts by Sulla was the wisest and most valuable part of his legislation.

Sulla's Abdication and Death.—After a reign of three years (B.C. 82-79), and after having placed the government securely in the hands of the senate, as he supposed, Sulla resigned the dictatorship. He retired to his country house at Puteoli on the Bay of Naples. He spent the few remaining months of his life in writing his memoirs, which have unfortunately been lost. He hastened his end by dissipation, and died the next year (B.C. 78). The senate decreed him a public funeral, the most splendid that Rome had ever seen. His body was burned in the Campus Martius. Upon the monument which was erected to his memory were inscribed these words: "No friend ever did him a kindness, and no enemy a wrong, without being fully repaid."

Sulla was a man of blood and iron. Cool and calculating, definite in his purpose, and unscrupulous in his methods, he was invincible in war and in peace. But the great part of the work which he seemed to accomplish so thoroughly did not long survive him. His great foreign enemy, Mithridates, soon renewed his wars with Rome. His boasted constitution fell in the next political conflict. The career of Sulla, like that of the Gracchi and of Marius, marks a stage in the decline of the republic and the establishment of the empire.

SELECTIONS FOR READING
Merivale, Gen. Hist., Ch. 32, "Rivalry of Marius and Sulla" (1).[1]
Mommsen, Vol. III., Bk. IV., Ch. 10, "The Sullan Constitution" (2).
Mommsen, abridged, Ch. 22, "Marius as a Revolutionist" (2).

How and Leigh, Ch. 39, "The Social War" (1).

Shuckburgh, Ch. 38, "Mithridates in Asia and Greece" (1).

Taylor, Ch. 11, "Cinna and Sulla" (1).

Beesly, Ch. 15, "Sulla's Reactionary Measures" (6).

Freeman, Essay on "Sulla" (3).

Plutarch, "Marius," "Sulla" (11).

SPECIAL STUDY

THE ROMAN SENATE.—Gow, pp. 193-199 (8); Pelham, pp. 159-167 (1); Shuckburgh, pp. 206-208, 397-399 (1); How and Leigh, p. 298 (1); Merivale, Gen. Hist., pp. 209-212 (1); Mommsen, Vol. 1., pp 406-412 (2); Ramsay and Lanciani, pp. 254-263 (8); Harper's Dict. Antiqq., "Senatus" (8).

[1] The figure in parenthesis refers to the number of the topic in the Appendix, where a fuller title of the book will be found.

CHAPTER XXI

THE TIMES OF POMPEY AND CAESAR

The Rise of Pompey, I.—The Growing Influence of Caesar, II.—Civil War between Pompey and Caesar, III.—
The Rule of Julius Caesar, IV.

I. THE RISE OF POMPEY

Failures of the Sullan Party.—When Sulla resigned his power and placed the government in the hands of his party, he no doubt thought that he had secured the state from any further disturbance. He had destroyed all opposition, he fancied, by wiping out the Marian party. But as soon as he died, the remnants of this party began to reappear on every side. With the restoration of the senate's power there also returned all the old evils of the senatorial rule. The aristocratic party was still a selfish faction ruling for its own interests, and with little regard for the welfare of the people. The separation between the rich and the poor became more marked than ever. Luxury and dissipation were the passion of one class, and poverty and distress the condition of the other. The feebleness of the new government was evident from the start, and Sulla was scarcely dead when symptoms of reaction began to appear.

The Revolt of Lepidus (B.C. 77).—The first attempt to overthrow the work of Sulla was made by the consul M. Aemilius Lepidus, a vain and petulant man, who aspired to be chief of the popular party. Lepidus proposed to restore to the tribunes the full power which Sulla had diminished, and then to rescind the whole Sullan constitution. But his colleague, Q. Lutatius Catulus,1 had no sympathy with his schemes and opposed him at every step. To prevent a new civil war the senate bound the two consuls by an oath not to take up arms. But Lepidus disregarded this oath, raised an army, and marched on Rome. He was soon defeated by Catulus with the aid of Cn. Pompey. It is well for us to notice that Pompey by this act came into greater prominence in politics as a supporter of the senate and the Sullan party.

The Sertorian War and Pompey (B.C. 80-72).—A much more formidable attempt at revolution was made by Q. Sertorius, who was one of the friends of Marius, and who had escaped to Spain during the Sullan proscriptions. Sertorius was a man of noble character, brave, prudent, generous, and withal a very able soldier. The native tribes of Spain were chafing under the Roman governors; and Spain itself had become the retreat of many Marian refugees. Sertorius, therefore, formed the plan of delivering Spain from the power of Rome, and setting up an independent republic. (For map of Spain, see p. 112.) He won the devotion and loyalty of the Spanish provincials, whom he placed on an equality with his Roman subjects. He organized the cities after the Italian model. He encouraged the natives to adopt the arts of civilization. He formed a school at Osca, where the young men were instructed in Latin and Greek. He also defeated the Roman legions under Q. Caecilius Metellus Pius, who had been sent against him.

The Roman senate was firmly convinced that something must be done to save the Spanish province. Pompey was therefore appointed proconsul in Spain—although he had never been consul or held any other civil office. Sertorius showed what kind of general he was when he defeated the young Pompey in the first battle, and might have destroyed his army if Metellus had not come to his assistance. But fortune at last frowned upon Sertorius and favored Pompey. Sertorius, in a fit of wrath, caused the boys in the school at Osca to be put to death. This cruel act aroused the indignation of the Spanish subjects. It was not long before he himself was murdered by one of his lieutenants. With Sertorius out of the way, Pompey obtained an easy victory; and Spain was reduced to submission.

War of the Gladiators, and Crassus (B.C. 73-71).—Before the war with Sertorius was ended, the senate was called upon to meet a far greater danger at home. In order to prepare the gladiators for their bloody contests in the arena, training schools had been established in different parts of Italy. At Capua, in one of these so-called schools (which were rather prisons), was confined a brave Thracian, Spartacus. With no desire to be "butchered to make a Roman holiday," Spartacus incited his companions to revolt. Seventy of them fled to the crater of Vesuvius and made it a stronghold. Reënforced by other slaves and outlaws of all descriptions, they grew into a motley mass of one hundred thousand desperate men. They ravaged the fields and plundered the cities, until all Italy seemed at their mercy. Four Roman armies were defeated in succession. With Pompey still absent in Spain, the senate sought some other leader to crush this fearful insurrection. The command fell to M. Crassus, who finally defeated Spartacus and his army. A remnant of five thousand men fled to the north, hoping to escape into Gaul; but they fell in with Pompey, who was just returning from Spain, and were destroyed. By this stroke of luck, Pompey had the assurance to claim that in addition to closing the war in Spain, he had also finished the war with the gladiators.

First Consulship of Pompey and Crassus (B.C. 70).—With their victorious legions, Pompey and Crassus now returned to the capital and claimed the consulship. Neither of these men had any great ability as a politician. But Crassus, on account of his wealth, had influence with the capitalists; and Pompey, on account of his military successes, was becoming a sort of popular hero, as Marius had been before him. The popular party was now beginning to gather up its scattered forces, and to make its influence felt. With this party, therefore, as offering the greater prospect of success, the two soldiers formed a coalition, and were elected consuls.

The chief event of the consulship of Pompey and Crassus was the complete overthrow of the Sullan constitution. The old power was given back to the tribunes. The legislative power was restored to the assembly, which now could pass laws without the approval of the senate. The exclusive right to furnish jurors in criminal cases was taken away from the senate; and henceforth the jurors (*iudices*) were to be chosen, one third from the senate, one third from the equites, and one third from the wealthy men below the rank of the equites (the so-called *tribuni aerarii*). Also, the power of the censors to revise the list of the senators, which Sulla had abolished, was restored; and as a result of this, sixty-four senators were expelled from the senate. By these measures the Sullan regime was practically destroyed, and the supremacy of the senate taken away. This was a great triumph for the popular party. After the close of his consulship, Pompey, with affected modesty, retired to private life.

Pompey and the War with the Pirates.—But Pompey was soon needed to rescue Rome from still another danger. Since the decline of the Roman navy the sea had become infested with pirates. These robbers made their home in Crete and Cilicia (see map, p. 142), from which they made their depredations. They had practically the control of the whole Mediterranean, and preyed upon the commerce of the world. They plundered the cities of nearly every coast. They even cut off the grain supplies of Rome, so that Italy was threatened with a famine. To meet this emergency a law was passed (*lex Gabinia*, B.C. 61) giving to Pompey for three years supreme control over the Mediterranean Sea and its coasts for fifty miles inland. He was given five hundred ships and as many soldiers as he might wish. The public treasuries and all the resources of the provinces were placed at his disposal.

Such extraordinary power had never before been given to any man, except Sulla. But Pompey fully satisfied the expectations of the people. Within ninety days from the time he set sail, he had cleared the whole Mediterranean Sea of its pirates. He had captured three thousand vessels, slain ten thousand of the enemy, and taken twenty thousand prisoners. Cicerosaid in his rhetorical way that "Pompey had made his preparations for the war at the end of the winter, began it in the early spring, and finished it in the middle of the summer." Pompey remained in the East to settle affairs in Cilicia, and perhaps to win fresh laurels as a soldier.

Pompey and the Conquest of the East.—The splendid success of Pompey against the pirates led his friends to believe that he was the only man who could bring to a close the long and tedious war against Mithridates. Since the death of Sulla the king of Pontus had continued to be a menace to Rome. The campaigns in the East had been conducted by L. Licinius Lucullus, who was a really able general, but who was charged with prolonging the war in order to enrich himself. There was some ground, too, for this charge: for, as it was afterward well said of him, "he transplanted the luxury of Asia to Rome." Lucullus had already gained several victories over Mithridates; but the war still lingered. A law was then passed at Rome (*lex Manilia*, B.C. 66) displacing Lucullus and giving to Pompey supreme control over all the Roman dominions in the East. Armed with this extensive authority, Pompey began the conquest of the East. He soon succeeded in defeating Mithridates, and in driving him from his kingdom. He then invaded Syria and took possession of that kingdom. He next entered Judea, and after a severe struggle succeeded in capturing Jerusalem (B.C. 63). All the eastern coasts of the Mediterranean were now subject to Pompey. Out of the conquered countries he formed four new provinces: (1) Bithynia with Pontus; (2) Syria; (3) Cilicia; and (4) Crete. When he returned to Italy he had the most successful and brilliant record that any Roman general had ever achieved.

II. THE GROWING INFLUENCE OF CAESAR

Rome during the Absence of Pompey.—During the absence of Pompey in the East (B.C. 67-61) the politics of the capital were mainly in the hands of three men— Marcus Porcius Cato, Marcus Tullius Cicero, and Gaius Julius Caesar. Cato was the grandson of Cato the Censor; and like his great ancestor he was a man of firmness and of the strictest integrity. He was by nature a conservative, and came to be regarded as the leader of the aristocratic party. He contended for the power of the senate as it existed in the days of old. But lacking the highest qualities of a statesman, he could not prevent the inroads which were being made upon the constitution.

On the other hand, Julius Caesar was coming to the front as the leader of the popular party. Though born of patrician stock, he was related by family ties to Marius and Cinna, the old leaders of the people. He was wise enough to see that the cause of the people was in the ascendancy. He aroused the sympathies of the Italians by favoring the extension of the Roman franchise to cities beyond the Po. He appealed to the populace by the splendor of the games which he gave as curule aedile. He allied himself to Crassus, whose great wealth and average ability he could use to good advantage.

Between these two party leaders stood Cicero, who, in spite of his vanity, was a man of great intellect and of excellent administrative ability; but being a moderate man, he was liable to be misjudged by both parties. He was also what was called a "new man" (*novus homo*), that is, the first of his family to obtain the senatorial rank. Cicero was made consul, and rose to the highest distinction during the absence of Pompey.

Cicero and the Catilinian Conspiracy.—If Cicero had done nothing else, he would have been entitled to the gratitude of his country for two acts—the impeachment of Verres and the defeat of Catiline. Cicero stood for law and order, and generally for constitutional government. By his impeachment of Verres, the corrupt governor of Sicily, he brought to light, as had never been done before, the infamous methods employed in the administration of the provinces. He not only brought to light this corruption; he also brought to justice one of the greatest offenders. Then by the defeat of Catiline during his consulship Cicero saved Rome from the execution of a most infamous plot. Catiline was a man of great influence with a certain class, and had already become quite a politician. He had been a partisan of Sulla; had held the office of praetor; and had twice been defeated for the consulship. But if one half of the accounts of him are true, he was a man of most abandoned and depraved character. When Cato threatened to prosecute him, he said that if a fire were kindled against him he would put it out, not with water, but by a general ruin. Ruined himself in fortune, he gathered about him the ruined classes—insolvent debtors, desperate adventurers, and the rabble of Rome. It is said that his plot involved the purpose to kill the consuls, massacre the senators, and to burn the city of Rome. The plot was discovered by Cicero, and was foiled. Cicero delivered in the senate an oration against Catiline, who was present and attempted to reply; but his voice was drowned with the cries of "Traitor," and he fled from the senate to his camp in Etruria. Here a desperate battle ensued; and Catiline was defeated and slain, with three thousand of his followers (B.C. 62). Five of his fellow-conspirators were condemned to death by the senate; and Cicero put the judgment into execution. This act afterward exposed Cicero to the charge of executing Roman citizens without a proper trial. But the people hailed Cicero as the savior of Rome, the Father of his Country.

It was charged that Caesar was implicated in the plot of Catiline; but this charge was answered when Cicero declared that Caesar had done all that a good citizen could do to crush it. The great success of Cicero gave to the senate and the moderate party a temporary advantage. But the senate under the leadership of Cato and Lucullus had not the skill to retain this advantage.

The First Triumvirate—Pompey, Caesar, and Crassus (B.C. 60).—Pompey soon returned to Italy from his victories in the East (B.C. 61). Like Marius returning from the Cimbric war, he was given a magnificent triumph. But like Sulla returning from the East, he was feared by those in power, lest he might use his victorious army to overthrow the existing government, and reign in its stead. To allay all suspicion, Pompey disbanded his army as soon as it touched the soil of Italy; and he hoped that his great services would give him the proud position of the first citizen of Rome. But in this he was disappointed. By disbanding his army, he had given up the source of his influence. Still, he hoped that the senate would at least confirm his arrangements in the East and reward his veterans by grants of land. In this, too, he was disappointed. Yielding to the influence of Lucullus, who had been deposed from the command in the East, the senate refused either to confirm his acts, or to reward his soldiers. Pompey had thus a serious grievance against the senate.

But this grievance of Pompey might not have been very dangerous, if the senate had not also offended Caesar. Caesar was rapidly gaining power and influence. He had held the offices of military tribune, quaestor, aedile, pontifex maximus, and praetor. Then as propraetor he had been sent to Spain, where he laid the basis of his military fame. On his return from Spain the senate thwarted him in his desire to have a triumph. In other ways Caesar was embarrassed by the senate. But he was beginning to feel his power, and was not the man to put up with petty annoyances. He accordingly entered into a coalition with Pompey, to which Crassus was also admitted. This coalition, or self-constituted league, is known as the "first triumvirate." It was formed for the purpose of opposing the senatorial party, and of advancing the personal designs of its members. By the terms of this compact Pompey was to have his acts confirmed and his veterans rewarded; Crassus was to have an opportunity to increase his fortune; and Caesar was to have the consulship, and afterward a command in Gaul. Pompey was ostensibly at the head of the league, but Caesar was its ruling spirit.

The Consulship of Caesar (B.C. 59).—The first fruit of the new alliance was the election of Caesar to the consulship. On his election Caesar went faithfully to work to fulfill his obligations to Pompey, and to strengthen his hold upon the people. He obtained, in the first place, the passage of an agrarian law which provided for the veterans of Pompey, and which also gave estates in Campania to the needy citizens of Rome. In the next place, he secured a law confirming all the acts of Pompey in the East. Finally, he obtained the passage of a law which pleased and conciliated the equites. The tax collectors had made a high offer for the privilege of collecting the taxes of Asia, and afterward concluded that they had made a bad bargain. Accordingly, Caesar took their part, and succeeded in remitting one third of what they had agreed to give.

These laws were bitterly opposed by the senators, but without success. Pompey was now satisfied; the people were pleased; and the capitalists were reconciled. The senate under its bad management was thus outgeneraled by Caesar; and it lost the temporary advantage it had gained during the consulship of Cicero. So completely did Julius Caesar overshadow his weak colleague, Bibulus, who was a partisan of the senate, that this term of office was humorously called the consulship of Julius and Caesar. At the close of his consulship Caesar obtained the government of Cisalpine Gaul and Illyricum, to which was added Transalpine Gaul (Narbonensis). This power was granted for five years. Caesar was thus furnished with an opportunity for the exercise of his military talents, and the building up of a powerful army devoted to his cause.

Clodius and the Banishment of Cicero.—Before Caesar departed for his provinces, he was careful to see that his interests would be looked after during his absence. He chose as his agent P. Clodius, an unscrupulous politician whose personal character was not above reproach, but whose hostility to the senate could be depended upon. To Clodius, who held the position of tribune, was given the task, first, of keeping hold of the populace; and, next, of getting out of the way as best he could the two most influential men in the senate, Cicero and Cato.

The first part of this task he easily accomplished by passing a law that grain should hereafter be distributed to the Roman people free of all expense.

To carry out the second part of his task was not so easy—to remove from the senate its chief leaders. Cato was disposed of, however, by a law annexing Cyprus (see map, p. 202) to the Roman dominion, and appointing him as its governor. Cicero was also got rid of by a law which Clodius succeeded in passing, and which provided that any magistrate who had put a Roman citizen to death without a trial should be banished. Cicero knew that this act was intended for him, and that it referred to his execution of the Catilinian conspirators. After vainly attempting to enlist sympathy in his own behalf, Cicero retired to Greece (B.C. 58) and devoted himself to literary pursuits. With their leaders thus removed, the senate was for a time paralyzed.

Renewal of the Triumvirate at Lucca (B.C. 56).—When Caesar had departed from Rome to undertake his work in Gaul, Clodius began to feel his own importance and to rule with a high hand. The policy of this able and depraved demagogue was evidently to govern Rome with the aid of the mob. He paraded the streets with armed bands, and used his political influence to please the rabble. Pompey as well as the senate became disgusted with the regime of Clodius. They united their influence, and obtained the recall of Cicero from exile. At the same time Cato retuned from his absence in Cyprus. On the return of the old senatorial leaders, it looked as though the senate would once more regain its power, and the triumvirate would go to pieces.

But the watchful eye of Caesar detected these symptoms of discontent, and a conference of the leaders took place at Lucca, a town in northern Italy (see map, p. 81), where a new arrangement was brought about. Caesar was now to be given an additional term of five years in Gaul, and to be elected consul at the end of that time; Pompey and Crassus were to receive the consulship; and at the close of their term of office Pompey was to have the provinces of Spain and Africa, and the money-loving Crassus was to receive the rich province of Syria. In this way they would divide the world among them. The terms of the agreement were apparently satisfactory to the parties concerned. Caesar now felt that matters at Rome were safe, at least until he could complete his work in Gaul and fortify his own power with a devoted and invincible army.

Caesar and his Province.—It is not easy for us to say exactly what was in the mind of Caesar when he selected Gaul for his province. It was at this time the most forbidding part of the Roman territory. It was the home of barbarians, with no wealth like that of Asia, and few relics of a former civilization like those of Spain and Africa. But there were three or four things, no doubt, that Caesar saw clearly.

In the first place, he saw that the power which should hereafter rule the Roman state must be a military power. Sulla had succeeded by the help of his army, and Pompey had failed by giving up his army. If he himself should ever establish his own power, it must be by the aid of a strong military force.

In the next place, he saw that no other province afforded the same political opportunities as those which Gaul presented. It is true that the distant province of Syria might open a way for the conquest of Parthia, and for attaining the glories of another Alexander. But Syria was too far removed from Roman politics; and Caesar's first ambition was political power, and not military glory.

Again, he saw that the conquest of Gaul was necessary for the protection of the Roman state. The invasions of the northern barbarians—the Gauls, the Cimbri and the Teutones had twice already threatened Rome with destruction. By its conquest Gaul might be made a barrier against barbarism.

Moreover, he saw that Rome was in need of new and fertile lands for colonization. Italy was overcrowded. The most patriotic men had seen the need of extra-Italian colonies. Gaius Gracchus had sought an outlet in Africa. He himself had advocated settlements in the valley of the Po. What Italy needed most, after a stable government, was an outlet for her surplus population. His own ambition and the highest interests of his country Caesar believed to be at one. By conquering Gaul he would be fighting not for Pompey or the senate, but for himself and Rome.

The Conquest of Gaul (B.C. 58-51).—The provinces over which Caesar was placed at first included Cisalpine Gaul, that is, the valley of the Po; Illyricum, that is, the strip of territory across the Adriatic Sea; and Narbonensis, that is, a small part of Transalpine Gaul lying about the mouth of the Rhone. Within eight years he brought under his power all the territory bounded by the Pyrenees, the Alps, the Rhine, and the Atlantic Ocean, or about what corresponds to the modern countries of France, Belgium, and Holland.

He at first conquered the Helvetii, a tribe lying on the outskirts of his own province of Narbonensis. He then met and drove back a great invasion of Germans, who, under a prince called Ariovistus, had crossed the Rhine, and threatened to overrun the whole of Gaul. He then pushed into the northern parts of Gaul, and conquered the Nervii and the neighboring tribes. He overcame the Veneti on the Atlantic coast, and conquered Aquitania. He also made two invasions into Britain (B.C. 55, 54), crossed the Rhine into Germany, and revealed to the Roman soldiers countries they had never seen before. After once subduing the various tribes of Gaul, he was finally caned upon to suppress a general insurrection, led by a powerful leader called Vercingetorix. The conquest of Gaul was then completed.

A large part of the population had been either slain in war or reduced to slavery. The new territory was pacified by bestowing honors upon the Gallic chiefs, and self-government upon the surviving tribes. The Roman legions were distributed through the territory; but Caesar established no military colonies like those of Sulla. The Roman arts and manners were encouraged; and Gaul was brought within the pale of civilization.

III. CIVIL WAR BETWEEN POMPEY AND CAESAR

Dissolution of the Triumvirate.—While Caesar was absent in Gaul, the ties which bound the three leaders together were becoming weaker and weaker. The position of Crassus tended somewhat, as long as he was alive, to allay the growing suspicion between the two great rivals. But after Crassus departed for the East to take control of his province in Syria, he invaded Parthia, was badly defeated, lost the Roman standards, and was himself killed (B.C. 53). The death of Crassus practically dissolved the triumvirate; or we might rather say, it reduced the triumvirate to a duumvirate. But the relation between the two leaders was now no longer one of friendly support, but one of mutual distrust.

The Sole Consulship of Pompey (B.C. 52)—The growing estrangement between Pompey and Caesar was increased when the senate appointed Pompey "sole consul." This was not intended as an affront to Caesar, but was evidently demanded to meet a

146

real emergency. The city was distracted by continual street fights between the armed bands of Clodius, the demagogue, and those of T. Annius Milo, who professed to be defending the cause of the senate. In one of these broils Clodius was killed. His excited followers made his death the occasion of riotous proceedings. His body was burned in the Forum by the wild mob, and the senate house was destroyed by fire. In the anarchy which followed, the senate felt obliged to confer some extraordinary power upon Pompey. On the proposal of Cato, he was appointed "consul without a colleague." Under this unusual title Pompey restored order to the state, and was looked upon as "the savior of society." He became more and more closely bound to the cause of the senate; and the senate recognized its obligations to him by prolonging his command in Spain for five years.

The Rupture between Pompey and Caesar.—It was a part of the agreement made at the conference of Lucca, we remember, that Caesar was to receive the consulship at the close of his command in Gaul. He naturally wished to retain the control of his army until he had been elected to his new office. The senate was determined that he should not, but should present himself at Rome as a private citizen before his election. Caesar well knew that he would be helpless as a private citizen in the presence of the enemies who were seeking to destroy him. Cato had already declared that he would prosecute him as soon as he ceased to be proconsul in Gaul. Caesar promised, however, to give up his province and his army, if Pompey would do the same; but Pompey refused. The senate then called upon Caesar to give up two of his legions on the plea that they were needed in the Parthian war. The legions were given up; but instead of being sent to the East they were stationed in Campania. Upon further demands, Caesar agreed to give up eight legions of his army, if he were allowed to retain two legions in Cisalpine Gaul until the time of his election. This the senate refused; and demanded that he must give up his province and his whole army by a certain day, or be declared a public enemy. The senate had offered him humiliation or war. He chose war, and crossed the Rubicon (B.C. 49), the stream which separated his province of Cisalpine Gaul from Italy.

Campaigns in Italy, Spain, and Greece.—The contest was now reduced to a struggle between the two greatest soldiers which Rome had ever produced. Caesar knew the value of time; at the instant when he decided upon war, he invaded Italy with a single legion. Pompey, unprepared for such a sudden move and not relying upon the two legions which the senate had taken from Caesar, was obliged to withdraw to Brundisium (see map, p. 114). Besieged in this place by Caesar, he skillfully withdrew his forces to Greece, and left Caesar master of Italy.

Caesar was now between two hostile forces, the army in Spain under Pompey's lieutenants, and the army in Greece under Pompey himself. He must now defeat these armies separately before they could be united against him. As he had no fleet with which to follow Pompey into Greece, he decided at once to attack the army in Spain. He dispatched his Gallic legions across the Pyrenees, while he secured himself at Rome. He entered the city, and dispelled the fear that there might be repeated the horrors of the first civil war. He showed that he was neither a Marius nor a Sulla. Rejoining his legions in Spain, he soon defeated Pompey's lieutenants. When he returned to Rome he found that he had been proclaimed dictator. He resigned this title and accepted the office of consul.

In the beginning of the next year (B.C. 48), with the few ships that he had collected, he transported his troops from Brundisium across the Adriatic to meet the army of Pompey. In the first conflict, at Dyrrachium, he was defeated. He then retreated across the peninsula (see map, p. 128) in the direction of Pharsalus in order to draw Pompey away from his supplies on the seacoast. The two generals met at Pharsalus (B.C. 48), when Caesar with about twenty thousand men completely defeated the army of Pompey, which numbered more than forty thousand. Pompey fled to Egypt, where he was treacherously murdered. Caesar had now accomplished the first part of his work, by taking possession of Italy and defeating the two armies of Pompey in Spain and Greece. He had established his title to supremacy. Especial honors were paid to him at Rome. He was made consul for five years, tribune for life, and dictator for one year.

Campaigns in Egypt, Asia, Africa, and Spain.—Caesar now entered upon the second part of his work—that of pacifying the provinces. While in Egypt, be became fascinated by the charms of Cleopatra, and settled a dispute in which she was involved. That country was disturbed by a civil war between this princess and her brother Ptolemy. Each claimed the right to the throne. Caesar defeated the forces of Ptolemy and assigned the throne to Cleopatra, under the protection of two Roman legions.

On his way back to Italy he passed through Asia Minor. Here he found Pharnaces, the son of the great Mithridates, stirring up a revolt in Pontus. At the battle of Zela (47 B.C.) he destroyed the armies of this prince, and restored the Asiatic provinces, recording his speedy victory in the famous words, "*Veni, vidi, vici.*"

The armies of Caesar had now swept over all the provinces of Rome, except Africa. Here the Pompeian leaders, assisted by the king of Numidia, determined to make a last stand against the conqueror. Their forces were under Cato, who held Utica, and Metellus Scipio, who commanded in the field. After subduing a mutiny of his tenth

legion by a single word,—calling the men "citizens," instead of "fellow-soldiers,"—
Caesar invaded Africa. The battle of Thapsus (B.C. 46) destroyed the last hope of the
Pompeian party. The republican forces were defeated; and Cato, the chief of the
senatorial party, committed suicide at Utica. In this war Numidia was conquered and
attached to the province of Africa. All resistance to Caesar's power was now at an
end, except a brief revolt in Spain, led by the sons of Pompey, which was soon put
down, the enemy being crushed (B.C. 45) at the battle of Munda (see map, p. 112).

IV. THE RULE OF JULIUS CAESAR

Caesar's Triumphs and Titles.—When Caesar returned to Rome after the battle of
Thapsus, he came not as the servant of the senate, but as master of the world. He
crowned his victories by four splendid triumphs, one for Gaul, one for Egypt, one for
Pontus, and one for Numidia. He made no reference to the civil war; and no citizens
were led among his captives. His victory was attended by no massacres, no
proscriptions, no confiscations. He was as generous in peace as he had been relentless
in war. Caesar was great enough to forgive his enemies. A general amnesty was
proclaimed; and friend and foe were treated alike. We may see the kind of power
which he exercised by the titles which he received. He was consul, dictator, controller
of public morals (*praefectus morum*), tribune, pontifex maximus, and chief of the
senate (*princeps senatus*). He thus gathered up in his own person the powers which
had been scattered among the various republican officers. The name of "imperator"
with which the soldiers had been accustomed to salute a victorious general, was now
made an official title, and prefixed to his name. In Caesar was thus embodied the one-
man power which had been growing up during the civil wars. He was in fact the first
Roman emperor.

Caesar's Political Reforms.—Caesar held his great power only for a short time.
But the reforms which he made are enough to show us his policy, and to enable us to
judge of him as a statesman. The first need of Rome was a stable government based
on the interest of the whole people. The senate had failed to secure such a
government; and so had the popular assemblies led by the tribunes. Caesar believed
that the only government suited to Rome was a democratic monarchy—a government
in which the supreme power should be held permanently by a single man, and
exercised, not for the benefit of himself or any single class, but for the benefit of the
whole state. Let us see how his changes accomplished this end.

In the first place, the senate was changed to meet this view. It had hitherto been a
comparatively small body, drawn from a single class and ruling for its own interests.
Caesar increased the number to nine hundred members, and filled it up with

representative men of all classes, not simply nobles, but also *ignobiles*—Spaniards, Gauls, military officers, sons of freedmen, and others. It was to be not a legislative body but an advisory body, to inform the monarch of the condition and wants of Italy and the provinces. In the next place, he extended the Roman franchise to the inhabitants beyond the Po, and to many cities in the provinces, especially in Transalpine Gaul and Spain. All his political changes tended to break down the distinction between nobles and commons, between Italians and the provincials, and to make of all the people of the empire one nation.

Caesar's Economic Reforms.—The next great need of Rome was the improvement of the condition of the lower classes. Caesar well knew that the condition of the people could not be changed in a day; but he believed that the government ought not to encourage pauperism by helping those who ought to help themselves. There were three hundred and twenty thousand persons at Rome to whom grain was distributed. He reduced this number to one hundred and fifty thousand, or more than one half. He provided means of employment for the idle, by constructing new buildings in the city, and other public works; and also by enforcing the law that one third of the labor employed on landed estates should be free labor. As the land of Italy was so completely occupied, he encouraged the establishment, in the provinces, of agricultural colonies which would not only tend to relieve the farmer class, but to Romanize the empire. He relieved the debtor class by a bankrupt law which permitted the insolvent debtor to escape imprisonment by turning over his property to his creditors. In such ways as these, while not pretending to abolish poverty, he afforded better means for the poorer classes to obtain a living.

His Reform of the Provincial System.—The despotism of the Roman republic was nowhere more severe and unjust than in the provinces. This was due to two things— the arbitrary authority of the governor, and the wretched system of farming the taxes. The governor ruled the province, not for the benefit of the provincials, but for the benefit of himself. It is said that the proconsul hoped to make three fortunes out of his province—one to pay his debts, one to bribe the jury if he were brought to trial, and one to keep himself. The tax collector also looked upon the property of the province as a harvest to be divided between the Roman treasury and himself. Caesar put a check upon this system of robbery. The governor was now made a responsible agent of the emperor; and the collection of taxes was placed under a more rigid supervision. The provincials found in Caesar a protector; because his policy involved the welfare of all his subjects.

His Other Reforms and Projects.—The most noted of Caesar's other changes was the reform of the calendar, which has remained as he left it, with slight change, down to the present day. He also intended to codify the Roman law; to provide for the founding of public libraries; to improve the architecture of the city; to drain the Pontine Marshes for the improvement of the public health; to cut a channel through the Isthmus of Corinth; and to extend the empire to its natural limits, the Euphrates, the Danube, and the Rhine. These projects show the comprehensive mind of Caesar. That they would have been carried out in great part, if he had lived, we can scarcely doubt, when we consider his wonderful executive genius and the works he actually accomplished in the short time in which he held his power.

The Assassination of Caesar.—If Caesar failed, it was because he did not adjust himself sufficiently to the conservative spirit of the time. There were still living at Rome men who were blindly attached to the old republican forms. To them the reforms of Caesar looked like a work of destruction, rather than a work of creation. They saw in his projects a scheme for reviving the kingship. It was said that when Caesar was offered a crown he looked at it wistfully; and that he had selected his nephew Octavius as his royal heir.

The men who hated Caesar, and who conspired to kill him, were men who had themselves received special favors from him. The leading conspirators, M. Brutus and C. Cassius, had both served in Pompey's army, and had been pardoned by Caesar and promoted to offices under his government. Joined by some fifty other conspirators, these men formed a plot to kill Caesar in the senate house. The story of his assassination has been told by Plutarch and made immortal by Shakespeare. When the appointed day came, the Ides of March (March 15, B.C. 44), Caesar was struck down by the daggers of his treacherous friends, and he fell at the foot of Pompey's statue. It has been said that the murder of Caesar was the most senseless act that the Romans ever committed. His death deprived Rome of the greatest man she ever produced. But the work of the conspirators did not destroy the work of Caesar.

SELECTIONS FOR READING

Liddell, Ch. 67, "The Second Civil War" (1).[2]

Shuckburgh, Ch. 42, "Pompey in the East" (1).

How and Leigh, Ch. 47, "Cicero and Catiline" (1).

Merivale, Gen. Hist., Ch. 40, "The First Triumvirate" (1).

Mommsen, Vol. IV., Bk. V., Ch. 11, "The Old Republic and New Monarchy" (2).

Mommsen, abridged, Ch. 35, "Joint Rule of Pompey and Caesar" (2).

Pelham, Bk. V., Ch. 1, "The Dictatorship of Julius" (1).1).

Shakespeare, "Julius Caesar" (36).

Plutarch, "Sertorius," "Lucullus," "Pompey," "Crassus," "Cato the Younger," "Caesar," "Cicero" (11).

SPECIAL STUDY

CAESAR'S CAMPAIGNS IN GAUL.—How and Leigh, Ch. 49 (1); Shuckburgh, Ch. 44 (1); Merivale, Gen. Hist., Ch. 41 (1); Merivale, Triumvirates, Ch. 5 (6); Merivale, Empire, Chs. 5-12 (7); Dodge, Julius Caesar, Chs. 8-14 (22).

[1] Son of the colleague of Marius (p. 165).

[2] The figure in parenthesis refers to the number of the topic in the Appendix, where a fuller title of the book will be found.

CHAPTER XXII

THE TIMES OF ANTONY AND OCTAVIUS

The Rise of Antony and Octavius, I.—Civil War between Antony and Octavius, II.—Review of the Period of the Civil Wars, III.

I. THE RISE OF ANTONY AND OCTAVIUS

Rome after the Death of Caesar.—The men who murdered Caesar considered themselves as "liberators" of the republic. Whatever may have been their motives, they seem to have taken little thought as to how Rome would be governed after they had killed their tyrant. If they thought that the senate would take up the powers it had lost, and successfully rule the republic, they were grievously mistaken. The only leading man of the senate who had survived the last civil war was Cicero; but Cicero with all his learning and eloquence could not take the place of Caesar. What Rome needed was what the liberators had taken from her, a master mind of broad views and of great executive power. We need not be surprised that the death of Caesar was followed by confusion and dismay. No one knew which way to look or what to expect. Soon there appeared new actors upon the scene, men struggling for the supreme power in the state—M. Antonius (Antony), the friend of Caesar and his fellow-consul; C. Octavius, his adopted son and heir; M. Aemilius Lepidus,1 his master of horse; Sextus Pompeius, his previous enemy and the son of his greatest rival; while Cicero still raised his voice in defense of what he regarded as his country's freedom.

The Supremacy of Antony.—The first to take advantage of the confusion which followed Caesar's death was Marcus Antonius. With the aid of Lepidus he got possession of Caesar's will and other papers, and seized his treasury. He influenced the senate to confirm all of Caesar's acts, and obtained permission to speak at his public funeral. He made a strong appeal to the populace to avenge the death of their great friend; and read the will of Caesar, which left his palace and gardens to the people, and a legacy to every citizen. Excited to fury by the eloquence of Antony, the people seized firebrands from the burning funeral pile, and rushed through the streets swearing vengeance to the so-called liberators. The liberators were obliged to flee from the city; and Antony was for the time supreme. As the senate had confirmed Caesar's acts, and as Antony had Caesar's papers, which were supposed to contain these acts, he assumed the role of Caesar's executor and did what he pleased. The chief liberators hastened to the provinces to which they had previously been assigned

154

by Caesar—Cassius to Syria, Marcus Brutus to Macedonia, and Decimus Brutus to Cisalpine Gaul.

The Rise of Octavius.—Antony's dream of power was soon disturbed by the appearance of the young Octavius, Caesar's grand-nephew and adopted son. Although a young man—only nineteen—he was a born politician, and soon became Antony's greatest rival. He assumed his adopted name, Gaius Julius Caesar Octavianus, and claimed his inheritance and the treasures which had fallen into Antony's hands. But Antony said that these were public moneys, and that they had been spent in the interests of the Roman state.

Octavius (as we shall continue to call him) now for the first time showed that adroit skill for which he was always distinguished. Antony had raised the false hopes of the people by reading Caesar's will, which promised a legacy to every citizen. The people had heard the will; but they had not yet received the promised legacies. To humiliate Antony and to insure his own popularity, the young Octavius sold his own estates, borrowed money of his friends, and paid the legacies which Caesar had promised to the people. By this act Octavius displaced Antony as the people's friend. The young heir grew so rapidly in popular favor that his influence was sought both by Cicero, who represented the senate, and by Antony, who represented himself.

Cicero's Attack upon Antony.—Cicero thought that everything should be done to weaken the power of Antony, and to prevent any possible coalition between him and the young Octavius. The hostility between Cicero and Antony grew to be bitter and relentless; and they were pitted against each other on the floor of the senate. But in a war of words Antony was no match for Cicero. By a series of famous speeches known as the "Philippics," the popularity of Antony was crushed; and he retired from Rome to seek for victory upon other fields. He claimed Cisalpine Gaul as his province. But this province was still held by Decimus Brutus, one of the liberators to whom the senate looked for military support.

When Antony attempted to gain possession of this territory, Cicero thought he saw an opportunity to use Octavius in the interests of the senate. Accordingly Antony was declared a public enemy; Octavius was made a senator with the rank of a consul, and was authorized to conduct the war against Antony. In this war—the so-called war of Mutina (B.C. 44-43)—Octavius was successful. As a reward for his victory he demanded of the senate that he receive a triumph and the consulship. Cicero had intended Decimus Brutus for this office, and the request of Octavius was refused. But the young heir, then twenty years of age, following the example of Caesar, enforced his claims with the sword; he took possession of the city, and obtained his election to the consulship. Octavius thus became the ruling man in Rome.

The Second Triumvirate—Antony, Octavius, and Lepidus (B.C. 43).—Cicero's attempt to defeat Antony by the aid of Octavius was not a successful piece of diplomacy. It resulted not only in alienating the young heir; but worse than that, it brought about the very coalition which Cicero was trying to prevent. Octavius had broken with the senate, and had obtained a complete victory. But he was not yet ready to break with Antony, who was supported by Lepidus, especially as the two chief liberators, Brutus and Cassius, were still in control of the eastern provinces. If he had had the military genius of Caesar, he might have destroyed all their armies in detail. But the young Octavius was not inclined to overrate his military abilities. He saw that it would be for his interest to make friends with Antony and Lepidus. A coalition was therefore formed between the three leaders, usually called the "second triumvirate." They agreed to divide the western provinces among themselves, and then to make a new division after they had driven Brutus and Cassius from the eastern provinces.

The Proscriptions; Murder of Cicero.—No government could be more despotic than that of the three masters who now governed Rome. They assumed the consular power for five years, with the right of appointing all magistrates. Their decrees were to have the force of law without the sanction of either the senate or the people. It is to the eternal disgrace of these men who professed to espouse the cause of Caesar, that they abandoned the humane policy of their great exemplar, and turned to the infamous policy of Marius and Sulla. Antony especially desired a proscription, as he was surrounded by thousands of personal enemies, chief among whom was Cicero, the author of the "Philippics." Octavius was reconciled to the horrible work as a matter of policy; and Lepidus acquiesced in it as a matter of indifference. It is said that three hundred senators and two thousand equites were outlawed, and their property confiscated. The triumvirs justified their atrocious acts as a retaliation for the murder of Caesar. Many of the proscribed escaped from Italy and found a refuge with Brutus and Cassius in the East. But a large number of persons were slain.

The world will always feel a painful interest in these black days, because it was then that Cicero lost his life. When the old man was warned of his danger, and urged to flee, he replied, "Let me die in my fatherland which I have so often saved." He was slain, and his head was sent to Antony, whose wife, Fulvia, is said to have pierced the lifeless tongue with a needle, in revenge for the words it had uttered against her husband. Thus perished the greatest orator of Rome. Cicero has been accused of timidity; but he remained at his post, the last defender of the republic. He has been charged with vacillation; but he lived in days when no man knew which way to turn for help. He failed as a politician, because he continually bungled in the fine arts of intrigue. He failed as a statesman, because he persisted in defending a lost cause. He appealed to reason, when the highest arbiter was the sword. But with all his faults, Cicero was, next to Cato, the most upright man of his time; and his influence has been, next to that of Caesar, the most enduring. To practical politics he contributed little; but his numerous writings have exercised a wonderful influence in the intellectual and moral education of the world.

War against the Liberators; Battle of Philippi (B.C. 42).—Having murdered their enemies at home, the triumvirs were now prepared to crush their enemies abroad. There were three of these enemies whom they were obliged to meet—Brutus and Cassius, who had united their forces in the East; and Sextus Pompeius, who had got possession of the island of Sicily, and had under his command a powerful fleet. While Lepidus remained at Rome, Antony and Octavius invaded Greece with an army of one hundred and twenty thousand men. Against them the two liberators, Brutus and Cassius, collected an army of eighty thousand men. The hostile forces met near Philippi (B.C. 42), a town in Macedonia on the northern coast of the Aegean Sea (see map, p. 128). Octavius was opposed to Brutus, and Antony to Cassius. Octavius was driven back by Brutus, while Antony, more fortunate, drove back the wing commanded by Cassius. As Cassius saw his flying legions, he thought that all was lost, and stabbed himself with the same dagger, it is said, with which he struck Caesar. This left Brutus in sole command of the opposing army; but he also was defeated in a second battle, and, following the example of Cassius, committed suicide. The double battle at Philippi decided the fate of the republic. As Cicero was its last political champion, Brutus and Cassius were its last military defenders; and with their death we may say that the republic was at an end.

II. CIVIL WAR BETWEEN ANTONY AND OCTAVIUS

New Division of the Provinces.—With the republic overthrown, it now remained to be seen who should be the master of the new empire, Antony or Octavius. Lepidus, although ambitious, was too weak and vacillating to be dangerous. The triumvirs were growing to be envious of each other; but they contrived to smother their jealousy, and made a new division of the empire. Antony was now to have the East, and Octavius the West. It was a question what to do with Lepidus, as he was accused of giving aid to the only remaining enemy of the triumvirs, that is, Sextus Pompeius. If he could prove himself innocent of the charge, he was to be given the small province of Africa. The real work of the triumvirate was to be done by Antony and Octavius. Antony was to take control of the eastern provinces, and to push the Roman conquests if possible into Parthia. Octavius was to preserve the peace of Italy and the western provinces, and to destroy the fleet of Sextus Pompeius, which was seriously interfering with Roman commerce

Octavius in the West.—Octavius proceeded to secure his position in the West by means of force and craft. He first put down an insurrection incited by the partisans of Antony. The young conqueror won the affections of the people, and tried to show them that peace and prosperity could come only through his influence. The next thing was to dispose of Sextus Pompeius and his hostile fleet. With the help of his friend and able general, Agrippa, and with the aid of a hundred ships lent him by Antony, Octavius destroyed the forces of Pompeius. The defeated general fled to the East, and was killed by the soldiers of Antony.

Octavius was then called upon to deal with a treacherous friend. This was the weak and ambitious Lepidus, who with twenty legions thought that he could defeat Octavius and become the chief man of Rome. But Octavius did not think the emergency grave enough to declare war. He defeated Lepidus without a battle. Unarmed and almost unattended he entered his rival's camp, and made an eloquent appeal to the soldiers. The whole army of Lepidus deserted to Octavius. Lepidus was deposed from his position as triumvir, but was generously allowed to retain the office of pontifex maximus on condition of remaining quiet. By the use of force and diplomacy Octavius thus baffled all his foes in the West, and he and Antony were now the undisputed rulers of the Roman world.

Antony in the East.—While everything in the West was turning in favor of Octavius, all things in the East were also contributing to his success. But this was due not so much to his own skill as to the weakness and folly of Antony. Octavius had tried to cement the league of the triumvirs by giving his sister Octavia to Antony in marriage. But Antony Soon grew tired of Octavia, and became fascinated by Cleopatra, the "Serpent of the Nile." His time was divided between campaigns in Parthia and dissipations in Egypt. His Parthian wars turned out to be failures; and his Egyptian entanglements resulted in his ruin. He aspired to the position of an Oriental monarch. He divided the Roman provinces with Cleopatra, who was called "the queen of kings." The Roman people were shocked when he desired his disgraceful acts to be confirmed by the senate. They could not help contrasting this weak and infatuated slave of Cleopatra with their own Octavius, the strong and prudent governor of the West. While Octavius was growing in popularity, Antony was thus becoming more and more an object of detestation.

Rupture between Antony and Octavius.—The strong feeling at Rome against

Antony, Octavius was able to use to his own advantage. But he wished it to appear that he was following, and not directing, the will of the people. He therefore made no attempt to force an issue with Antony, but bided his time. The people suspected Antony of treasonable designs, as they saw his military preparations, which might be used to enthrone himself as king of the East, or to install Cleopatra as queen of Rome.

All doubt as to Antony's real character and purpose was settled when his will was found and published. In it he had made the sons of Cleopatra his heirs, and ordered his own body to be buried at Alexandria beside that of the Egyptian queen. This was looked upon as an insult to the majesty of Rome. The citizens were aroused. They demanded that war be declared against the hated triumvir. Octavius suggested that it would be more wise to declare war against Cleopatra than against Antony and the deluded citizens who had espoused his cause. Thus what was really a civil war between Octavius and Antony assumed the appearance of a foreign war between Rome and Egypt. But Antony well understood against whom the war was directed; and he replied by publicly divorcing Octavia, and accepting his real position as the public enemy of Rome.

Defeat of Antony; Battle of Actium (B.C. 31).—When war was declared, Antony and Cleopatra united their forces against Rome. Antony gathered together an immense army of eighty thousand men, and occupied the western coasts of Greece, where he could either threaten Italy or resist the approach of Octavius. His main army was posted at Actium (see map, p. 128), south of the strait leading into the Gulf of Ambracia. His fleet of five hundred heavy ships was for the most part moored within the gulf. Octavius, with the aid of his trusted general Agrippa, succeeded in transporting an army of fifty thousand men to the coast of Epirus, and took up a position north of the strait and opposite the land forces of Antony. His fleet of two hundred and fifty light galleys was stationed outside of the strait to await the approach of the enemy's vessels. Antony, on the advice of his ablest officers, desired that the battle should be waged with the land forces. But Cleopatra, proud of her navy, insisted that it should be fought on the sea. The contest was therefore decided by a naval battle. As the fleet of Antony emerged from the strait, it was immediately attacked by Octavius and Agrippa. But scarcely had the battle begun when Cleopatra with her squadron withdrew from the line, and was quickly followed by Antony. Their sailors fought on until their fleet was destroyed. The battle at Actium closed the political career of Antony, and left Octavius the sole master of the Roman world. The date of this battle may be taken to mark the beginning of the empire.

The Triumph of Octavius.—Before returning to Rome Octavius restored order to the eastern provinces, and followed the fugitives to Egypt. The arts by which Cleopatra had fascinated Caesar and enslaved Antony, she tried to use upon her new Roman guest. But Octavius did not fall into the tempter's snare. The Egyptian queen found in the Roman sovereign a nature as crafty as her own. Octavius kept his thoughts upon the prosperity and honor of Rome, and no allurements could draw him away from his high mission. Antony, defeated and ruined, committed suicide; and Cleopatra followed his example rather than be led a captive in a Roman triumph. Together this wretched pair were laid in the mausoleum of the Ptolemies. Egypt was annexed as a province of the new empire (B.C. 30). Octavius returned to Rome (B.C. 29), where he was given the honors of a triple triumph—for Dalmatia (where he had gained some previous victories), for Actium, and for Egypt. The temple of Janus was now closed for the first time since the second Punic war; and the Romans, tired of war and of civil strife, looked upon the triumph of Octavius as the dawn of a new era of peace and prosperity.

III. REVIEW OF THE PERIOD OF THE CIVIL WARS

Progress of Rome.—As we look back over the period which we have just completed, we may ask the question whether Rome had made any progress since the days of her great conquests. More than a hundred years had passed away since the beginning of the commotions under the Gracchi. During this time we have seen the long conflict between the senate and the people; we have seen the republic gradually declining and giving way to the empire. But we must not suppose that the fall of the republic was the fall of Rome. The so-called republic of Rome was a government neither by the people nor for the people. It had become the government of a selfish aristocracy, ruling for its own interests. Whether the new empire which was now established was better than the old republic which had fallen, remains to be seen. But there are many things in which we can see that Rome was making some real progress.

Appearance of Great Men.—The first thing that we notice is the fad that during this period of conflict Rome produced some of the greatest men of her history. It is in the times of stress and storm that great men are brought to the front; and it was the fierce struggles of this period which developed some of the foremost men of the ancient world—men like the two Gracchi, Marius, Sulla, Cato, Cicero, and Julius Caesar. Whatever we may think of their opinions, of the methods which they used, or of the results which they accomplished, we cannot regard them as ordinary men.

Extension of the Franchise.—Another evidence of the progress of Rome was the extension of the rights of citizenship, and the bringing into the state of many who had hitherto been excluded. At the beginning of this period only the inhabitants of a comparatively small part of the Italian peninsula were citizens of Rome. The franchise was restricted chiefly to those who dwelt upon the lands in the vicinity of the capital. But during the civil wars the rights of citizenship had been extended to all parts of Italy and to many cities in Gaul and Spain.

Improvement in the Roman Law.—We have already seen the improvement which Sulla made in the organization of the criminal courts for the trial of public crimes. But there were also improvements made in the civil law, by which the private rights of individuals were better protected. Not only were the rights of citizens made more secure, but the rights of foreigners were also more carefully guarded. Before the social war, the rights of all foreigners in Italy were protected by a special praetor (*praetor peregrinus*); and after that war all Italians became equal before the law. There was also a tendency to give all foreigners in the provinces rights equal to those of citizens, so far as these rights related to persons and property.

Progress in Architecture.—That the Romans were improving in their culture and taste is shown by the new and splendid buildings which were erected during this period. While some public buildings were destroyed by the riots in the city, they were replaced by finer and more durable structures. Many new temples were built—temples to Hercules, to Minerva, to Fortune, to Concord, to Honor and Virtue. There were new basilicas, or halls of justice, the most notable being the Basilica Julia, which was commenced by Julius Caesar. A new forum, the Forum Julii, was also laid out by Caesar, and a new theater was constructed by Pompey. The great national temple of Jupiter Capitolinus, which was burned during the civil war of Marius and Sulla, was restored with great magnificence by Sulla, who adorned it with the columns of the temple of the Olympian Zeus brought from Athens. It was during this period that the triumphal arches were first erected, and became a distinctive feature of Roman architecture.

Advancement in Literature.—The most important evidence of the progress of the Romans during the period of the civil wars is seen in their literature. It was at this time that Rome began to produce writers whose names belong to the literature of the world. Caesar wrote his "Commentaries on the Gallic War," which is a fine specimen of clear historical narrative.Sallust wrote a history of the Jugurthine War and an account of the conspiracy of Catiline, which give us graphic and vigorous descriptions of these events. Lucretius wrote a great poem "On the Nature of Things," which expounds the Epicurean theory of the universe, and reveals powers of description and imagination rarely equaled by any other poet, ancient or modern. Catullus wrote lyric poems of exquisite grace and beauty. Cicero was the most learned and prolific writer of the age;

his orations, letters, rhetorical and philosophical essays furnish the best models of classic style, and have given him a place among the great prose writers of the world.

Decay of Religion and Morals.—While the Romans, during this period, showed many evidences of progress in their laws, their art, and their literature, they were evidently declining in their religious and moral sense. Their religion was diluted more and more with Oriental superstitions and degrading ceremonies. In their moral life they were suffering from the effects of their conquests, which had brought wealth and the passion for luxury and display. Ambition and avarice tended to corrupt the life of the Roman people. The only remedy or this condition of religious and moral decay was found in the philosophy of the Greeks, which, however, appealed only to the more educated classes.[2]

SELECTIONS FOR READING

Abbott, Ch. 7, "The Period of Transition" (13).

Merivale, Empire, Vol. III., Ch. 25, "Cicero and the 'Philippics'" (7).

Leighton, Ch. 28, "Last Days of the Republic" (1).

Schmitz, Ch. 39, "Rome during the Later Republic" (1).

Taylor, Ch. 16, "Struggle for the Crown" (1).

Seeley, Essay, "The Great Roman Revolution" (7).

Shakespeare, "Antony and Cleopatra" (37).

Plutarch, "Antony," "Brutus" (11).

SPECIAL STUDY

CHARACTER OF CICERO.—Plutarch, "Cicero" (11); Mommsen, IV., pp. 724-726 (2); Merivale, Empire, Vol. III., pp. 148-153 (1); Forsyth, II., Ch. 25 (23). See also Appendix (23) "Cicero."

[1] Son of the Lepidus who opposed the Sullan party (p. 180).

[2] Roman education was patterned in many respects after that of the Greeks; for its general character, see p. 260.

[3] The figure in parenthesis refers to the number of the topic in the Appendix, where a fuller title of the book will be found.

CHAPTER XXIII

THE REIGN OF AUGUSTUS (B.C. 31-A.D. 14)

The New Imperial Government, I.—Augustus and the Roman World, II.—The Age of Augustus, III.

I. THE NEW IMPERIAL GOVERNMENT

Beginning of the Empire.—We have taken the date of the battle of Actium (B.C. 31) to mark the beginning of the empire, because Octavius then became the sole and undisputed master of the Roman world. But it is not so important for us to fix upon a particular date for the beginning of the empire, as it is to see that some form of imperialism had come to be a necessity. During the whole period of the civil wars we have seen the gradual growth of the one-man power. We have seen it in the tribunate under the Gracchi; in the successive consulships of Marius; in the perpetual dictatorship of Sulla; in the sole consulship of Pompey; in the absolute rule of Julius Caesar. The name of "king" the Romans hated, because it brought to mind the memory of the last Tarquin. But the principle of monarchy they could not get rid of, because they had found no efficient form of government to take its place. The aristocratic government under the senate had proved corrupt, inefficient, and disastrous to the people. A popular government without representation had shown itself unwieldy, and had become a prey to demagogues. There was nothing left for the Romans to do except to establish some form of monarchy which would not suggest the hated name of king.

The Policy of Augustus.—There was no other man so well fitted to put the new monarchy into an attractive form as Octavius, whom we may now call by his official title of Augustus. We have been accustomed to think of this man as merely a shrewd politician. But when we contrast the distracted condition of Rome during the last hundred years with the peace and prosperity which he brought with him, we shall be inclined to look upon him as a wise and successful statesman. His whole policy was a policy of conciliation. He wished to wipe out the hatreds of the civil war. He regarded himself as the chief of no party, but as the head of the whole state. He tried to reconcile the conservative and the progressive men of his time. All the cherished forms of the republic he therefore preserved; and he exercised his powers under titles which were not hateful to the senate or the people.

The Titles and Powers of Augustus.—Soon after returning to Rome, Augustus resigned the powers which he had hitherto exercised, giving "back the commonwealth into the hands of the senate and the people" (B.C. 27). The first official title which he then received was the surname *Augustus*, bestowed by the senate in recognition of his dignity and his services to the state, He then received the proconsular power (*imperium proconsulare*) over all the frontier provinces, or those which required the presence of an army. He had also conferred upon himself the tribunician power *tribunicia potestas*, by which he became the protector of the people. He moreover was made pontifex maximus, and received the title of *Pater Patriae*. Although Augustus did not receive the permanent titles of consul and censor, he occasionally assumed, or had temporarily assigned to himself, the duties of these offices. He still retained the title of *Imperator*, which gave him the command of the army. But the title which Augustus chose to indicate his real position was that of *Princeps Civitatis*, or "the first citizen of the state," The new "prince" thus desired himself to be looked upon as a magistrate rather than a monarch—a citizen who had received a trust rather than a ruler governing in his own name.

Augustus and the Senate.—Augustus showed his conciliatory policy in fixing the position which the senate was to assume in the new government. He did not adopt fully the plan either of Sulla or of Julius Caesar; but reconciled as far as possible their different ideas. He restored to the senate the dignity which it had in the time of Sulla. He did this by excluding the provincials and freedmen whom Caesar had introduced into it, and by reducing its number from nine hundred to six hundred members. But still he did not confer upon it the great legislative power which Sulla intended it should have; he rather made it a kind of advisory-body, according to Caesar's idea. In theory the senate was to assist the emperor in matters of legislation; but in fact it was simply to approve the proposals which he submitted to it.

The Assemblies of the People.—Augustus did not formally take away from the popular assemblies their legislative power, but occasionally submitted to them laws for their approval. This was, however, hardly more than a discreet concession to custom. The people in their present unwieldy assemblies, the emperor did not regard as able to decide upon important matters of state. Their duties were therefore practically restricted to the election of the magistrates, whose names he usually presented to them.

The Republican Magistrates.—In accordance with his general policy Augustus did not interfere with the old republican offices, but allowed them to remain as undisturbed as possible. The consuls, praetors, quaestors, and other officers continued to be elected just as they had been before. But the emperor did not generally use these magistrates to carry out the details of his administration. This was performed by other officers appointed by himself. The position of the old republican magistrates was rather one of honor than one of executive responsibility.

The Army.—While the emperor knew that his power must have some military support, he was careful not to make the army a burden to the people. He therefore reduced the number of legions from fifty to twenty-five. As each legion contained not more than six thousand men, the whole army did not exceed one hundred and fifty thousand soldiers. These legions were distributed through the frontier provinces; the inner provinces and Italy were thus not burdened by the quartering of troops. To support the imperial authority at home, and to maintain public order, Augustus organized a body of nine thousand men called the "praetorian guard," which force was stationed at different points outside of Rome.

II. AUGUSTUS AND THE ROMAN WORLD

Rome, Italy, and the Provinces.—We can get some further idea of the policy of Augustus by looking at the way in which he governed the different parts of the Roman world. The whole empire may be regarded as made up of three parts—Rome, Italy, and the provinces. We are now to look at the improvements which he made in these three spheres of administration.

The Administration of Rome.—We have read enough of the distracted condition of the Roman city during the last hundred years to see the need of some improvement. Augustus met this need by creating certain new officers to keep the city under better control. In the first place, he established a city police under the charge of a chief (*praefectus urbi*), to preserve order and prevent the scenes of violence which had been of such frequent occurrence. In the next place, he created a fire and detective department under the charge of another chief (*praefectus vigilum*), to have jurisdiction over all incendiaries, burglars, and other night-prowlers. He then placed the grain supply under a regular officer (*praefectus annonae*) who was to superintend the transport of grain from Egypt, and was held responsible for its proper distribution. Moreover, he broke up the "secret clubs" which had been hotbeds of disorder, and substituted in their place more orderly societies under the supervision of the government. For administrative purposes the city was divided into fourteen districts, or wards. By these arrangements, life and property became more secure, and the populace became more orderly and law-abiding.

The Administration of Italy.—Italy was now extended to the Alps, the province of Cisalpine Gaul having lately been joined to the peninsula. The whole of Italy was divided by Augustus into eleven "regions," or administrative districts. In order to maintain the splendid system of roads which had been constructed during the republican period, the emperor appointed a superintendent of highways (*curator* *viarurn*) to keep them in repair. He also established a post system by which the different parts of the peninsula could be kept in communication with one another. He suppressed brigandage by establishing military patrols in the dangerous districts. It was his policy to encourage everywhere the growth of a healthy and vigorous municipal life. To relieve the poverty of Italy he continued the plan of Julius Caesar in sending out colonies into the provinces, where there were better opportunities to make a living.

The Administration of the Provinces.—During the reign of Augustus the number of provinces was increased by taking in the outlying territory south of the Rhine and the Danube. The new frontier provinces were Rhaetia, Noricum, Pannonia, and Moesia. The provinces were not only increased in number, but were thoroughly reorganized. They were first divided into two groups,—the *senatorial*, or those which remained under the control of the senate; and the *imperial*, or those which passed under the control of the emperor. The latter were generally on the frontiers, and required the presence of an army and a military governor. The governors of the imperial provinces were lieutenants (*legati*) of the emperor. Appointed by him, and strictly responsible to him, they were no longer permitted to prey upon their subjects, but were obliged to rule in the name of the emperor, and for the welfare of the people. The senatorial provinces, on the other hand, were still under the control of proconsuls and propraetors appointed by the senate. But the condition of these provinces was also greatly improved. The establishment of the new government thus proved to be a great benefit to the provincials. Their property became more secure, their commerce revived, their cities became prosperous, and their lives were made more tolerable.

The Finances of the Empire.—With the division of the provinces, the administration of the finances was also divided between the senate and the emperor. The revenues of the senatorial provinces went into the treasury of the senate, or the *aerarium*; while those of the imperial provinces passed into the treasury of the emperor, or the *fiscus*. The old wretched system of farming the revenues, which had disgraced the republic and impoverished the provincials, was gradually abandoned. The collection of the taxes in the senatorial as well as the imperial provinces was placed in the charge of imperial officers. It was not long before the cities themselves were allowed to raise by their own officers the taxes due to the Roman government. Augustus also laid the foundation of a sound financial system by making careful estimates of the revenues and expenditures of the state; and by raising and expending the public money in the most economical and least burdensome manner.

The Frontiers of the Empire.—By the wars of Augustus, the boundaries of the empire were extended to the Rhine and the Danube (including the Alpine region) on the north, to the Atlantic Ocean on the west, to the desert of Africa on the south, and nearly to the Euphrates on the east. The only two great frontier nations which threatened to disturb the peace of Rome were the Parthians on the east and the Germans on the north. The Parthians still retained the standards lost by Crassus; but Augustus by his skillful diplomacy was able to recover them without a battle. He abandoned, however, all design of conquering that Eastern people. But his eyes looked longingly to the country of the Germans. He invaded their territory; and after a temporary success his general, Varus, was slain and three Roman legions were utterly destroyed by the great German chieftain Arminius at the famous battle of the Teutoberg forest (9 A.D.). The frontiers remained for many years where they were fixed by Augustus; and he advised his successors to govern well the territory which he left to them rather than to increase its limits.

III. THE AGE OF AUGUSTUS

The Advisers of Augustus.—The remarkable prosperity that attended the reign of Augustus has caused this age to be called by his name. The glory of this period is largely due to the wise policy of Augustus himself; but in his work he was greatly assisted by two men, whose names are closely linked to his own. These men were Agrippa and Maecenas.

Agrippa had been from boyhood one of the most intimate friends of Augustus, and during the trying times of the later republic had constantly aided him by his counsel and his sword. The victories of Augustus before and after he came to power were largely due to this able general. By his artistic ability Agrippa also contributed much to the architectural splendor of Rome.

The man who shared with Agrippa the favor and confidence of Augustus was Maecenas, a wise statesman and patron of literature. It was by the advice of Maecenas that many of the important reforms of Augustus were adopted and carried out. But the greatest honor is due to Maecenas for encouraging those men whose writings made this period one of the "golden ages" of the world's literature. It was chiefly the encouragement given to architecture and literature which made the reign of Augustus an epoch in civilization.

Encouragement to Architecture.—It is said that Augustus boasted that he "found Rome of brick and left it of marble." He restored many of the temples and other buildings which had either fallen into decay or been destroyed during the riots of the civil war. On the Palatine hill he began the construction of the great imperial palace, which became the magnificent home of the Caesars. He built a new temple of Vesta, where the sacred fire of the city was kept burning. He erected a new temple to Apollo, to which was attached a library of Greek and Latin authors; also temples to Jupiter Tonans and to the Divine Julius. One of the noblest and most useful of the public works of the emperor was the new Forum of Augustus, near the old Roman Forum and the Forum of Julius. In this new Forum was erected the temple of Mars the Avenger (*Mars Ultor*), which Augustus built to commemorate the war by which he had avenged the death of Caesar. We must not forget to notice the massive Pantheon, the temple of all the gods, which is to-day the best preserved monument of the Augustan period. This was built by Agrippa, in the early part of Augustus's reign (B.C. 27), but was altered to the form shown above by the emperor Hadrian (p. 267).

Patronage of Literature.—But more splendid and enduring than these temples of marble were the works of literature which this age produced. At this time was written Vergil's "Aeneid," which is one of the greatest epic poems of the world. It was then that the "Odes" of Horace were composed, the race and rhythm of which are unsurpassed. Then, too, were written the elegies of Tibullus, Propertius, and Ovid. Greatest among the prose writers of this time was Livy, whose "pictured pages" tell of the miraculous origin of Rome, and her great achievements in war and in peace. During this time also flourished certain Greek writers whose works are famous. Dionysius of Halicarnassus wrote a book on the antiquities of Rome, and tried to reconcile his countrymen to the Roman sway. Strabo, the geographer, described the subject lands of Rome in the Augustan age. The whole literature of this period was inspired with a growing spirit of patriotism, and an appreciation of Rome as the great ruler of the world.

Religious and Social Reforms.—With his encouragement of art and literature Augustus also tried to improve the religious and moral condition of the people. The old religion was falling into decay. With the restoration of the old temples, he hoped to bring the people back to the worship of the ancient gods. The worship of Juno, which had been neglected, was restored, and assigned to the care of his wife, Livia, as the representative of the matrons of Rome. Augustus tried to purify the Roman religion by discouraging the introduction of the foreign deities whose worship was corrupt. He believed that even a great Roman had better be worshiped than the degenerate gods and goddesses of Syria and Egypt; and so the Divine Julius was added to the number of the Roman gods. He did not favor the Jewish religion; and Christianity had not yet been preached at Rome.

With the attempt to restore the old Roman religion, he also wished to revive the old morality and simple life of the past. He himself disdained luxurious living and foreign fashions. He tried to improve the lax customs which prevailed in respect to marriage and divorce, and to restrain the vices which were destroying the population of Rome. But it is difficult to say whether these laudable attempts of Augustus produced any real results upon either the religious or the moral life of the Roman people.

Death and Character of Augustus.—Augustus lived to the age of seventy-five; and his reign covered a period of forty-five years. During this time he had been performing "the difficult part of ruling without appearing to rule, of being at once the autocrat of the civilized world and the first citizen of a free commonwealth." His last words are said to have been, "Have I not played my part well?" But it is not necessary for us to suppose that Augustus was a mere actor. The part which he had to perform in restoring peace to the world was a great and difficult task. In the midst of conflicting views which had distracted the republic for a century, he was called upon to perform a work of reconciliation. And it is doubtful whether any political leader ever performed such a work with greater success. When he became the supreme ruler of Rome he was fully equal to the place, and brought order out of confusion. He was content with the substance of power and indifferent to its form. Not so great as Julius Caesar, he was yet more successful. He was one of the greatest examples of what we may call the "conservative reformer," a man who accomplishes the work of regeneration without destroying existing institutions.

SELECTIONS FOR READING

Capes, Early Empire, Ch. I, "Augustus" (7).[1]

Pelham, Bk. V., Ch. 3, "Foundation of the Principate" (1).

Bury, Roman Empire, Ch. 2, "The Principate" (7).

Taylor, Ch. 18, "The Princeps and the Government" (1).

Merivale, Gen. Hist., Ch. 52, "Provinces under Augustus" (1).

Freeman, Hist. Geog., Ch. 3, "Formation of the Roman Empire" (14).

Abbott, Ch. 12, "The Establishment of the Empire" (13).

SPECIAL STUDY

THE WRITERS OF THE AUGUSTAN AGE.—Bury, Roman Empire, Ch. 11 (7); Lawton, Bk. III. (17); Cruttwell, Part II. (17). See also Appendix (17) "Literature."

[1] The figure in parenthesis refers to the number of the topic in the Appendix, where a fuller title of the book will be found.

CHAPTER XXIV

THE JULIAN EMPERORS—TIBERIUS TO NERO

The Reign of Tiberius (A.D. 14-37), I.—The Reign of Caligula (A.D. 37-41), II.—The Reign of Claudius (A.D. 41-54), III.—The Reign of Nero (A.D. 54-68), III.

I. THE REIGN OF TIBERIUS (A.D. 14-37)

The Character of Tiberius.—The system established by Augustus was put to a severe test by the character of the men who immediately followed him. The emperors who made up the Julian line were often tyrannical, vicious, and a disgrace to Rome. That the empire was able to survive at all is, perhaps, another proof of the thoroughness of the work done by the first emperor. Of the four Julian emperors who succeeded Augustus, Tiberius was perhaps the ablest. He had already shown his ability as a general; and having been adopted by Augustus and associated with him in the government, he was prepared to carry out the policy already laid down. But in his personal character he presented a strong contrast to his predecessor. Instead of being generous and conciliatory, he was cruel and tyrannical to those with whom he was brought into personal relations. But we must distinguish between the way in which he treated his enemies and the way in which he ruled the empire. He had a certain sense of duty, and tried to maintain the authority which devolved upon him. If he could not accomplish this by the winning ways of Augustus, he could do it by more severe methods.

Campaigns of Germanicus.—The first duty which fell to Tiberius was to gain the support of the army. The legions on the Rhine and the Danube were at first not disposed to accept his authority. Those on the Danube were soon subdued by Drusus, the son of Tiberius, who took advantage of an eclipse of the moon to appeal to the superstitious dread of the soldiers. The legions on the Rhine were more determined, and desired to place their favorite general, Germanicus (a nephew of Tiberius), on the throne in place of Tiberius. But Germanicus, loyal to his chief, resisted this first attempt of the army to enthrone an emperor. To turn their minds from thoughts of treason, he planned the invasion and conquest of Germany. Three successful campaigns were made across the Rhine. A portion of the German territory was occupied, and the lost standards of Varus were recovered. These campaigns in Germany were cut short by Tiberius, who recalled Germanicus from the Rhine, and sent him to the East to oppose the Parthians. Whether this act was inspired by envy or by wisdom on the part of Tiberius, we cannot say. After a brief and unsuccessful career in the East, Germanicus died, whether as the result of natural causes or as the result of foul play, we are also at a loss to determine.

Despotic Measures of Tiberius.—While Tiberius pursued in many respects the policy of Augustus, he adopted certain measures which showed that he had little sympathy with the "disguises of monarchy." In the first place, he extinguished the political rights of the people by taking away from the assemblies what little legislative power had been left to them; and also by transferring to the senate the election of the regular magistrates. The popular assemblies were thus reduced to a mere shadow.

In the next place, he gave a new meaning to the law of treason (*lex maiestatis*). This law had hitherto referred only to actual crimes against the state. Now it was made to include any words or conduct, looks or gestures, which could be interpreted as hostile to the emperor. This is what we call "constructive treason"; and at Rome, as in any other country where it has been tolerated, it became an instrument of despotism. Again, in order to punish his enemies, Tiberius encouraged the practice of "delation"; that is, he offered rewards to all persons who would give information regarding offenders. There thus sprang up at Rome a class of informers (*delatores*), who acted as professional spies, or inquisitors, to detect the enemies of the emperor.

Finally, we may mention another change made by Tiberius. This was the bringing together of the praetorian cohorts into one camp near Rome, to protect the person of the emperor and thus to secure more strongly his power.

The Influence of Sejanus.—The removal of the praetorian camp to Rome was done at the suggestion of Sejanus, a wily and unscrupulous officer, who had obtained command of these cohorts. As Tiberius was suspicious of everyone else he selected Sejanus as his trusted adviser. Sejanus was to Tiberius what Agrippa or Maecenas had been to Augustus. But unlike those imperial friends, Sejanus was desirous of power and was treacherous to his master. To secure his position, Sejanus caused the murder of Drusus, the son of Tiberius. He even induced the emperor himself to retire from Rome to the island of Capreae in the Bay of Naples, and to leave him in control of the government. The schemes and crimes of Sejanus formed a large part of this despotic reign. When his treason was discovered by Tiberius, he was deposed from his place and strangled in prison. The fall of Sejanus was followed by the prosecution of his fellow-conspirators, or those who were suspected of plotting against the emperor. Although these prosecutions were made under the forms of law, the law was the *lex maiestatis*; and the methods of its execution produced a reign of terror at Rome.

Prosperity of the Provinces.—The cruel tyranny of Tiberius was restricted mainly to the city of Rome, and to those persons whom he suspected as his persona enemies.

The provinces were relieved from this suspicion, and hence they continued to be prosperous as they had been under Augustus. Indeed, Tiberius seemed to be especially anxious regarding their welfare. Like Augustus he tried to protect them from unjust government and oppressive taxation. His favorite maxim is said to have been, "A good shepherd should shear his flock, and not flay them." While he prosecuted his own enemies, he also brought to justice the provincial governors who were guilty of extortion. It is said that while he was hated at Rome, he was loved in the provinces. When many cities of Asia were destroyed by an earthquake, he sent to them relief in the form of money and remitted their taxes for five years. When he died, his faults were exaggerated by the Roman historians, and his virtues were extolled by the provincials.

II. THE REIGN OF CALIGULA (A.D. 37-41)

The Early Promise of Caligula.—Tiberius had made no provision for a successor. Hence the choice lay entirely with the senate, which selected a favorite of the army. This was Gaius Caesar, the son of the famous general, Germanicus. He was familiarly called by the soldiers "Caligula,"1 by which name he is generally known. He was joyfully welcomed by the people, and gave promise of a successful reign. He declared his intention of devoting himself to the public welfare. But the high hopes which he raised at his accession were soon dashed to the ground, when it was discovered that the empire was in the hands of a man who had lost his reason. The brief career of Caligula may be of interest as showing the vagaries of a diseased and unbalanced mind; but they have no special political importance, except as proving that the empire could survive even with a mad prince on the throne.

His Insanity and Extravagances.—Caligula was subject in childhood to epileptic fits, and his mind was evidently diseased. When he was placed in the high position of emperor his brain was turned and he revealed all the grotesque symptoms of insanity. He believed himself a god. He wasted the money of the treasury in senseless projects. He built a bridge from the Palatine hill, where he resided, to the Capitoline, that he might be "next door neighbor to Jupiter." To lead his army over the sea he constructed a bridge three miles long over the Gulf of Baiae, a part of the Bay of Naples, and conducted his soldiers over it in a triumphal procession. He professed to lead an expedition against Britain; and when he had collected his soldiers on the seashore as if for embarkation, he suddenly issued an order to them to gather the shells from the beach and carry them to Rome as "the spoils of the ocean." The senate was directed to deposit these spoils among the treasures of the Capitol. It is said that he nominated his horse for consul. In order to exceed the luxuries of Lucullus, he expended an amount equal to $240,000 on a single meal. He threatened to set up his own image in the temple at Jerusalem and to compel the Jews to worship it. Numerous other stories of a similar kind are told of this delirious man—stories which are more suited to illustrate a treatise on insanity than to burden the pages of history.

Significance of his Reign.—The reign of Caligula, which was fortunately limited to the brief space of four years, shows to us the perils inherent in a despotic form of government that permitted a madman to rule the civilized world. The Roman Empire had no provision by which any prince could be held responsible, either to law or to reason. A cruel tyrant could revel in blood, or a maniac could indulge in the wildest excesses without restraint. The only limit to such a despotism was assassination; and by this severe method the reign of Caligula was brought to an end.

III. THE REIGN OF CLAUDIUS (A.D. 41-54)

His Elevation by the Praetorians.—Claudius was the first emperor proclaimed by the army. The murder of Caligula had been provoked by an insult given to an officer of the praetorian guard. When the senate hesitated to choose a successor, the praetorians, accidentally finding Claudius in the palace, and recognizing him as the brother of Germanicus, assumed the right to name him as emperor. The senate was obliged to submit; and for a long time after this the praetorians continued to exercise the right of naming the prince. Claudius is usually represented as a weak imbecile; but his reign stands out in refreshing contrast to the cruel tyranny of Tiberius and the wild extravagances of Caligula.

The Emperor's Household.—Claudius was naturally weak and timid, and came under the influence of the members of his household—his wives and freedmen. The intrigues and crimes of his wife Messalina, and of his niece Agrippina, whom he married after the death of Messalina, were a scandal to Roman society. So far as he was influenced by these abandoned women, his reign was a disgrace. But the same can scarcely be said of the freedmen of his household—Narcissus, his secretary; Pallas, the keeper of accounts; and Polybius, the director of his studies. These men were educated Greeks, and although they were called menials, he took them into his confidence and received benefit from their advice. Indeed, it has been said that "from Claudius dates the transformation of Caesar's household servants into ministers of state."

His Public Works.—Claudius followed the example of Augustus in the execution of works of public utility. He constructed the Claudian aqueduct, which brought water to the city from a distance of forty-five miles. For the purpose of giving Rome a good harbor where the grain supplies from Egypt might be landed, he built the *Portus*

Romanus at the mouth of the Tiber near Ostia. To improve the agriculture of the Marsians, he constructed a great tunnel to drain the Fucine Lake, a work which required the labor of thirty thousand men for eleven years. He celebrated the completion of this work by a mimic naval battle on the waters of the lake.

The Conquest of Southern Britain.—But the most important event of the reign of Claudius was the invasion and partial conquest of Britain. Since the invasion of Julius Caesar a hundred years before, the Romans had taken little interest in this island. With the aid of his lieutenants, Aulus Plautius and Vespasian, Claudius now effected a permanent landing in Britain. He was opposed by the famous Celtic chief Caractacus, but succeeded in subduing the southern part of the island. Britain was thus opened to the benefits of Roman civilization.

His Care of the Provinces.—It is to the credit of Claudius that he was greatly interested in the condition of the provinces. He spent much time in regulating the affairs of the East. The kingdom of Thrace was changed into a province, and governed by a Roman procurator. Lycia, in Asia Minor, also was made a province, as well as Mauretania in Africa. One of the most important changes which he made was the restoration of the kingdom of the Jews to Herod Agrippa. This he did out of respect for this people, and to allay the bad feeling which had been stirred up during the previous reign. But Claudius especially showed his interest in the provinces by extending to them the rights of Roman citizenship. The *civitas* was granted to a large part of Gaul, thus carrying out the policy which had been begun by Julius Caesar. If we except the scandals of the court, the reign of Claudius may be regarded as inspired by prudence and a wise regard for the welfare of his subjects.

IV. THE REIGN OF NERO (A.D. 54-68)

The "Quinquennium Neronis."—Nero was the grandson of Germanicus and a descendant of Augustus. He was proclaimed by the praetorians and accepted by the senate. He had been educated by the great philosopher Seneca; and his interests had been looked after by Burrhus, the able captain of the praetorian guards. His accession was hailed with gladness. He assured the senate that he would not interfere with its powers. The first five years of his reign, which are known as the "Quinquennium Neronis," were marked by a wise and beneficent administration. During this time he yielded to the advice and influence of Seneca and Burrhus, who practically controlled the affairs of the empire and restrained the young prince from exercising his power to the detriment of the state. Under their influence delation was forbidden, the taxes were reduced, and the authority of the senate was respected.

Tyranny and Crimes of Nero.—But Nero's worst foes were those of his own household, especially his unscrupulous and ambitious mother, Agrippina. The intrigues of this woman to displace Nero and to elevate Britannicus, the son of Claudius, led to Nero's first domestic tragedy—the poisoning of Britannicus. He afterward yielded himself to the influence of the infamous Poppaea Sabina, the most beautiful and the wickedest woman of Rome. At her suggestion, he murdered first his mother, and then his wife. He discarded the counsels of Seneca and Burrhus, and accepted those of Tigellinus, a man of the worst character. Then followed a career of wickedness, extortion, atrocious cruelty, which it is not necessary to describe, but which has made his name a synonym for all that is vicious in human nature, and despicable in a ruler.

Burning and Rebuilding of the City.—In the tenth year of his reign occurred a great fire which destroyed a large part of the city of Rome. It is said that out of the fourteen regions, six were reduced to ashes. Many ancient temples and public buildings were consumed, such as the temple of Jupiter Stator ascribed to Romulus, and the temples of Vesta and Diana, which dated from the time of the kings. The reports which have come to us of the conduct of Nero during this great disaster are very diverse. Some represent him as gloating over the destruction of the city and repeating his own poem on the "Sack of Troy." Other reports declare that he never showed himself in a more favorable light, exerting himself to put out the flames, opening the public buildings and the imperial palace for the shelter of the homeless, and relieving the suffering by reducing the price of grain. But it is charged that if he performed these charities, it was to relieve himself of the suspicion of having caused the conflagration. Whatever may be the truth as to his conduct, the burning of Rome resulted in rebuilding the city on a more magnificent scale. The narrow streets were widened, and more splendid buildings were erected. The vanity of the emperor was shown in the building of an enormous and meretricious palace, called the "golden house of Nero," and also in the erection of a colossal statue of himself near the Palatine hill. To meet the expenses of these structures the provinces were obliged to contribute; and the cities and temples of Greece were plundered of their works of art to furnish the new buildings.

First Persecution of the Christians.—In order to shield himself from the suspicion of firing the city, Nero accused the Christians and made them the victims of his cruelty. Nothing can give us a more vivid idea of this first persecution than the account of the Roman historian Tacitus, which is of great interest to us because it contains the first reference found in any pagan author to Christ and his followers. This passage shows not only the cruelty of Nero and the terrible sufferings of the early

Christian martyrs, but also the pagan prejudice against the new religion.

Tacitus says: "In order to drown the rumor, Nero shifted the guilt on persons hated for their abominations and known as Christians, and punished them with exquisite tortures. Christ, from whom they derive their name, had been punished under Tiberius by the procurator Pontius Pilate. Checked for a time, this pernicious religion broke out again not only in Judea but in Rome. Those who confessed their creed were first arrested; and then by their information a large number were convicted, not so much on the charge of burning the city, as of hating the human race. In their deaths they were made the subjects of sport; for they were covered with the skins of wild beasts, worried to death by dogs, nailed to crosses, burned to serve for torches in the night. Nero offered his own gardens for this spectacle. The people were moved with pity for the sufferers; for it was felt that they were suffering to gratify Nero's cruelty, not from considerations for the public welfare." ("Annals," Bk. XV., Ch. 44.)

General Condition of the Empire.—In spite of such enormous crimes as those practiced by Nero, the larger part of the empire was beyond the circle of his immediate influence, and remained undisturbed. While the palace and the city presented scenes of intrigue and bloodshed, the world in general was tranquil and even prosperous. Except the occasional extortion by which the princes sought to defray the expenses of their debaucheries, Italy and the provinces were reaping the fruits of the reforms of Julius Caesar and Augustus. During this early period, the empire was better than the emperor. Men tolerated the excesses and vices of the palace, on the ground that a bad ruler was better than anarchy.

SELECTIONS FOR READING

Pelham, Bk. V., Ch. 4, "The Julian Line" (1).[2]

Capes, Early Empire, Ch. 2, "Tiberius," Ch. 3, "Caligula," Ch. 4, "Claudius," Ch. 5, "Nero" (7).

Bury, Empire, Ch. 13, Sect. 1, "Civil Government of Tiberius" (7).

Merivale, Empire, Vol. IV., Ch. 39, "Unity of the Empire" (7). Cruttwell, Bk. III., Ch. 3, "Seneca" (17).

Suetonius, "Tiberius," "Caligula," "Claudius," "Nero" (11).

Tacitus, Annals, Bk. I., Chs. 11-15, Tiberius and the Senate (4).

SPECIAL STUDY

THE LAW OF "MAIESTAS" AND DELATION.—Leighton, p. 442 (1); Bury, Empire, pp. 194, 195 (7); Capes, Early Empire, pp. 57-61 (7); Merivale, Gen. Hist., pp. 446, 447 (1); Merivale, Empire, Vol. V., pp. 114-130 (7).

[1] *Caligula* is the diminutive of *caliga*, the name given to a soldier's boot, such as is shown in

the appended illustration. Hence Caligula might be translated "Little Boots."

[2] The figure in parenthesis refers to the number of the topic in the Appendix, where a fuller title of the book will be found.

CHAPTER XXV

THE FLAVIAN EMPERORS—VESPASIAN TO DOMITIAN

The Disputed Succession, I.—The Reign of Vespasian (A.D. 69-79), II.—The Reign of Titus (A.D. 79-81), III.—
Life and Manners of the Romans, IV.—The Reign of Domitian (A.D. 81-96), V.

I. THE DISPUTED SUCCESSION

Extinction of the Julian Line.—With the death of Nero, the imperial line which traced its descent from Julius Caesar and Augustus became extinct. We are now about to discover one of the great defects of the empire as established by Augustus. With all his prudence, Augustus had failed to provide a definite law of succession. In theory the appointment of a successor depended upon the choice of the senate, with which he was supposed to share his power. But in fact it depended quite as much upon the army, upon which his power rested for support. Whether the appointment was made by the senate or by the army, the choice had hitherto always fallen upon some member of the Julian family. But with the extinction of the Julian line, the imperial office was open to anyone.

The War of Succession.—Under such circumstances we could hardly expect anything else than a contest for the throne. Not only the praetorian guards, but the legions in the field, claimed the right to name the successor. The rival claims of different armies to place their favorite generals on the throne led to a brief period of civil war—the first to break the long peace established by Augustus.

Galba (A.D. 68-69).—At the time of Nero's death, the Spanish legions had already selected their commander, Galba, for the position of emperor. Advancing upon Rome, this general was accepted by the praetorians and approved by the senate. He was a man of high birth, and with a good military record. But his career was a brief one. The legions on the Rhine revolted against him. The praetorians were discontented with his severity and small donations: He soon found a rival in Otho, the husband of the infamous Poppaea Sabina who had disgraced the reign of Nero. Otho enlisted the support of the praetorians, and Galba was murdered to give place to his rival.

Otho (A.D. 69).—The brief space of three months, during which Otho was emperor, cannot be called a reign, but only an attempt to reign. On his accession the new aspirant to the throne found his right immediately disputed by the legions of Spain and Gaul, which proclaimed Vitellius. The armies of these two rivals met in northern Italy, and fortune declared in favor of Vitellius.

Vitellius (A.D. 69).—No sooner had Vitellius begun to revel in the luxuries of the palace, than the standard of revolt was again raised, this time by the legions of the East in favor of their able and popular commander, Vespasian. The events of the previous contest were now repeated; and on the same battlefield in northern Italy where Otho's army had been defeated by that of Vitellius, the forces of Vitellius were now defeated by those of Vespasian. Afterward a severe and bloody contest took place in the streets of Rome, and Vespasian made his position secure.

The only significance of these three so-called reigns, and the civil wars which attended them, is the fact that they showed the great danger to which the empire was exposed by having no regular law of succession.

II. THE REIGN OF VESPASIAN (A.D. 69-79)

Beginning of a New Era.—The accession of Vespasian was the beginning of a new era for Rome. Indeed, the next century may be regarded as the most prosperous in her whole history. The ideals of Julius Caesar and Augustus seemed to be realized. The hundred and eleven years which elapsed from the beginning of Vespasian's reign to the death of Marcus Aurelius, have been called the happiest in the history of mankind. The new emperor belonged to the Flavian family, which furnished three rulers, Vespasian, Titus, and Domitian. Vespasian was an able and efficient prince. He rescued Rome from the bankrupt condition into which it had been plunged by his predecessors. He retrenched the expenses of the court and set the example of moderation. He appointed good governors for the provinces, and extended the Latin right, that is, the *commercium*, to the people of Spain.

Roman Civilization in Gaul.—The first duty of Vespasian was to suppress a revolt in Gaul which, under Claudius Civilis, threatened to deprive Rome of that province. After three defeats Civilis was obliged to give up his ambitious scheme, and Gaul again was pacified. Nowhere in the West, outside of Italy, did the civilization of Rome take a firmer hold. Gaul became the seat of Roman colonies; its cities were united by Roman roads; and the Roman language, literature, law, manners, and art found there a congenial home. The ruins which we find to-day in France, of the ancient buildings, baths, aqueducts and amphitheaters, show how completely the province of Gaul was Romanized.

Destruction of Jerusalem (A.D. 70).—The most unfortunate event in the reign of Vespasian was the revolt of the Jews, which finally resulted in the destruction of Jerusalem. There had been many changes in the government of Judea since its first conquest by Pompey. Some of these changes had been made to reconcile the Jews to the Roman sway. But there had been many things to awaken the opposition of the people; for example, the unreasonable prejudice against them at Rome, the insane attempt of Caligula to place his statue in their temple, as well as the harsh government of Nero. At last the Jews were provoked into a general rebellion. Vespasian was conducting the war against them when he was proclaimed emperor by his legions. The war was then left in the hands of his son Titus, who, in spite of desperate resistance, captured and destroyed the sacred city. The Jews were left without a national home; and Judea became a separate province of the empire. The representation of the golden candlestick cut upon the arch of Titus is a striking memorial of this unfortunate war.

The Public Buildings.—By the strictest economy Vespasian was able to replenish the treasury; and by the means thus obtained he spent large sums upon the public buildings of Rome. He restored the Capitoline temple, which had been destroyed during the late civil war. He laid out a new Forum which bore his name. He built a temple to Peace, the goddess whom he delighted to honor. But the most memorable of his works was the Flavian Amphitheater, or as it is sometimes called, the Colosseum. This stupendous building occupied about six acres of ground, and was capable of seating nearly fifty thousand spectators. The sports which took place in this great structure were the most popular of all the Roman amusements.

Amusements of the Romans.—The chief public amusements of the Romans were those which took place in the circus, the theater, and the amphitheater.

The greatest circus of Rome was the Circus Maximus. It was an inclosure about two thousand feet long and six hundred feet wide. Within it were arranged seats for different classes of citizens, a separate box being reserved for the imperial family. The games consisted chiefly of chariot races. The excitement was due to the reckless and dangerous driving of the charioteers, each striving to win by upsetting his competitors. There were also athletic sports; running, leaping, boxing, wrestling, throwing the quoit, and hurling the javelin. Sometimes sham battles and sea fights took place.

The Romans were not very much addicted to the theater, there being only three principal structures of this kind at Rome, those of Pompey, Marcellus, and Balbus. The theater was derived from the Greeks and was built in the form of a semicircle, the seats being apportioned, as in the case of the circus, to different classes of persons. The shows consisted largely of dramatic exhibitions, of mimes, pantomimes, and dancing. It is said that the poems of Ovid were acted in pantomime.

The most popular and characteristic amusements of the Romans were the sports of the amphitheater. This building was in the form of a double theater, forming an entire circle or ellipse. Such structures were built in different cities of the empire, but none equaled the colossal building of Vespasian. The sports of the amphitheater were chiefly gladiatorial shows and the combats of wild beasts. The amusements of the

Romans were largely sensational, and appealed to the tastes of the populace. Their influence was almost always bad, and tended to degrade the morals of the people.

III. THE REIGN OF TITUS (A.D. 79-81)

"Delight of Mankind."—Vespasian had prepared for his death by associating with the government his son, Titus; so the change to the new reign was attended by no war of succession or other disturbance. The great aim of Titus was to make himself loved by the people. He was lavish in the giving of public shows. He dedicated the great amphitheater built by his father with a magnificent naval spectacle. He ruled with so much kindness and moderation that he became the most popular of the emperors, and was called the "Delight of Mankind." It is related that one evening he remembered that he had bestowed no gift upon any one, and in regret exclaimed to his friends, "I have lost a day."

Destruction of Herculaneum and Pompeii.—But the reign of Titus, delightful as it was, was marked by two great calamities. One was a great fire which consumed the new temple of the Capitoline Jupiter, which his father had just erected; and which also injured the Pantheon, the baths of Agrippa, and the theaters of Pompey and Marcellus. But the greatest calamity of this reign was due to the terrible eruption of Mt. Vesuvius, which destroyed the two cities of Herculaneum and Pompeii; situated on the Bay of Naples (see map, p. 233). The Romans had never suspected that this mountain was a volcano, although a few years before it had been shaken by an earthquake. The scenes which attended this eruption are described by the younger Pliny, whose uncle, the elder Pliny, lost his life while investigating the causes of the eruption. The buried city of Pompeii has been exhumed, and its relics reveal in a vivid way the private life and customs of the Roman people.

IV. LIFE AND MANNERS OF THE ROMANS

Houses of the Romans.—The uncovered ruins of Pompeii show to us a great many houses, from the most simple to the elaborate "House of Pansa." The ordinary house (*domus*) consisted of front and rear parts connected by a central area, or court. The front part contained the entrance hall (*vestibulum*); the large reception room (*atrium*); and the private room of the master (*tablinum*), which contained the archives of the family. The large central court was surrounded by columns (*peristylum*). The rear part contained the more private apartments—the dining room (*triclinium*), where the members of the family took their meals reclining on couches; the kitchen (*culina*); and the bathroom (*balneum*). The Romans had no stoves like ours, and rarely did they have any chimneys. The house was warmed by portable furnaces (*foculi*), like fire pans, in which coal or charcoal was burned, the smoke escaping through the doors or an open place in the roof; sometimes hot air was introduced by pipes from below. The rooms were lighted either by candles (*candelae*) made of tallow or wax; or by oil lamps (*lucernae*) made of terra cotta, or of bronze, worked sometimes into exquisite designs.

Meals.—There were usually three daily meals: the breakfast (*ientaculum*), soon after rising; the luncheon, or midday meal (*prandium*); and the chief meal, or dinner (*cena*), in the afternoon. The food of the poorer classes consisted of a kind of porridge, or breakfast food (*farina*), made of a coarse species of wheat (*far*), together with ordinary vegetables, such as turnips and onions, with milk and olives. The wealthy classes vied with one another in procuring the rarest delicacies from Italy and other parts of the world.

Dress.—The characteristic dress of the men was the *toga*, a loose garment thrown abouy the person in ample folds, and covering a closer garment called the tunic (*tunica*). The Romans wore sandals on the feet, but generally no covering for the head. The dress of a Roman matron consisted of three parts: the close-fitting *tunica*; the *stola*, a gown reaching to the feet; and the *palla*, a shawl large enough to cover the whole figure. The ladies took great pains in arranging the hair, and possessed the usual fondness for ornaments—necklaces, bracelets, earrings, and costly jewels,

Writing Materials.—For writing the Romans used different materials: first, the tablet (*tabula*), or a thin piece of board covered with wax, which was written upon with a sharp iron pencil (*stylus*); next, a kind of paper (*charta*) made from the plant called *papyrus*; and, finally, parchment (*membrana*) made from the skins of animals. The paper and parchment were written upon with a pen made of reed sharpened with a penknife, and ink made of a mixture of lampblack. When a book (*liber*) was written, the different pieces of paper or parchment were pasted together in a long sheet and rolled upon a round stick. When collected in a library (*bibliotheca*), the rolls were arranged upon shelves or in boxes.

The Employments of the Romans comprised many of the chief occupations and trades with which we are familiar to-day, including professional, commercial, mechanical, and agricultural pursuits. To the learned professions belonged the priest, the lawyer, the physician, and the teacher. The commercial classes included the merchant, the banker, the broker, the contractor, to whom may also be added the taxgatherer of earlier times. The mechanical trades comprised a great variety of occupations, such as the making of glass, earthenware, bread, cloth, wearing apparel, articles of wood, leather, iron, bronze, silver, and gold. The artisans were often organized into societies or guilds (*collegia*) for their mutual benefit; these guilds were very ancient, their origin being ascribed to Numa. The agriculturists of Rome comprised the large landowners, who were regarded as a highly respectable class, and the small proprietors, the free laborers, and the slaves, the last mentioned forming a great part of the tillers of the soil. In general, the Roman who claimed to be respectable disdained all manual labor, and resigned such labor into the hands of slaves and freedmen.

Marriage.—The marriage customs comprised, first, the ceremony of betrothal (*sponsalia*), which included the formal consent of the bride's father, and an announcement in the form of a festival or the presentation of the betrothal ring; secondly, the marriage ceremony, which might be either a religious ceremony, in which a consecrated cake was eaten in the presence of the priest (*confarreatio*), or a secular ceremony, in which the. father gave away his daughter by the forms of a legal sale (*coemptio*). In the time of the empire it was customary for persons to be married without these ceremonies, by their simple consent, During this time, also, divorces became common and the general morals of society became corrupt.

Life in the Towns.—The towns of the empire were in their general appearance reflections of the capital city on the Tiber. Each town had its forum, its temples, its courthouse (*basilica*) and its places of entertainment, Its government seemed to be copied after the old city government of Rome. It had its magistrates, chief among whom were two men (*duumviri*), something like the old consuls. It had its municipal council or senate (*curia*), controlled by a municipal aristocracy (*curiales*). Its people delighted in the same kind of shows and amusements that we have seen at Rome (p. 249). At Pompeii we find in the *graffiti*, or writings left upon the walls of buildings, some remarkable evidences of the ordinary life of the townsmen. Some of these writings hardly rise above the dignity of mere scribblings. They are most numerous upon the buildings in those places frequented by the crowds. There we find advertisements of public shows, memoranda of sales, cookery receipts, personal lampoons, love effusions, and hundreds of similar records of the common life of this ancient people.

If we should attempt to draw a distinction among the various towns of the empire, we might observe that the people of the Western towns became more Romanized than those of the Eastern towns. The Latin language prevailed in the West, and the Greek language in the East. But still the Latin was used as the official language in the East as well as in the West; and, on the other hand, the knowledge of the Greek was a mark of culture in the West as in the East.

V. THE REIGN OF DOMITIAN (A.D. 81-96)

Exceptional Tyranny of Domitian.—The happy period begun by Vespasian and Titus was interrupted by the exceptional tyranny of Domitian, the younger brother of Titus. Domitian seemed to take for his models Tiberius and Nero. He ignored the senate and the forms of the constitution. He revived the practice of delation, and was guilty of confiscations and extortions. He teased and irritated all classes, He persecuted the Jews and the Christians. Like Tiberius, he was suspicious, and lived in perpetual fear of assassination. His fears were realized; a conspiracy was organized against him, and he was murdered by a freedman of the palace.

Agricola in Britain.—The chief event of importance in the reign of Domitian was the extension of the Roman power in Britain. Agricola had already been appointed governor of Britain by Vespasian; but it was not until this time that his arms were crowned with marked success. The limits of the province were now pushed to the north, and a new field was opened for the advance of civilization. Britain became dotted with Roman cities, united by great military roads. As in Gaul, the Roman law and customs found a home, although they did not obtain so enduring an influence as in the continental provinces.

The Silver Age of Roman Literature.—The period of Roman literature which followed the age of Augustus is often called "the Silver Age." The despotic rule of the Julian emperors had not been favorable to literature. Only two names of that period stand out with prominence, those of Seneca, the Stoic philosopher, and Lucan, who wrote an epic poem describing the civil war between Pompey and Caesar. Under the Flavians occurred a revival of letters, which continued under the subsequent emperors. Among the most noted writers who flourished at this time were Juvenal, the satirist; Tacitus, the historian; Suetonius, the biographer of the "Twelve Caesars"; Martial, the epigrammatist; Quintilian, the rhetorician; and Pliny the Younger, the writer of epistles. Although the writings of the Silver Age do not equal those of the age of Augustus in grace of style, they show quite as much vigor and originality.

SELECTIONS FOR READING

Capes, Early Empire, Ch. 9, "Vespasian," Ch. 10, "Titus," "Domitian" (7).[1]

Merivale, Gen. Hist., Ch. 60, "The Wars of Succession" (1).

Bury, Empire, Ch. 31, "Roman Life and Manners" (7).

Thomas, Ch. 1, "At Pompeii"; Ch. 8, "Country Life" (16)

Merivale, Empire, Vol. IV., Ch. 41, "Life in Rome" (7).

Inge, Ch. 9, "Amusements" (16).

Guhl and Koner, pp. 553-564, "Amphitheatrical Games" (16).

Preston and Dodge, II., "The House and Every Day Life" (16).

See also Appendix (16), "Life and Manners."

SPECIAL STUDY

THE ROMAN HOUSE.—Inge, pp. 245-258 (16); Eschenburg, pp. 290-292 (8); Guhl and Koner, pp. 365-375, 437-460 (16); Harper's Dict. Antiqq., "Domus" (8); Becker, Gallus, pp. 231-314 (16).

[1] The figure in parenthesis refers to the number of the topic in the Appendix, where a fuller title of the book will be found.

CHAPTER XXVI

THE FIVE GOOD EMPERORS,—NERVA TO MARCUS AURELIUS

The Reign of Nerva (A.D. 96-98), I.—The Reign of Trajan (A.D. 98-117), II.—The Reign of Hadrian (A.D. 117-138), III.—The Reign of Antoninus Pius (A.D. 138-161), IV.—The Reign of Marcus Aurelius (A.D. 161-180), V.

I. THE REIGN OF NERVA (A.D. 96-98)

Prosperity of the Empire.—With the death of Domitian the empire came back into the hands of wise and beneficent rulers. The "five good emperors," as they are usually called, were Nerva, Trajan, and Hadrian (who were related to one another only by adoption), and the two Antonines, Antoninus Pius and Marcus Aurelius. The period of general prosperity which began under Vespasian continued under these emperors. It is during this time that we are able to see Roman civilization at its best, its highest stage of development. Nerva was chosen neither by the praetorians nor by the legions, but by the senate. Within the brief time that he sat upon the throne, he could do little except to remedy the wrongs of his predecessor. He forbade the practice of delation, recalled the exiles of Domitian, relieved the people from some oppressive taxes and was tolerant to the Christians. His wise and just reign is praised by all ancient writers. In order to prevent any trouble at his death, he adopted Trajan as his successor and gave him a share in the government.

Nerva's Attempt to relieve the Poor.—One of the characteristic features of Nerva's short reign was his attempt to relieve the poor. In the first place, he bought up large lots of land from the wealthy landlords, and let them out to the needy citizens. It is noteworthy that he submitted this law to the assembly of the people. In the next place, he showed his great interest in the cause of public education. He set apart a certain fund, the interest of which was used to educate the children of poor parents. This interest in providing for the care and education of the poorer classes was continued by his successors.

Roman Education.—Education among the Romans, though not usually endowed by the state, was very general and was highly appreciated. Its main features were derived from the Greeks. It was intended to develop all the mental powers, and to train a man for public life. Children—both boys and girls—began to attend school at six or seven years of age. The elementary studies were reading, writing, and arithmetic. The children were tempted to learn the alphabet by playing with pieces of ivory with the letters marked upon them. They were taught writing by a copy, set upon their tablets; and arithmetic by means of the calculating board (*abacus*) and counters (*calculi*). The higher education comprised what were called the liberal arts (*artes liberales*), including the Latin and Greek languages, composition and oratory, and mental and moral philosophy. An important part of education consisted in public recitals and declamations, which were intended to train young men for the forum, and which were often held in the temples. The state sometimes patronized education, as we have already seen in the case of Nerva. Hadrian afterward instituted a public school in a building called the Athenaeum. Public fees were sometimes paid to the instructors (*professores*) in addition to the fees of the pupils.

II. THE REIGN OF TRAJAN (A.D. 98-117)

The Greatness of Trajan.—After Julius Caesar and Augustus, Trajan may be called, in many respects, the greatest of the Roman sovereigns. Adopted by Nerva, he was accepted by the senate. He made himself popular with the army and with the great body of the people. He was a Spaniard by birth; and the fact that he was the first emperor who was not a native of Italy, shows that the distinction between Romans and provincials was passing away. He was a brave general, a wise statesman, and a successful administrator. He continued the efforts of Nerva to remedy the evils which the early despotism had brought upon Rome. To the people he restored the elective power; to the senate, liberty of speech and of action; to the magistrates, their former authority. He abolished the law of treason (*lex maiestatis*), and assumed his proper place as the chief magistrate of the empire. He was a generous patron of literature and of art. He also desired to relieve the condition of the poor. It is said that five thousand children received from him their daily allowance of food. So highly was Trajan esteemed by the Romans that to his other imperial titles was added that of "Optimus" (the Best).

A LIST OF THE CHIEF ROMAN PROVINCES
WITH THE DATES OF THEIR ACQUISITION OR ORGANIZATION

I. EUROPEAN PROVINCES
1. *Western.*
   Spain (B.C. 205-19).
   Gaul (B.C. 120-17).
   Britain (A.D. 43-84).
2. *Central.*
   Rhaetia et Vindelicia (B.C. 15).
   Noricum (B.C. 15).
   Pannonia (A.D. 10).
3. *Eastern.*
   Illyricum (B.C. 167-59).
   Macedonia (B.C. 146).

III. ASIATIC PROVINCES
1. *In Asia Minor.*
   Asia proper (B.C. 133).
   Bithynia et Pontus (B.C. 74, 65).
   Cilicia (B.C. 67).
   Galatia (B.C. 25).
   Pamphylia et Lycia (B.C. 25, A.D. 43).
   Cappadocia (A.D. 17).
2. *In Southwestern Asia.*
   Syria (B.C. 64).
   Judea (B.C. 63-A.D. 70).

191

Achaia (B.C. 146).	Arabia Petraea (A.D. 105).
Moesia (B.C. 20).	Armenia (A.D. 114).
Thrace (A.D. 40).	Mesopotamia (A.D. 115).
Dacia (A.D. 107).	Assyria (A.D. 115).
II. AFRICAN PROVINCES	IV. ISLAND PROVINCES
Africa proper (B.C. 146).	Sicily (B.C. 241).
Cyrenaica and Crete (B.C. 74, 63).	Sardinia et Corsica (B.C. 238).
	Cyprus (B.C. 58).
Numidia (B.C. 46).	
Egypt (B.C. 30).	Total, 32.
Mauretania (A.D. 42).	

NOTE.—Many of these chief provinces were subdivided into smaller provinces. each under a separate governor—making the total number of provincial governors more than one hundred. For a complete list of the Roman provinces in A.D. 117, see Leighton, p. xxix.

The Conquests of Trajan.—Since the death of Augustus there had been made no important additions to the Roman territory, except Britain. But under Trajan the Romans became once more a conquering people. The new emperor carried his conquests across the Danube and acquired the province of Dacia. He then extended his arms into Asia, and brought into subjection Armenia, Mesopotamia, and Assyria, as the result of a short war with the Parthians. Under Trajan the boundaries of the empire reached their greatest extent.

His Public Works and Buildings.—Rome and Italy and the provinces all received the benefit of his wise administration; and the empire reached its highest point of material grandeur. Roads were constructed for the aid of the provincials. He restored the harbors of Italy, and improved the water supply of Rome. He built two new baths, one of which was for the exclusive use of women. The greatest monument of Trajan was the new Forum, in which a splendid column was erected to commemorate his victories.

Roman Art.—During this period Roman art reached its highest development. The art of the Romans, as we have before noticed, was modeled in great part after that of the Greeks. While lacking the fine sense of beauty which the Greeks possessed, the Romans yet expressed in a remarkable degree the ideas of massive strength and of imposing dignity. In their sculpture and painting they were least original, reproducing the figures of Greek deities, like those of Venus and Apollo, and Greek mythological scenes, as shown in the wall paintings at Pompeii. Roman sculpture is seen to good advantage in the statues and busts of the emperors, and in such reliefs as those on the arch of Titus and the column of Trajan.

But it was in architecture that the Romans excelled; and by their splendid works they have taken rank among the world's greatest builders. We have already seen the progress made during the later Republic and under Augustus. With Trajan, Rome became a city of magnificent public buildings. The architectural center of the city was the Roman Forum (see frontispiece), with the additional Forums of Julius, Augustus, Vespasian, Nerva, and Trajan (see map, p. 303). Surrounding these were the temples, the basilicas or halls of justice, porticoes, and other public buildings. The most conspicuous buildings which would attract the eyes of one standing in the Forum were the splendid temples of Jupiter and Juno upon the Capitoline hill. While it is true that the Romans obtained their chief ideas of architectural beauty from the Greeks, it is a question whether Athens, even in the time of Pericles, could have presented such a scene of imposing grandeur as did Rome in the time of Trajan and Hadrian, with its forums, temples, aqueducts, basilicas, palaces, porticoes, amphitheaters, theaters, circuses, baths, columns, triumphal arches, and tombs.

III. THE REIGN OF HADRIAN (A.D. 117-138)

The Statesmanship of Hadrian.—At the death of Trajan, his adopted son Hadrian was proclaimed by the praetorian guards. But Hadrian did not regard this as a constitutional act; and he requested to be formally elected by the senate, In some respects he was similar to Trajan, with the same generous spirit and desire for the welfare of the people, and with the same wish to add to the architectural splendor of Rome. He was, like Trajan, a friend of literature and a patron of the fine arts, But he differed from Trajan in not thinking that the greatness of Rome depended upon military glory. He believed that the army should be maintained; but that foreign conquest was less important than the prosperity of his subjects. In his political ideas and administrative ability he was a type of the true statesman. He is said to have been a man of wider acquirements and greater general capacity than any previous ruler since Julius Caesar. He was in the best sense liberal and cosmopolitan. He was tolerant of the Christians, and put himself in sympathy with the various races and creeds which made up the empire. Against the Jews only, who rose in revolt during his reign, did he show a spirit of unreasonable severity.

His Abandonment of Trajan's Conquests.—Hadrian did not believe that the mission of Rome was to conquer the world, but to civilize her own subjects. He therefore voluntarily gave up the extensive conquests of Trajan in the East, the provinces of Armenia, Mesopotamia, an Assyria. He declared that the Eastern policy of Trajan was a great mistake. He openly professed to cling to the policy of Augustus, which was to improve the empire rather than to enlarge it.

The Imperial Council.—Another evidence of the statesmanship of Hadrian is seen in the fact that he was willing, to take advice. While he is said to have shown on some occasions an exceptional irritability of temper, he is represented as a man distinguished on the whole by "an a ability rarely equaled by the Roman princes" (Merivale). He paid great deference to the senate; and the body of imperial counselors (*consilium principis*), which had been occasionally consulted by the previous emperors, became from his time a permanent institution. The emperor was not now the victim of unworthy advisers, as in the time of Tiberius, but was surrounded by men noted for their learning and wisdom. These men were often trained lawyers, who were skilled in the rules of justice.

The Perpetual Edict of Salvius Julianus.—Perhaps the most important event in the reign of Hadrian was his compilation of the best part of the Roman law. Since the XII. Tables there had been no collection of legal rules. That ancient code was framed upon the customs of a primitive people. It did not represent the actual law by which justice was now administered. A new and better law had grown up in the courts of the praetors and of the provincial governors. It had been expressed in the edicts of these magistrates; but it had now become voluminous and scattered. Hadrian delegated to one of his jurists, Salvius Julianus, the task of collecting this law into a concise form, so that it could be used for the better a ministration of justice throughout the empire. This collection was called the Perpetual Edict (*Edictum Perpetuum*).

The Visitation of the Provinces.—Hadrian showed a stronger sympathy with the provinces than any of his predecessors, and under his reign the provincials attained a high degree of prosperity and happiness. He conducted himself as a true sovereign and friend of his people. To become acquainted with their condition and to remedy their evils, he spent a large part of his time in visiting the provinces. Of his long reign of twenty-one years, he spent more than two thirds outside of Italy. He made his temporary residence in the chief cities of the empire,—in York, in Athens, in Antioch, and in Alexandria—where he was continually looking after the interests of his subjects. In the provinces, as at Rome, he constructed many magnificent public works; and won for himself a renown equal, if not superior, to that of Trajan as a great builder. Rome was decorated with the temple of Venus and Roma, and the splendid mausoleum which to-day bears the name of the Castle of St. Angelo. Hadrian also built strong fortifications to protect the frontiers, one of these connecting the head waters of the Rhine and the Danube, and another built on the northern boundary of Britain.

Life in the Provinces: Travel, Correspondence, Commerce.—The general organization of the provinces remained with few changes. There were still the two classes, the senatorial, governed by the proconsuls and propraetors, and the imperial, governed by the *legati*, or the emperor's lieutenants. The improvement which took place under the empire in the condition of the provinces was due to the longer term of office given the governors, the more economic management of the finances, and the abolition of the system of farming the revenues.

The good influence of such emperors as Hadrian is seen in the new spirit which inspired the life of the provincials. The people were no longer the prey of the taxgatherer, as in the times of the later republic. They could therefore use their wealth to improve and beautify their own cities. The growing public spirit is seen in the new buildings and works, everywhere erected, not only by the city governments, but by the generous contributions of private citizens. The relations between the people of different provinces were also becoming closer by the improvement of the means of communication. The roads were now extended throughout the empire, and were used not merely for the transportation of armies, but for travel and correspondence. The people thus became better acquainted with one another. Many of the highways were used as post-roads, over which letters might be sent by means of private runners or government couriers.

The different provinces of the empire were also brought into closer communication by means of the increasing commerce, which furnished one of the most honored pursuits of the Roman citizen. The provinces encircled the Mediterranean Sea, which was now the greatest highway of the empire. The sea was traversed by merchant ships exchanging the products of various lands. The provinces of the empire were thus joined together in one great commercial community.

IV. THE REIGN OF ANTONINUS PIUS (A.D. 138-161)

The Virtues of Antoninus.—If we desired to find in Roman history a more noble character than that of Hadrian, we should perhaps find it in his adopted son and successor, Antoninus, surnamed Pius. The description given of him by his son, Marcus Aurelius, is worthy to be read by the young people of all times. "In my father," he says, "I saw mildness of manners, firmness of resolution, contempt of vain glory. He knew when to rest as well as to labor. He taught me to forbear from all improper indulgences, to conduct myself as an equal among equals, to lay on my friends no burden of servility. From him I learned to be resigned to every fortune and to bear myself calmly and serenely; to rise superior to vulgar applause, and to despise vulgar criticism; to worship the gods without superstition and to serve mankind without ambition. He was ever prudent and moderate; he looked to his duty only, and not to the opinions that might be formed of him. Such was the character of his life and manners—nothing harsh, nothing excessive, nothing rude, nothing which showed roughness and violence."

The "Reign without Events."—The reign of Antoninus, although a long one of twenty-three years, is known in history as the uneventful reign. Since much that is usually called "eventful" in history is made up of wars, tumults, calamities, and discords, it is to the greatest credit of Antoninus that his reign is called uneventful. We read of no conquests, no insurrections, no proscriptions, no extortions, no cruelty. His reign is an illustration of the maxim, "Happy is the people which has no history." Although not so great a statesman as Hadrian, he yet maintained the empire in a state of peace and prosperity. He managed the finances with skill and economy. He was kind to his subjects; and interfered to prevent the persecution of the Christians at Athens and Thessalonica.

His Influence upon Law and Legislation.—If we should seek for the most distinguishing feature of his reign, we should doubtless find it in the field of law. His high sense of justice brought him into close relation with the great jurists of the age, who were now beginning to make their influence felt. With them he believed that the spirit of the law was more important than the letter. One of his maxims was this: "While the forms of the law must not be lightly altered, they must be interpreted so as to meet the demands of justice." He laid down the important principle that everyone should be regarded as innocent until proved guilty. He mitigated the evils of slavery, and declared that a man had no more right to kill his own slave than the slave of another. It was about the close of his reign that the great elementary treatise on the Roman law, called the "Institutes" of Gaius, appeared.

Roman Jurisprudence.—Some one has said that the greatest bequests of antiquity to the modern world were Christianity, Greek philosophy, and the Roman law. We should study the history of Rome to little purpose if we failed to take account of this, the highest product of her civilization. It is not to her amphitheaters, her circuses, her triumphal arches, or to her sacred temples that we must look in order to see the most distinctive and enduring features of Roman life. We must look rather to her basilicas—that is, her courthouses where the principles of justice were administered to her citizens and her subjects in the forms of law.

The Government and Administration.—It was during the period of the Antonines that the imperial government reached its highest development. This government was, in fact, the most remarkable example that the world has ever seen of what we may call a "paternal autocracy"—that is government in the hands of a single ruler, but exercised solely for the benefit of the people. In this respect the ideals of Julius and Augustus seem to have been completely realized. The emperor was looked upon as the embodiment of the state, the personification of law, and the promoter of justice, equality, and domestic peace. Every department of the administration was under his control. He had the selection of the officials to carry into execution his will. The character of such a government the Romans well expressed in their maxim, "What is pleasing to the prince has the force of law."

V. THE REIGN OF MARCUS AURELIUS (A.D. 161-180)

Philosopher on the Throne.—Marcus Aurelius was the adopted son of Antoninus Pius, and came to the throne at his father's death. The new emperor was first of all a philosopher. He had studied in the school of the Stoics, and was himself the highest embodiment of their principles. He was wise brave, just, and temperate. The history of the pagan world presents no higher example of uprightness and manhood. In whatever he did he acted from a pure sense of duty. But his character as a man was no doubt greater than his ability as a statesman. So far as we know, Marcus Aurelius never shrank from a known duty, private or public; but it is not so clear that his sense of personal duty was always in harmony with the best interests of the empire.

Misfortunes of his Reign.—In judging of this great man we must not forget that his reign was a time of great misfortunes. Rome was afflicted by a deadly plague and famine, the most terrible in her history. From the East it spread over the provinces, carrying with it death and desolation. One writer affirms, with perhaps some exaggeration, that half the population of the empire perished. The fierce barbarians of the north were also trying to break through the frontiers, and threatening to overrun the provinces. But Marcus Aurelius met all these dangers and difficulties with courage and patience.

His Persecution of the Christians.—The most striking example of the fact that the emperor's sense of duty was not always in harmony with the highest welfare of the people is shown in his persecution of the Christians. The new religion had found its way throughout the eastern and western provinces. It was at first received by the common people in the cities. As it was despised by many, it was the occasion of bitter opposition and often of popular tumults. The secret meetings of the Christians had given rise to scandalous stories about their practices. They were also regarded as responsible in some way for the calamities inflicted by the gods upon the people. Since the time of Nero, the policy of the rulers toward the new sect had varied. But the best of the emperors had hitherto been cautious like Trajan, or tolerant like Hadrian, or openly friendly like Antoninus. But Marcus Aurelius sincerely believed that the Christians were the cause of the popular tumults, and that the new sect was dangerous to the public peace. He therefore issued an order that those who denied their faith should be let alone, but those who confessed should be put to death. The most charitable judgment which can be passed upon this act is that it was the result of a great mistake made by the emperor regarding the character of the Christians and their part in disturbing the peace of society.

Encroachments upon the Frontiers.—During this reign the peace of the empire was first seriously threatened by invasions from without. The two great frontier enemies of Rome were the Parthians on the east and the Germans on the north. The Parthians were soon repelled. But the barbarians from the north, the Marcomanni and Quadi, continued their attacks for fourteen years. Pressed by the Slavonians and the Turanians on the north and east, these tribes were the forerunners of that great migration of the northern nations which finally overran the empire. With courage and a high sense of his mission the emperor struggled against these hordes, and succeeded for the most part in maintaining the northern frontier. He died in his camp at Vienna, at his post of duty. However much we may condemn his policy with reference to the Christians, we must always admire him for the purity of his life and his nobility as a man.

Roman Philosophy.—Marcus Aurelius expressed in his life and writings the highest ideas of Roman philosophy. The Romans cannot, however, be said to have shown any originality in their philosophical systems. These they derived almost entirely from the Greeks. The two systems which were most popular with them were Epicureanism and Stoicism. The Epicureans believed that happiness was the great end of life. But the high idea of happiness advocated by the Greek philosophers became degraded into the selfish idea of pleasure, which could easily excuse almost any form of indulgence. In Rome we see this idea of life exercising its influence especially upon the wealthy and indolent classes. The Stoics, on the other hand, believed that the end of life was to live according to the highest law of our nature. This doctrine tended to make strong and upright characters. It could not well have a degrading influence; so we find some of the noblest men of Rome adhering to its tenets—such men as Cato, Cicero, Seneca, and Marcus Aurelius. The Stoic philosophy also exercised a great and beneficial influence upon the Roman jurists, who believed that the law of the state should be in harmony with the higher law of justice and equity.

SELECTIONS FOR READING

Capes, Antonines, Ch. 1, "Nerva," Ch. 2, "Trajan," Ch. 3, "Hadrian," Ch. 4, "Antoninus Pius," Ch. 5, "Marcus Aurelius" (7).[1]

Pelham, Bk. VI., Ch. 1, "The Antonines" (1).

Bury, Empire, Ch. 30, "Roman World under the Empire" (7).

Dyer, City, Sect. 4, "Rome from Augustus to Hadrian" (9).

Merivale, Empire, Vol. IV., Ch. 40, "Great Cities of the Empire" (7).

Merivale, Gen. Hist., Ch. 79, "The City of Rome" (1).

Farrar, chapter on "Marcus Aurelius" (18).

SPECIAL STUDY

THE FORUMS OF ROME.—Bury, Empire, see index, "Forum" (7); Burn, Chs. 2, 4 (9); Parker, Arch, Hist., Ch. 11 (9);.Hare, Ch. 4 (14); Middleton, Ancient Rome, Chs. 5, 6, 8 (9); Lanciani, Rums, pp. 232-254 (9).

[1] The figure in parenthesis refers to the number of the topic in the Appendix, where a fuller title of the book will be found.

CHAPTER XXVII

THE DECLINE OF THE EMPIRE

The Times of the Severi, I.—The Disintegration of the Empire, II.—The Illyrian Emperors, III.

I. THE TIMES OF THE SEVERI

Review of the Early Empire.—As we review the condition of the Roman world since the time of Augustus, we can see that the fall of the republic and the establishment of the empire were not an evil, but a great benefit to Rome. In place of a century of civil wars and discord which closed the republic, we see more than two centuries of internal peace and tranquillity. Instead of an oppressive and avaricious treatment of the provincials, we see a treatment which is with few exceptions mild and generous. Instead of a government controlled by a proud and selfish oligarchy, we see a government controlled, generally speaking, by a wise and patriotic prince. From the accession of Augustus to the death of Marcus Aurelius (B.C. 31—A.D. 180), a period of two hundred and eleven years, only three emperors who held power for any length of time—Tiberius, Nero, and Domitian—are known as tyrants; and their cruelty was confined almost entirely to the city, and to their own personal enemies. The establishment of the empire, we must therefore believe, marked a stage of progress and not of decline in the history of the Roman people.

Symptoms of Decay.—But in spite of the fact that the empire met the needs of the people better than the old aristocratic republic, it yet contained many elements of weakness, The Roman people themselves possessed the frailties of human nature, and the imperial government was not without the imperfection of all human institutions. The decay of religion and morality among the people was a fundamental cause of their weakness and ruin. If we were asked what were the symptoms of this moral decay, we should answer: the selfishness of classes; the accumulation of wealth, not as the fruit of legitimate industry, but as the spoils of war an of cupidity; the love of gold and the passion for luxury; the misery of poverty and its attendant vices and crimes; the terrible evils of slave labor; the decrease of the population; and the decline of the patriotic spirit. These were moral diseases, which could hardly be cured by any government.

Military Despotism.—The great defect of the imperial government was the fact that its power rested upon a military basis, and not upon the rational will of the people. It is true that many of the emperors were popular and loved by their subjects. But back of their power was the army, which knew its strength, and which now more than ever before asserted its claims to the government. This period, extending from the death of Marcus Aurelius to the accession of Diocletian (A.D. 180-284), has therefore been aptly called "the period of military despotism." It was a time when the emperors were set up by the soldiers, and generally cut down by their swords. During this period of one hundred and four years, the imperial title was held by twenty-nine different rulers,1 some few of whom were able and high-minded men, but a large number of them were weak and despicable. Some of them held their places for only a few months. The history of this time contains for the most part only the dreary records of a declining government. There are few events of importance, except those which illustrate the tyranny of the army and the general tendency toward decay and disintegration.

After the reign of Commodus, the unworthy son of Marcus, the soldiers became the real sovereigns of Rome. His successor Pertinax was dispatched by their swords; and the empire was offered to the one who would give them the largest donation. This proved to be a rich senator by the name of Didius Julianus, who offered for the vacant throne a sum equal to $15,000,000. He held this place for about two months. In the meantime three different armies—in Britain, in Pannonia, and in Syria—each proclaimed its own leader as emperor.

Septimius Severus (A.D. 193-211).—The commander of the army in the neighboring province of Pannonia was the first to reach Rome; and was thus able to secure the throne against his rivals. The reign of Septimius is noted for the reforming of the praetorian guard, which Augustus had organized and Tiberius had encamped near the city. In place of the old body of nine thousand soldiers, Septimius organized a Roman garrison of forty thousand troops selected from the best soldiers of the legions. This was intended to give a stronger military support to the government; but in fact it gave to the army a more powerful influence in appointment of the emperors. Septimius destroyed his enemies in the senate, and took away from that body the last vestige of its authority. He was himself an able soldier and made several successful campaigns m the East.

Edict of Caracalla (A.D. 212).—The Roman franchise, which had been gradually extended by the previous emperors, was now conferred upon all the free inhabitants of the Roman world. This important act was done by Caracalla, the worthless son and tyrannical successor of Septimius Severus. The edict was issued to increase the revenue by extending the inheritance tax, which had heretofore rested only upon citizens. Notwithstanding the avaricious motive of the emperor this was in the line of earlier reforms and effaced the last distinction between Romans and provincials. The name of Caracalla is infamous, not only for his cruel proscriptions, but especially for his murder of Papinian, the greatest of the Roman jurists, who refused to defend his crimes.

Alexander Severus (A.D. 222-235).—After the brief reign of Macrinus, and the longer reign of the monster Elagabalus, the most repulsive of all the emperors, the throne was occupied by a really excellent man, Alexander Severus. In a corrupt age, he was a prince of pure and blameless life. He loved the true and the good of all times. It is said that he set up in his private chapel the images of those whom he regarded as the greatest teachers of mankind, including Abraham and Jesus Christ. He tried as best he could to follow the example of the best of the emperors. He selected as his advisers the great jurists, Ulpian and Paullus. The most important event of his reign was his successful resistance to the Persians, who had just established a new monarchy on the ruins of the Parthian kingdom (A.D. 226).

II. THE DISINTEGRATION OF THE EMPIRE

Foreign Enemies of Rome.—Never before had the Roman Empire been beset by such an array of foreign enemies as it encountered during the third century. On the east was the new Persian monarchy established under a vigorous and ambitious line of kings, called the Sassanidae. The founder of this line, Artaxares (Ardashir), laid claim to all the Asiatic provinces of Rome as properly belonging to Persia. The refusal of this demand gave rise to the war with Alexander Severus, just referred to, and to severe struggles with his successors.

But the most formidable enemies of Rome were the German barbarians on the frontiers of the Rhine and the Danube. On the lower Rhine near the North Sea were several tribes known as the Chatti, Chauci, and the Cherusci, who came to be united with other tribes under the common name of "Franks." On the upper Rhine in the vicinity of the Alps were various tribes gathered together under the name of Alemanni (all men). Across the Danube and on the northern shores of the Black Sea was the great nation of the Goths, which came to be the terror of Rome. Under a succession of emperors whose names have little significance to us, the Romans engaged in wars with these various peoples—not now wars for the sake of conquest and glory as in the time of the republic, but wars of defense and for the sake of existence.

Invasion of the Goths in the East.—The Goths made their first appearance upon the Roman territory m the middle of the third century (A.D. 250). At this time they invaded Dacia, crossed the Danube, and overran the province of Moesia. In a great battle in Moesia perished the brave emperor Decius, descendant of the Decius Mus who devoted his life at Mt. Vesuvius in the heroic days of the republic. His successor,

Gallus, purchased a peace of the Goths by the payment of an annual tribute. It was not many years after this that the same barbarians, during the reigns of Valerian and Gallienus (A.D. 253-268), made a more formidable invasion, this time by way of the Black Sea and the Bosphorus. With the aid of their ships they crossed the sea, besieged and plundered the cities of Asia Minor. They destroyed the splendid temple of Diana at Ephesus; they crossed the Aegean Sea into Greece, and threatened Italy; and finally retired with their spoils to their homes across the Danube.

Invasion of the Franks and Alemanni in the West.—In the meantime the western provinces were invaded by the barbarians who lived across the Rhine. The Franks entered the western regions of Gaul, crossed the Pyrenees, and sacked the cities of Spain; while the Alemanni entered eastern Gaul and invaded Italy as far as the walls of Ravenna. It was then that the Roman garrison, which took the place of the old praetorian guard, rendered a real service to Rome by preventing the destruction of the city.

Attacks of the Persians in Asia.—But all the disasters of Rome did not come from the north. The new Persian monarchy, under its second great king, Sapor, was attempting to carry out the policy of Artaxares and expel the Romans from their Asiatic provinces. Sapor at first brought under his control Armenia, which had remained an independent kingdom since the time of Hadrian. He then overran the Roman provinces of Syria, Cilicia, and Cappadocia; Antioch and other cities of the coast were destroyed and pillaged; and the emperor Valerian was made a prisoner. The story of Sapor's pride and of Valerian's disgrace has passed into history; to humiliate his captive, it is said, whenever the Persian monarch mounted his horse, he placed his foot on the neck of the Roman emperor.

The Time of the "Thirty Tyrants."—In the midst of these external perils Rome beheld another danger which she had never seen before, at least to the same extent, and that was the appearance of usurpers in every part of the empire—in Asia, in Egypt, in Greece, in Illyricum, and in Gaul. This is called the time of the "thirty tyrants"; although Gibbon counts only nineteen of these so-called tyrants during the reign of Gallienus. If we should imagine another calamity in addition to those already mentioned, it would be famine and pestilence—and from these, too, Rome now suffered. From the reign of Decius to the reign of Gallienus, a period of about fifteen years, the empire was the victim of a furious plague, which is said to have raged in every province, in every city, and almost in every family. With invasions from without and revolts and pestilence within, Rome never before seemed so near to destruction.

III. THE ILLYRIAN EMPERORS

Partial Recovery of the Empire.—For a period of eighty-eight years—from the death of Marcus Aurelius (A.D. 180) to the death of Gallienus (A.D. 268)—the imperial government had gradually been growing weaker until it now seemed that the empire was going to pieces for the want of a leader. But we have before seen Rome on the verge of ruin—in the early days of the Gauls, during the invasion of Hannibal, and under the attacks of the Cimbri. As in those more ancient times, so now the Romans showed their remarkable fortitude and courage in the presence of danger. Under the leadership of five able rulers—Claudius II., Aurelian, Tacitus, Probus, and Carus—they again recovered; and they maintained their existence for more than two hundred years in the West and for more than a thousand years in the East. Let us see how Rome recovered from her present disasters, and we may also understand how the early empire as established by Augustus was changed into the new empire established by Diocletian and Constantine.

Claudius II. and the Defeat of the Goths (A.D. 268-270).—One of the reasons of the recent revolts in the provinces had been general distrust of the central authority at Rome. If the Roman emperor could not protect the provinces, the provinces were determined to protect themselves under their own rulers. When a man should appear able to defend the frontiers the cause of these revolts would disappear. Such a man was Claudius II., who came from Illyricum. He aroused the patriotism of his army and restored its discipline. Paying little attention to the independent governors, he pushed his army into Greece to meet the Goths, who had again crossed the Danube and had advanced into Macedonia. By a series of victories he succeeded in delivering the empire from these barbarians, and for this reason he received the name of Claudius Gothicus.

Aurelian and the Restored Empire (A.D. 270-275).—The fruits of the victories of Claudius were reaped by his successor Aurelian, who became the real restorer of the empire. He first provided against a sudden descent upon the city by rebuilding the walls of Rome, which remain to this day and are known as the walls of Aurelian. He then followed the prudent policy of Augustus by withdrawing the Roman army from Dacia and making the Danube the frontier of the empire. He then turned his attention to the rebellious provinces; and recovered Gaul, Spain, and Britain from the hand of the usurper Tetricus. He finally restored the Roman authority in the East; and destroyed the city of Palmyra, which had been made the seat of an independent kingdom, where ruled the famous Queen Zenobia.

The "Silent Invasions."—The successors of Aurelian—Tacitus, Probus, and

Carus—preserved what he himself had achieved. The integrity of the empire was in general maintained against the enemies from without and the "tyrants" from within. It is worthy of notice that at this time a conciliatory policy toward the barbarians was adopted, by granting to them peaceful settlements in the frontier provinces. This step began what are known as the "silent invasions." Not only the Roman territory, but the army and the offices of the state, military and civil, were gradually opened to the Germans who were willing to become Roman subjects.

The New Class of "Coloni."—It became a serious question what to do with all the newcomers who were now admitted into the provinces. The most able of the barbarian chiefs were sometimes made Roman generals. Many persons were admitted to the ranks of the army. Sometimes whole tribes were allowed to settle upon lands assigned to them. But a great many persons, especially those who had been captured in war, were treated in a somewhat novel manner. Instead of being sold as slaves they were given over to the large landed proprietors, and attached to the estates as permanent tenants. They could not be sold off from these estates like slaves; but if the land was sold they were sold with it. This class of persons came to be called *coloni*. They were really serfs bound to the soil. The *colonus* had a little plot of ground which he could cultivate for himself, and for which he paid a rent to his landlord. But the class of *coloni* came to be made up not only of barbarian captives, but of manumitted slaves, and even of Roman freemen, who were not able to support themselves and who gave themselves up to become the serfs of some landlord. The *coloni* thus came to form a large part of the population in the provinces.

This new class of persons, which held such a peculiar position in the Roman empire, has a special interest to the general historical student; because from them were descended, in great part, the class of serfs which formed a large element of European society after the fall of Rome, during the middle ages.

Transition to the Later Empire.—The successful efforts of the last five rulers showed that the Roman Empire could still be preserved if properly organized and governed. In the hands of weak and vicious men, like Commodus and Elagabalus, the people were practically left without a government, and were exposed to the attacks of foreign enemies and to all the dangers of anarchy. But when ruled by such men as Claudius II. and Aurelian they were still able to resist foreign invasions and to repress internal revolts. The events of the third century made it clear that if the empire was to continue and the provinces were to be held together there must be some change in the imperial government. The decline of the early empire thus paved the way for a new form of imperialism.

SELECTIONS FOR READING

Pelham, Bk. VI., Ch. 2, "The Empire in the Third Century" (1).[2]

Merivale, Empire, Vol. VII., Ch. 68, "Symptoms of Decline" (7).

Merivale, Gen. Hist., Ch. 69, "The Barbarian Confederations" (1).

Gibbon, Decline, Ch. 10, "Emperor Decius, etc." (7).

Gibbon, abridged, Ch. 2, "Septimius Severus" (7).

Dyer, City, Sect. 5, "From Hadrian to Constantine" (9).

Curteis, Ch. 3, "The Barbarians on the Frontiers" (7).

SPECIAL STUDY

ROMAN SLAVERY.—Inge, pp. 159-171 (16); Guhl and Koner, pp. 511-533 (16); Eschenburg, pp. 288-290 (8); Harper's Dict. Antiqq., "Servus" (8); Ramsay and Lanciani, pp. 124-133 (8); Becker, Gallus, pp. 199-225 (16); Blair, Inquiry (21).

[1] The following table shows the names of these emperors and the dates of their accession:—

	A.D.			A.D.		A.D.
Commodus			Gordianus I. & II.		Claudius II	
Pertinax	193		Pupienus &	237	Aurelian	268
Julianus	193		Balbinus	238	Tacitus	270
Septimius	193		Gordianus III.	238	Florianus	275
Severus	211		Philippus	244	Probus	276
Caracalla &	217		Decius	249	Carus	276
Geta	218		Gallus	251	Carinus &	282
Macrinus	222		Aemilianus	253	Numerian	
Elagabalus	235		Valerian	253		283
Alexander			Gallienus			
Severus	235			260		
Maximinus						

[2] The figure in parenthesis refers to the number of the topic in the Appendix, where a fuller title of the book will be found.

CHAPTER XXVIII

THE REORGANIZATION OF THE EMPIRE

The Reign of Diocletian (A.D. 284-305), I.—The Reign of Constantine (A.D. 313-337), II.—The Successors of Constantine (337-395), III.

I. THE REIGN OF DIOCLETIAN (A.D. 284-305)

The New Imperialism.—The accession of Diocletian brings us to a new era in the history of the Roman Empire. It has been said that the early empire of Augustus and his successors was an absolute monarchy *disguised* by republican forms. This is in general quite true. But the old republican forms had for a long time been losing their hold, and at the time of Diocletian they were ready to be thrown away entirely. By the reforms of Diocletian and Constantine there was established a new form of imperialism—an absolute monarchy *divested* of republican forms. Some of their ideas of reform no doubt came from the new Persian monarchy, which was now the greatest rival of Rome. In this powerful monarchy the Romans saw certain elements of strength which they could use in giving new vigor to their own government. By adopting these Oriental ideas, the Roman Empire may be said to have become Orientalized.

The Policy of Diocletian.—Diocletian was in many respects a remarkable man. Born of an obscure family in Dalmatia (part of Illyricum), he had risen by his own efforts to the high position of commander of the Roman army in the East. It was here that he was proclaimed emperor by his soldiers. He overcame all opposition, assumed the imperial power, and made his residence not at Rome, but in Nicomedia, a town in Asia Minor (see map, p. 294). His whole policy was to give dignity and strength to the imperial authority. He made of himself an Oriental monarch. He assumed the diadem of the East. He wore the gorgeous robes of silk and gold such a were worn by eastern rulers. He compelled his subjects to salute him with low prostrations, and to treat him not as a citizen, but as a superior being. In this way he hoped to make the imperial office respected by the people and the army. The emperor was to be the sole source of power, and as such was to be venerated and obeyed.

The "Augusti" and "Caesars."—Diocletian saw that it was difficult for one man alone to manage all the affairs of a great empire. It was sufficient for one man to rule over the East, and to repel the Persians. It needed another to take care of the West and to drive back the German invaders. He therefore associated with him his trusted friend and companion in arms, Maximian. But he was soon convinced that even this division

209

of power was not sufficient. To each of the chief rulers, who received the title of *Augustus*, he assigned an assistant, who received the title of *Caesar*. The two Caesars were Galerius and Constantius; and they were to be regarded as the sons and successors of the chief rulers, the Augusti. Each Caesar was to recognize the authority of his chief; and all were to be subject to the supreme authority of Diocletian himself. The Roman world was divided among the four rulers as follows:

The Last Persecution of the Christians.—Diocletian himself was not a cruel and vindictive man, and was at first favorably disposed toward the Christians. But in the latter part of his reign he was induced to issue an edict of persecution against them. It is said that he was led to perform this infamous act by his assistant Galerius, who had always been hostile to the new religion, and who filled the emperor's mind with stories of seditions and conspiracies. An order was issued that all churches should be demolished, that the sacred Scriptures should be burned, that all Christians should be dismissed from public office, and that those who secretly met for public worship should be punished with death. The persecution raged most fiercely in the provinces subject to Galerius; and it has been suggested that the persecution should be known by his name rather than by the name of Diocletian.

Effects or Diocletian's Policy.—The general result of the new policy of Diocletian was to give to the empire a strong and efficient government. The dangers which threatened the state were met with firmness and vigor. A revolt in Egypt was quelled, and the frontiers were successfully defended against the Persians and the barbarians. Public works were constructed, among which were the great Baths of Diocletian at Rome. At the close of his reign he celebrated a triumph in the old capital.

Abdication of Diocletian.—After a successful reign of twenty-one years Diocletian voluntarily gave up his power, either on account of ill health, or else to see how his new system would work without his own supervision. He retired to his native province of Dalmatia, and spent the rest of his days in his new palace at Salona on the shores of the Adriatic. He loved his country home; and when he was asked by his old colleague Maximian to resume the imperial power, he wrote to him, "Were you to come to Salona and see the vegetables which I raise in my garden with my own hands, you would not talk to me of empire." But before he died (A.D. 313) Diocletian saw the defects of the system which he had established. Rivalries sprang up among the different rulers, which led to civil war. At one time there were six emperors who were trying to adjust between themselves the government of the empire. Out of this conflict Constantine arose as the man destined to carry on and complete the work of Diocletian.

II. THE REIGN OF CONSTANTINE (A.D. 313-337)

Accession and Policy of Constantine.—By a succession of victories over his different rivals, which it is not necessary for us to recount, Constantine became the sole ruler, and the whole empire was reunited under his authority. He was a man of wider views than Diocletian, and had even a greater genius for organization. The work which Diocletian began, Constantine completed. He in fact gave to Roman imperialism the final form which it preserved as long as the empire existed, and the form in which it exercised its great influence upon modern governments. We should remember that it was not so much the early imperialism of Augustus as the later imperialism of Constantine which reappeared in the empires of modern Europe. This fact will enable us to understand the greatness of Constantine as a statesman and a political reformer. His policy was to centralize all power in the hands of the chief ruler; to surround his person with an elaborate court system and an imposing ceremonial; and to make all officers, civil and military, responsible to the supreme head of the empire.

Conversion of Constantine.—Constantine is generally known as the "first Christian emperor." The story of his miraculous conversion is told by his biographer, Eusebius. It is said that while marching against his rival Maxentius, he beheld in the heavens the luminous sign of the cross, inscribed with the words, "By this sign conquer." As a result of this vision, he accepted the Christian religion; he adopted the cross as his battle standard; and from this time he ascribed his victories to God, and not to himself. The truth of this story has been doubted by some historians; but that Constantine looked upon Christianity in an entirely different light from his predecessors, and that he was an avowed friend of the Christian church, cannot be denied. His mother, Helena, was a Christian, and his father, Constantius, had opposed the persecutions of Diocletian and Galerius. He had himself, while he was ruler in only the West, issued an edict of toleration (A.D. 313) to the Christians in his own provinces.

Adoption of Christianity.—The attitude of the Roman government toward Christianity varied at different times. At first indifferent to the new religion, it became hostile and often bitter during the "period of persecutions" from Nero to Diocletian. But finally under Constantine Christianity was accepted as the religion of the people and of the state. A large part of the empire was already Christian, and the recognition of the new religion gave stability to the new government. Constantine, however, in accepting Christianity as the state religion, did not go to the extreme of trying to uproot paganism. The pagan worship was still tolerated, and it was not until many years after this time that it was proscribed by the Christian emperors. For the purpose of settling the disputes between the different Christian sects, Constantine called (A.D. 325) a large council of the clergy at Nice (*Nicaea*), which decided what should thereafter be regarded as the orthodox belief.

Removal of the Capital to Constantinople (A.D. 328).—The next important act of Constantine was to break away from the traditions of the old empire by establishing a new capital. The old Roman city was filled with the memories of paganism and the relics of the republic. It was the desire of Constantine to give the empire a new center of power, which should be favorably situated for working out his new plans, and also for defending the Roman territory. He selected for this purpose the site of the old Greek colony, Byzantium, on the confines of Europe and Asia. This site was favorable alike for defense, for commerce, and for the establishment of an Oriental system of government. Constantine laid out the city on an extensive scale, and adorned it with new buildings and works of art. The new capital was called, after its founder, the city of Constantine, or Constantinople.

The New Court Organization.—Constantine believed with Diocletian that one of the defects of the old empire was the fact that the person of the emperor was not sufficiently respected. He therefore not only adopted the diadem and the elaborate robes of the Asiatic monarchs, as Diocletian had done, but reorganized the court on a thoroughly eastern model. An Oriental court consisted of a large retinue of officials, who surrounded the monarch, who paid obeisance to him and served him, and who were raised to the rank of nobles by this service. All the powers of the monarch were exercised through these court officials.

These Oriental features were now adopted by the Roman emperor. The chief officers of the court comprised the grand chamberlain, who had charge of the imperial palace; the chancellor, who had the supervision of the court officials and received foreign ambassadors; the quaestor, who drew up and issued the imperial edicts; the treasurer-general, who had control of the public revenues; the master of the privy purse, who managed the emperor's private estate; and the two commanders of the bodyguard. The imperial court of Constantine furnished the model of the royal courts of modern times.

The New Provincial System.—Another important reform of Constantine was the reorganization of the Roman territory in a most systematic manner. This was based upon Diocletian's division, but was much more complete and thorough. The whole empire was first divided into four great parts, called "praefectures," each under a praetorian prefect subject to the emperor. These great territorial divisions were (1) the Praefecture of the East; (2) the Praefecture of Illyricum; (3) the Praefecture of Italy;

(4) the Praefecture of Gaul. Each praefecture was then subdivided into dioceses, each under a diocesan governor, called a vicar, subject to the praetorian prefect. Each diocese was further subdivided into provinces, each under a provincial governor called a consular, president, duke, or count. Each province was made up of cities and towns, under their own municipal governments. Each city was generally governed by a city council (*curia*) presided over by two or four magistrates (*duumviri, quattuorviri*). It had also in the later empire a defender of the people (*defensor populi*), who, like the old republican tribune, protected the people in their rights. The new divisions of the empire may be indicated as follows:

The New Military Organization.—Scarcely less important than the new provincial system was the new military organization. One of the chief defects of the early empire was the improper position which the army occupied in the state. This defect is seen in two ways. In the first place, the army was not subordinate to the civil authority. We have seen how the praetorian guards really became supreme, and brought about that wretched condition of things, a military despotism. In the next place, the military power was not separated from the civil power. In the early empire, every governor of a province had not only civil authority, but he also had command of an army, so that he could resist the central government if he were so disposed. But Constantine changed all this. He abolished the Roman garrison or praetorian guard. He gave to the territorial governors only a civil authority; and the whole army was organized under distinct officers, and made completely subject to the central power of the empire. This change tended to prevent, on the one hand, a military despotism; and, on the other hand, the revolt of local governors.

The military ability of Constantine cannot be questioned. In commemoration of his early victories, the senate erected in the city of Rome a splendid triumphal arch, which stands to-day as one of the finest specimens of this kind of architecture.

Effect of Constantine's Reforms.—If we should take no account of the effects of Constantine's reforms upon the liberties of the Roman people, we might say that his government was a great improvement upon that of Augustus. It gave new strength to the empire, and enabled it to resist foreign invasions. The empire was preserved for several generations longer in the West, and for more than a thousand years longer in the East. But the expenses necessary to maintain such a system, with its elaborate court and its vast number of officials, were great. The taxes were oppressive. The members of every city council (*curiales*) were held responsible for the raising of the revenues. The people were burdened, and lost their interest in the state. Constantine also, like Augustus, failed to make a proper provision for his successor. At his death

(A.D. 337) his three sons divided the empire between them, and this division gave rise to another period of quarrels and civil strife.

III. THE SUCCESSORS OF CONSTANTINE (337-395)

Attempt to Restore Paganism.—The first event of grave importance after the reign of Constantine was the attempt of the Emperor Julian (A.D. 360-363) to restore the old pagan religion, for which attempt he has been called "the Apostate." Julian was in many respects a man of ability and energy. He repelled the Alemanni who had crossed the Rhine, and made a vigorous campaign against the Persians. But he was by conviction a pagan, and in the struggle between Christianity and paganism he took the part of the ancient faith. He tried to undo the work of Constantine by bringing back paganism to its old position. He did not realize that Christianity was the religion of the future, and was presumptuous in his belief that he could accomplish that in which Marcus Aurelius and Diocletian had failed. He may not have expected to uproot the new religion entirely; but he hoped to deprive it of the important privileges which it had already acquired. The religious changes which he was able to effect in his brief reign were reversed by his successor Jovian (A.D. 363-364), and Christianity afterward remained undisturbed as the religion of the empire.

Revolt of the Goths.—After the death of Jovian the empire was divided between Valentinian and his younger brother Valens, the former ruling in the West, and the latter in the East. Valentinian died (A.D. 375), leaving his sons in control of the West, while Valens continued to rule in the East (till 378). It was during this latter period that a great event occurred which forewarned the empire of its final doom. This event was the irruption of the Huns into Europe. This savage race, emerging from the steppes of Asia, pressed upon the Goths and drove them from their homes into the Roman territory. It was now necessary for the Romans either to resist the whole Gothic nation, which numbered a million of people, or else to receive them as friends, and give them settlements within the empire. The latter course seemed the wiser, and they were admitted as allies, and given new homes south of the Danube, in Moesia and Thrace. But they were soon provoked by the ill-treatment of the Roman officials, and rose in revolt, defeating the Roman army in a battle at Adrianople (A.D. 378) in which Valens himself was slain.

Reign of Theodosius and the Final Division of the Empire (379-395).— Theodosius I. succeeded Valens as emperor of the East. He was a man of great vigor and military ability, although his reign was stained with acts of violence and injustice. He continued the policy of admitting the barbarians into the empire, but converted them into useful and loyal subjects. From their number he reënforced the ranks of the imperial armies, and jealously guarded them from injustice. When a garrison of Gothic soldiers was once mobbed in Thessalonica, he resorted to a punishment as revengeful as that of Marius and as cruel as that of Sulla. He gathered the people of this city into the circus to the number of seven thousand, and caused them to be massacred by a body of Gothic soldiers (A.D. 390). For this inhuman act he was compelled to do penance by St. Ambrose, the bishop of Milan—which fact shows how powerful the Church had become at this time, to compel an emperor to obey its mandates. Theodosius was himself an ardent and orthodox Christian, and went so far as to be intolerant of the pagan religion, and even of the worship of heretics. In spite of his shortcomings he was an able monarch, and has received the name of "Theodosius the Great." He conquered his rivals and reunited for a brief time the whole Roman world under a single ruler. But at his death (A.D. 395), he divided the empire between his two sons, Arcadius and Honorius, the former receiving the East, and the latter, the West.

SELECTIONS FOR READING

Gibbon, Decline, Ch. 17, "Foundation of Constantinople" (7).[1]

Gibbon, abridged, Ch. 7, "Reign of Diocletian" (7).

Stanley, Lect. 6, "The Emperor Constantine" (12).

Merivale, Gen. Hist., Ch. 73, "Reign of Julian" (1).

Seeley, Essay, "The Later Empire" (7).

SPECIAL STUDY

THE ROMAN BATHS.—Inge, pp. 232-236 (16); Bury, Empire, pp. 609-612 (7); Parker, Arch. Hist., Ch. 10 (9); Guhl and Koner, pp. 396-406 (16); Harper's Dict. Antiqq., "Balneae" (8); Ramsay and Lanciani, pp. 487-490 (8); Becker, Gallus, pp. 366-387 (16).

[1] The figure in parenthesis refers to the number of the topic in the Appendix, where a fuller title of the book will be found.

CHAPTER XXIX

THE EXTINCTION OF THE WESTERN EMPIRE
The Great Invasions, I.—The Fall of the Western Empire, II.

I. THE GREAT INVASIONS

The Divided Empire.—The death of Theodosius in A.D. 395 marks an important epoch, not only in the history of the later Roman Empire but in the history of European civilization. From this time the two parts of the empire—the East and the West—became more and more separated from each other, until they became at last two distinct worlds, having different destinies. The eastern part, the history of which does not belong to our present study, maintained itself for about a thousand years with its capital at Constantinople, until it was finally conquered by the Turks (A.D. 1453). The western part was soon overrun and conquered by the German invaders, who brought with them new blood and new ideas, and furnished the elements of a new civilization. We have now to see how the Western Empire was obliged finally to succumb to these barbarians, who had been for so many years pressing upon the frontiers, and who had already obtained some foothold in the provinces.

The General Stilicho.—When the youthful Honorius was made emperor in the West, he was placed under the guardianship of Stilicho, an able general who was a barbarian in the service of Rome. As long as Stilicho lived he was able to resist successfully the attacks upon Italy. The first of these attacks was due to jealousy and hatred on the part of the Eastern emperor. The Goths of Moesia were in a state of discontent, and demanded more extensive lands. Under their great leader, Alaric, they entered Macedonia, invaded Greece, and threatened to devastate the whole peninsula. The Eastern emperor, Arcadius, in order to relieve his own territory from their ravages, turned their faces toward Italy by giving them settlements in Illyricum, and making their chief, Alaric, master-general of that province. From this region they invaded Italy, and ravaged the plains of the Po. But they were defeated by Stilicho in the battle of Pollentia (A.D. 403), and forced to return again into Illyricum. The generalship of Stilicho was also shown in checking an invasion made by a host of Vandals, Burgundians, Suevi, and Alani under the lead of Radagaisus (A.D. 406). Italy seemed safe as long as Stilicho lived; but he was unfortunately put to death to satisfy the jealousy of his ungrateful master, Honorius (A.D. 408).

Invasion of Italy by the Goths.—With Stilicho dead, Italy was practically defenseless. Alaric at the head of the Visigoths (West Goths) immediately invaded the peninsula, and marched to Rome. He was induced to spare the city only by the payment of an enormous ransom. But the barbarian chief was not entirely satisfied with the payment of money. He was in search of lands upon which to settle his people. Honorius refused to grant this demand, and after fruitless negotiations with the emperor, Alaric determined to enforce it by the sword. He took the city of Rome and sacked it (A.D. 410). For three days the city was given up to plunder. He then overran southern Italy and made himself master of the peninsula. He soon died, and his successor, Adolphus (Ataulf), was induced to find in Gaul and Spain the lands which Alaric had sought in Italy.

The Rule of Placidia.—The great invasions which began during the reign of Honorius (A.D. 395-423) continued during the reign of Valentinian III. (A.D. 425-455). As Valentinian was only six years of age when he was proclaimed emperor, the government was carried on by his mother, Placidia, who was the sister of Honorius and daughter of Theodosius the Great. Placidia was in fact for many years during these eventful times the real ruler of Rome. Her armies were commanded by Aëtius and Boniface, who have been called the "last of the Romans."

Invasion of the Huns under Attila.—The next great invasion of the Western Empire was made by the Huns under Attila. This savage people from Asia had already gained a foothold in eastern Europe north of the Danube. Under their great chieftain, Attila, who has been called "the Scourge of God," they invaded Gaul, and devastated the provinces; they laid siege to the city of Orleans, but were finally defeated by the Roman general Aëtius, with the aid of the Visigoths. The battle was fought near Châlons (A.D. 451), and has been called one of the great decisive battles of the world, because it relieved Europe from the danger of Tartar domination. Attila later invaded Italy, but retired without attacking Rome.

Notwithstanding the brilliant service which Aëtius had rendered, he was made the victim of court intrigue, and was murdered by his jealous prince Valentinian III. The fate of Aëtius, like that of Stilicho before him, shows the wretched condition into which the imperial government had fallen.

Invasion of the Vandals under Genseric.—The Vandals who had fought under Radagaisus had, upon the death of that leader, retreated into Spain, and had finally crossed over into Africa, where they had erected a kingdom under their chief Genseric. They captured the Roman city of Carthage and made it their capital; and they soon obtained control of the western Mediterranean. On the pretext of settling a quarrel at Rome, Genseric landed his army at the port of Ostia, took possession of the city of Rome, and for fourteen days made it the subject of pillage (A.D. 455). By this act of Genseric, the city lost its treasures and many of its works of art, and the word "vandalism" came to be a term of odious meaning.

Occupation of Britain by the Saxons.—While the continental provinces were thus overrun by the Goths, the Huns, and the Vandals, the Roman army was withdrawn from the island of Britain. For many years it was left to govern itself. But the tribes of northern Germany, the Jutes and the Saxons, saw in it a desirable place of settlement, and began their migration to the island (A.D. 449).

In the various ways which we have thus briefly described, the provinces of the Western Empire—Spain, Africa, Gaul, and Britain—became for the most part occupied by German barbarians, and practically independent of the imperial authority at Rome.

II. THE FALL OF THE WESTERN EMPIRE

Ricimer and the Last Days of the Empire.—The authority of the Western Roman emperors became limited to Italy, and even here it was reduced to a mere shadow. The barbarians were the real power behind the throne. The Roman armies were made up mostly of barbarians, under the control of barbarian generals; and even the direction of affairs at the capital was in the hands of barbarian chiefs. The place which Stilicho the Vandal had held under Honorius, was filled by Ricimer the Goth during the last years of the empire. This chieftain commanded the foreign troops in the pay of Rome. He received the Roman title of "patrician," which at this time was equivalent to regent of the empire. For seventeen years (455-472) Ricimer exercised absolute authority, setting up and deposing emperors at his will. The Roman Empire in the West had in fact already passed away, and nothing was now left but to extinguish its name.

Odoacer deposes Romulus Augustulus (A.D. 476).—The part which Ricimer had played as "king-maker" was now assumed by Orestes the Pannonian, who received the title of patrician. Orestes placed upon the throne his son, Romulus Augustulus, a boy six years of age. The brief reign of this prince has no other significance than the fact that it was the last. The barbarian mercenaries demanded one third of the lands of Italy, and on the refusal of Orestes, they placed their cause in the hands of Odoacer (a Herulian, or a Rugian chief). Romulus was obliged to resign his title as emperor, and word was sent to the Eastern ruler that there was no need of another separate emperor in the West. Odoacer was given the title of patrician, and ruled over Italy as the vicar of the Eastern emperor. The West was then deprived of the imperial title; and this event is called the "fall of the Western Roman Empire."

Relation of the West to the Eastern Empire.—If we were asked to define the relation between the East and the West after the deposition of Romulus Augustulus, we might be in doubt how to answer the question. Since Odoacer was made a Roman ruler under the title of patrician, and since he recognized the authority of the Eastern emperor, we might say that the Western Empire was not destroyed, but was simply reunited once more to the Eastern Empire. This would be true so far as it referred to a mere matter of legal form. But as a matter of historical fact this event does not mark a return to the old system of things which existed before the death of Theodosius, but marks a real separation between the history of the East and the history of the West.

Transition to a New Civilization in the West.—The West had gradually become peopled with various German tribes. In Africa were the Vandals; in Spain and southern Gaul, the Visigoths; in northwestern Spain, the Suevi; in southeastern Gaul, the Burgundians; in Britain, the Saxons and the Jutes; in Italy, the Heruli. Only in the northern part of Gaul was the shadow of the Roman authority preserved by the governor, Syagrius, who still maintained himself for ten years longer against the invaders, but was at last conquered by the Franks under Clovis (A.D. 486). The chiefs of the new German kingdom had begun to exercise an independent authority and the Roman people had become subject to new rulers. The customs and manners of the Romans, their laws and their language, were still preserved, but upon them became engrafted new customs, new ideas, and new institutions. As the fall of the old republic was a transition to the empire, and as the decline of the early empire was a transition to a new phase of Imperialism; so now the fall of the Roman Empire in the West was in reality a transition to a new state of things out of which has grown our modern civilization.

SELECTIONS FOR READING

Pelham, Bk. VII., Ch. 2, "Extinction of the Western Empire" (1)[1]

Merivale, Gen. Hist., Ch. 77, "Loss of the Western Provinces" (1).

Freeman, Ch. 4, "Dismemberment of the Empire" (14).

Gibbon, Decline, Ch. 31, "Invasion of Italy" (7).

Gibbon, abridged, Ch. 15, "Western Empire under Honorius" (7).

Lord, Ch. 11, "Fall of Rome" (3).

SPECIAL STUDY

CAUSES OF THE FALL OF THE EMPIRE.—Seeley, Essay II. (7); Leighton, Ch. 37 (1); Lord, Ch. 12 (3); Hodgkin, Italy, Vol. II., Ch. 9 (7); Bury, Later Empire, Bk. I., Ch. 3 (7).

[1] The figure in parenthesis refers to the number of the topic in the Appendix, where a fuller title of the book will be found.

APPENDIX

A CLASSIFIED LIST OF BOOKS UPON ROMAN HISTORY, FOR READING AND REFERENCE

N.B.—This list includes only English works and English translations.

I. GENERAL AND MISCELLANEOUS WORKS

(1) Roman History, Compends.

Gilman, A. Story of Rome. N.Y. 1892. (Story of the Nations.)

How, W.W., and Leigh, H.D. History of Rome to the Death of Caesar. N.Y. 1896.

Leighton, R.F. History of Rome. N.Y. 1890.

Liddell, H.G. History of Rome. N.Y. 1868.

Matheson, P.E. Skeleton Outlines of Roman History. (Chronologically arranged.) Lond. 1890.

Merivale, C. General History of Rome. N.Y. 1880.

Pelham, H.F. Outlines of Roman History. 4th Ed. N.Y. 1907.

Shuckburgh, E.S. History of Rome to the Battle of Actium. N.Y. 1894.

Schmitz, L. History of Rome. Andover, 1847.

Taylor, T.M. Constitutional and Political History of Rome. Lond. 1899.

(2) General Treatises.

Arnold, T. History of Rome. N.Y. 1866. 3 vols. in one.

Duruy, V. History of Rome and the Roman People. Ed. J.P. Mahaffy. Bost. 1883. 8 vols.

Ihne, W. History of Rome. English Edition. Lond. 1882. 5 vols.

Mommsen, T. History of Rome. Tr. W.P. Dickson. N.Y. 1871. 4 vols. Abridged by C. Bryans and F.J.R. Hendy. N.Y. 1889.

Niebuhr, B.G. History of Rome. Tr. L.C. Hare and C. Thirwall. Phil. 1844. 5 vols. in two. Epitomized by T. Twiss. Oxf. 1845.

—— Lectures on Roman History. Tr. L. Schmitz. Lond. 1849. 3 vols.

(3) Miscellaneous Works.

Fowler, W.W. The City-state of the Greeks and the Romans. N.Y. 1893.

Freeman, E.A. Historical Essays. 2d series. N.Y. 1873.

Munro, D.C. Source Book of Roman History. Bost. 1904.

(4) Original Histories.

Ammianus Marcellinus. Roman History. (Bohn.)

Appian. Roman History. Tr. H. White. N.Y. 1899. 2 vols.

Caesar. Commentaries. (Harper's Classical Library.)

Livy. History of Rome. (Harper's Classical Library.) 2 vols. (Bohn.) 4 vols.

Polybius. Histories. Tr. E.S. Shuckburgh. Lond. 1889). 2 vols.

Sallust. Works. (Harper's Classical Library; Bohn.)

Tacitus. Works. (Harper's Classical Library; Bohn.) 2 vols.

See also (11) Biography, "Plutarch," "Suetonius."

II. SPECIAL PERIODS

(5) The Kingdom (B.C. 753-510).

Dyer, T.H. History of the Kings of Rome. Lond. 1868.

Ihne, W. Early Rome. N.Y. (Epochs of Anc. History.)

Lewis, G.C. An Inquiry into the Credibility of Early Roman History. Lond. 1855. 2 vols.

Newman, F.W. Regal Rome. Redfield, 1852.

(6) The Republic (B.C. 510-31).

Arnold, T. History of the Later Roman Commonwealth. N.Y. 1846.

—— Second Punic War. Ed. W.T. Arnold. Lond. 1886.

Beesly, A.H. The Gracchi, Marius, and Sulla. N.Y.

Heitland, W.E. Roman Republic. 3 vols. Camb. 1909.

Long, G. Civil Wars of Rome: Select Lives from Plutarch, newly trans., with notes. Lond. 1844-48. 5 vols.

—— Decline and Fall of the Roman Republic. Lond. 1864. 5 vols.

Merivale, C. The Roman Triumvirates. N.Y. (Epochs of Anc. History.)

Michelet, J. History of the Roman Republic. Tr. W. Hazlitt. Lond. 1847.

Smith, R.B. Rome and Carthage. N.Y. (Epochs of Anc. History.)

(7) The Empire (B.C. 31-A.D. 476).

Bury, J.B. History of the Roman Empire from its Foundation to the Death of Marcus Aurelius. N.Y. 1893.

—— History of the Later Roman Empire. Lond. 1889. 2 vols.

Capes, W.W The Early Empire. N.Y. (Epochs of Anc. Hist.)

—— Age of the Antonines. N.Y. (Epochs of Anc. History.)

Curteis, A.M. History of the Roman Empire, A.D. 395-800. Lond. 1875.

Gibbon, E. The History of the Decline and Fall of the Roman Empire. Phil. 6

vols. Abridged by W. Smith. N.Y. 1869.

Hodgkin, T. Italy and her invaders. Oxf. 1888-1890. 8 vols.

Jones, H.S. Roman Empire. N.Y. 1908.

Merivale, C.A History of the Romans under the Empire. N.Y. 1866. 7 vols.

Seeley, J.R. Roman Imperialism and Other Lectures and Essays. Bost. 1871.

III. SPECIAL TOPICS

(8) Antiquities.

Adam, A. Roman Antiquities. Ed. J. Boyd. Phil. 1872.

Eschenburg, J.J. Manual of Classical Literature (Antiquities). Tr. N.W. Fiske. Phil. 1864.

Fuss, J.D. Roman Antiquities. Eng. Trans. 1840.

Gow, J. Companion to School Classics. N.Y. 1889.

Harper's Dictionary of Classical Literature and Antiquities. Ed. H.T. Peck. N.Y. 1897.

Ramsay, W., and Lanciani, R. Manual of Roman Antiquities. Lond. 1894.

Rich, A. Dictionary of Roman and Greek Antiquities. Lond. 1873.

Seyffert, O. Dictionary of Classical Antiquities. Ed. H. Nettleship and J. E. Sandys. Lond. 1891.

Smith, W. Dictionary of Greek and Roman Antiquities. 3d edition. Land. 1890. 2 vols.

See also (16) Life and Manners.

(9) Archaeology.

Burn, R. Old Rome: a Handbook to the Ruins of the City and the Campagna. Lond. 1880.

—— Ancient Rome and its Neighborhood. Lond. 1895.

Dyer, T. H. A History of the City of Rome. Lond. 1883.

Lanciani, R. Ancient Rome in the Light of Recent Discoveries. Bost. 1891.

—— Ruins and Excavations of Ancient Rome. Bost. 1897.

Middleton, J. H. Ancient Rome in 1888. Edin. 1888.

—— Remains of Ancient Rome. Lond. 1892.

Parker, J.H. Archaeology of Rome. Oxf. 1876-79. 11 vols.

—— Architectural History of the City of Rome. Abridged from his "Archaeology of Rome." Lond. 1881.

(10) Art.

De Forest, J. B. Short History of Art. N. Y. 1881. (p. 85 *et seq*. "Roman Art.")

Fergusson, J. History of Architecture. Lond. 1871. 4 vols. (Pt. I., Bk. 4, "Etruscan and Roman Architecture.")

Lübke, W. History of Art. Tr. F.E. Burnett. Lond. 1888. 2 vols. (Ch. III., "Roman Art.")

Mitchell, L.M. History of Ancient Sculpture. N. Y. 1883.

Rosengarten, K. Handbook of Architectural Styles. Tr. W. Collett-Sanders. N.Y. 1876. (Bk. VII., "Roman Architecture.")

(11) Biography, General.

De Quincey, T. The Caesars. Lond. 1880.

Gould, S. Baring-. Tragedy of the Caesars. N.Y. 1892. 2 vols.

Herbert, H.W. Captains of the Roman Republic. N. Y. 1854.

Plutarch. Lives. (Bohn.)

Smith, W. Dictionary of Greek and Roman Biography and Mythology. Lond. 1880. 3 vols.

Suetonius. The Twelve Caesars. (Bohn.)

See also IV. Biography. Individuals.

(12) Christianity and Rome.

Carr, A. The Church and the Roman Empire. N.Y. 1887. (Epochs of Church Hist.)

Fisher, G.P. Beginnings of Christianity. N.Y. 1877.

Hardy, E.G. Christianity and the Roman Government. Lond. 1894.

Merivale, C. Conversion of the Roman Empire. N.Y. 1870.

Ramsay, W.M. The Church in the Roman Empire. N.Y. 1893.

Renan, E. Influence of Rome upon Christianity. N.Y.

Stanley, A.P. History of the Eastern Church. N.Y. 1884.

Uhlhorn, G. Conflict of Christianity with Heathenism. N.Y. 1879.

(13) Constitutional Antiquities.

Abbott, F.F. Roman Political Institutions. Bost. 1902.

Granrud, J.E. Roman Constitutional History. Bost. 1902.

Greenidge, A.H.J. Roman Public Life. Lond. 1901.

(14) Geography and Description.

Boissier, G. Country of Horace and Virgil. Tr. D. H. Fisher. Lond. 1896.

Burn, R. Rome and the Campagna. Camb. 1876.

Cramer, J.A. Description of Ancient Italy. Oxf. 1826. 2 vols.

Freeman, E.A. Historical Geography of Europe. N.Y. 1881. 2 vols.

Hare, A.J.C. Walks in Rome. N.Y.

Kiepert, H. Atlas Antiquus. Bost.

Murray, J. Handbook of Rome and its Environs. Lond.

Schmidt, H.I. Course of Ancient Geography. N.Y. 1860.

Story, W.W. Roba di Roma. Lond. 1884. 2 vols.

(15) Law.

Hadley, J. Introduction to Roman Law. N.Y.

Mackenzie, Lord. Studies in Roman Law. Lond. 1870.

Maine, H.S. Ancient Law. N. Y. 1884.

Morey, W.C. Outlines of Roman Law; Comprising its Historical Growth and General Principles. N. Y.

Muirhead, J. Historical Introduction to the Private Law of Rome. Ed. H. Goudy. Lond. 1899.

Ortolan, E. History of Roman Legislation. Tr. Pritchard and Nasmith. Lond. 1871.

(16) Life and Manners.

Becker, W.A. Gallus; or, Roman Scenes of the Time of Augustus. Tr. F. Metcalfe. Lond. 1866.

Church, A.J. Pictures from Roman Life and Story. N.Y. 1892.

—— Roman Life in the Days of Cicero. N.Y. 1884.

Dill, S. Roman Society in the Last Century of the Western Empire. Lond. and N. Y. 1898.

Elliot, F. M. Roman Gossip. N.Y. 1894.

Guhl, E., and Koner, W. The Life of the Greeks and Romans. Tr. F. Hueffer. Lond.

Inge, W.R. Society in Rome under the Caesars. N.Y. 1892.

Preston, H.W., and Dodge, L. Private Life of the Romans. Bost.

Shumway, E.S. A Day in Ancient Rome. Bost. 1893.

Thomas, E. Roman Life under the Caesars. N.Y. 1899.

See also (8) Antiquities.

(17) Literature.

Cruttwell, C.T. History of Roman Literature. N.Y. 1877.

Lawton, W.C. Classical Latin Literature. N.Y. 1904.

Simcox, G.A. History of Latin Literature. Lond. 1883. 2 vols.

Teuffel, W.S. History of Roman Literature. Tr. G.C. Warr. N.Y. 1891-92. 2 vols.

(18) Philosophy.

Enfield, W. History of Philosophy. Lond. 1837. (Bk. III., "Philosophy of the Romans.")

Farrar, F.W. Seekers after God. N.Y. 1883.

(19) Provinces.

Arnold, W.T. Roman System of Provincial Administration. Lond. 1879.

Mommsen, T. Provinces of the Roman Empire. N.Y. 1887. 2 vols.

(20) Religion.

Clarke, J.F. Ten Great Religions. Bost. 1871. (Ch. VIII., "Religion of Rome.")

Coulanges, F. de. Ancient City. Tr. W. Small. Bost. 1877.

Guerber, H.A. Myths of Greece and Rome. N.Y. 1893.

Murray, A.S. Manual of Mythology. N.Y. 1874.

(21) Slavery.

Blair, W. Inquiry into the State of Slavery amongst the Romans. Edin., 1833.

IV. BIOGRAPHY. INDIVIDUALS

(22) Caesar, Julius.

Abbott, J. History of Julius Caesar. N.Y. 1849.

Dodge, T.A. Caesar. Bost. 1892.

Fowler, W.W. Julius Caesar and the Foundation of the Roman Imperial System. N.Y. 1892.

Froude, J.A. Caesar; a Sketch. N.Y. 1880.

Napoleon, Louis. History of Julius Caesar. N.Y. 1865. 2 vols.

Williams, J. Life of Julius Caesar. Lond. 1854.

(23) Cicero.

Boissier, G. Cicero and his Friends. Tr. A. D. Jones. Lond.1897.

Davidson, J.L.S. Cicero and the Fall of the Roman Republic. N.Y. 1894.

Forsyth, W. Life of Cicero. N.Y. 1865. 2 vols.

Middleton, C., and others. Life and Letters of Cicero. Lond. 1876.

Newman, J.H. Historical Sketches. (In vol. 2.) N.Y. 1891.

Trollope, A. Life of Cicero. N.Y. 1881. 2 vols.

(24) Constantine.

Cutts, E. L. Constantine the Great. Lond. 1881.

(25) Hannibal.

Abbott, J. History of Hannibal. N.Y. 1849.

Arnold, T. Life of Hannibal. Bost. 1860.

Dodge, T.A. Hannibal. Bost. 1891.

Henty, G.A. The Young Carthaginian. N.Y. 1887.

(26) Julian.

Gardner, A. Julian, Philosopher and Emperor. N.Y. 1895.

Neander, J.A.W. Emperor Julian and his Generation. N.Y. 1850.

(27) Marcus Aurelius.

Watson, P.B. Marcus Aurelius Antoninus. N.Y. 1884.

V. HISTORICAL FICTION

NOTE.—Dramas are indicated thus, [D.]; novels, [N.]; poems, [P.].

1. *The Early Republic*

(28) Brutus the Elder.

Payne, J. H. Brutus; or the Fall of Tarquin. [D.]

(29) Horatius Cocles.

Macaulay, T.B. Horatius. (In Lays of Ancient Rome.) [P.]

(30) Coriolanus.

Shakespeare, W. Coriolanus. [D.]

(31) Appius Claudius.

Chaucer, G. The Phisiciens Tale. (In Canterbury Tales.) [P.]

Knowles, J.S. Virginius. [D.]

Macaulay, T.B. Virginia. (In Lays of Ancient Rome.) [P.]

2. *The Later Republic*

(32) Gracchus.

Knowles, J. S. Caius Gracchus. [D.]

(33) Marius.

Otway, T. Caius Marius. [D.]

(34) Spartacus.

Eckstein, E. Prusias. [N.]

(35) Catiline.

Herbert, H.W. The Roman Traitor. [N.]

Jonson, B. Catiline his Conspiracy. [D.]

(36) Caesar.

Beaumont, F., and Fletcher, J. The False One. [D.]

Lucan. Pharsalia. (Bohn.) [P.]

Shakespeare, W. Julius Caesar. [D.]

(37) Antony.

Hemans, F.D. Last Banquet of Antony and Cleopatra. [P.]

Shakespeare, W. Antony and Cleopatra. [D.]

3. *The Early Empire*

(38) Augustus.

Jonson, B. The Poetaster. [D.]

(39) Tiberius.

Graham, J.W. Neara. [N.]

Jonson, B. Seianus his Fall. [D.]

(40) Nero.

Baillie, J. The Martyr. [D.]

Church, A.J. Burning of Rome. [N.]

Eckstein, E. Nero: a Romance. [N.]

Sienkiewicz, H. Quo Vadis. [N.]

Story, W.W. Nero: a Historical Play. [D.]

(41) Vitellius.

Melville, G.J.W. The Gladiators. [N.]

(42) Titus.

Lytton, Bulwer. The Last Days of Pompeii. [N.]

Otway, T. Titus and Berenice. [D.]

(43) Domitian.

Eckstein, E. Quintus Claudius. [N.]

Marks, M.A.M. Masters of the World.

Massinger, P. The Roman Actor. [D.]

(44) Trajan.

Lockhart, J.G. Valerius. [N.]

(45) Hadrian.

Richardson, B.W. Son of a Star. [N.]

(46) Aurelian.

Ware, W. Aurelian; or, Rome in the Third Century. [N.]

—— Zenobia; or, the Fall of Palmyra. [N.]

4. *The Later Empire*

(47) Diocletian.

Crake, A.D. The Victor's Laurel. [N.]

Eckstein, E. The Chaldean Magician. [N.]

Massinger, P. The Virgin Martyr. [D.]

(48) Constantine.

Bayle, A. Thalia. [N.]

Crake, A.D. Evanus. [N.]

Lytton, Bulwer. Licinius. [P.]

Rounds, N.C. Arius the Libyan. [N.]

(49) Julian.

Bungener, L.L.F. Julian, the Close of an Era. [N.]

De Vere, A. Julian the Apostate. [P.]

Lee, E.B. Parthenia; or, the Last Days of Paganism. [N.]

Ware, W. Julian; or, Scenes in Judea. [N.]

(50) Theodosius.

Massinger, P. The Emperour of the East. [D.]

(51) Valentinian.

Beaumont, F., and Fletcher, J. Tragedy of Valentinian. [D.]

Printed in Great Britain
by Amazon